THE EASTERN BAND OF CHEROKEES 1819–1900

THE

EASTERN BAND OF CHEROKEES
1819-1900

by JOHN R. FINGER

THE UNIVERSITY OF TENNESSEE PRESS / KNOXVILLE

The paper in this book meets the guidelines for permanence and durability of the Committee on Production Guidelines for Book Longevity of the Council on Library Resources. Binding materials have been chosen for durability.

Library of Congress Cataloging in Publication Data

Finger, John R., 1939–
    The Eastern Band of Cherokees, 1819–1900.

    Bibliography: p.
    Includes index.
    1. Cherokee Indians—History.   I. Title.
E99.C5F56   1984   973'.0497   83–10284
ISBN 0–87049–409–0
ISBN 0–87049–410–4 (pbk.)

Dedicated with love and gratitude to my parents,
William Donovan Finger
and
Annada Tackett Finger

CONTENTS

Preface   *page* xi

1. Origins   3

2. Resisting Removal   20

3. An Anomalous Status   41

4. A Traditional Way of Life   60

5. The Civil War   82

6. Troubled Times   101

7. A Changing Society   126

8. Always a Cherokee   147

   Notes   179

   Bibliography   225

   Index   242

ILLUSTRATIONS

MAPS

1. Cherokee Nation, 1819–1838 — *page* 12
2. Western North Carolina, 1840 — 30
3. Lands of the Eastern Band, 1881 — 123
4. Qualla Boundary, 1881 — 124

PHOTOGRAPHS AND DRAWINGS

William Holland Thomas, 1858 — 57
Sawanugi, a Cherokee Ballplayer, 1888 — 75
Scratching a Ballplayer — 76
Cherokee Women and Children Watching the Ballplay, 1900 — 77
Cherokee Ballplayers in Action, 1900 — 78
Ballplayers Wrestling — 79
"Thomas's Rebel Indians Murdering Union Men" — 92
Cherokee Veterans of the Thomas Legion — 99
Chief Nimrod J. Smith, ca. 1890 — 141
James Mooney — 154
James Blythe, 1888 — 159
Walini, a Cherokee Woman — 160
Cherokee Councilmen, 1891 — 161
Bird Town Day School, ca. 1890 — 163
Eastern Cherokee Training School at Yellow Hill (Cherokee) — 164
Eastern Cherokee Training School, ca. 1890 — 165
Boys' Dormitory at Eastern Training School, ca. 1890 — 166
Cherokee Training School, 1893 — 167
Teacher and Pupils at Training School, 1893 — 168
Swimmer — 177

PREFACE

Why another book on the Cherokees? It is a predictable question and brings to mind another predictable inquiry of about eight years ago. When I first taught a course on the history of Indian-white relations, a student asked me how the Eastern Band of Cherokees had managed to avoid removal to the West during the 1830s. Although my university is only seventy-five miles from the Band's reservation in western North Carolina, I was unprepared for such an obvious question and had to take refuge in the kind of generalities academicians occasionally employ as a smokescreen to disguise their ignorance. I related a rather uncertain story about a Cherokee martyr who gave himself up for execution by the United States Army on condition that his people could remain in their mountain homeland. Even then, several aspects of the tale seemed implausible, and so I began looking into the legendary sacrifice of Tsali. The scope of my investigation soon broadened.

It surprised me that the only history of the Eastern Band was James Mooney's brief account, which appeared in 1900 as part of his larger anthropological work. This seemed odd, for the Cherokee majority, those who moved to present-day Oklahoma, have been the subjects of an impressive literature. Only in recent years have historians recognized the need for studies dealing with the Eastern Band and other remnant Indian groups that continued to reside in the Southeast after the removal era.[1] Some scholars, however, questioned whether there was sufficient evidence from which to reconstruct such histories. Mattie Russell's pioneering dissertation on William Holland Thomas had revealed extensive archival materials relating to the Band, but no one had used the wealth of pertinent records accumulated by the Bureau of Indian Affairs. It is my hope that this book will demonstrate the variety of sources available and also represent a significant step toward satisfying the long-standing need for a history of the Eastern Band.

I chose 1819 as my starting point because a treaty of that year led to the separation of a number of Indians from the main body of Cherokees, and these became the progenitors of the Eastern Band. The year 1900 was selected as a termination date both for its convenience and significance. This book is the first of two planned volumes on the Eastern Cherokees, and 1900 marks the midpoint of their history as well as an important transition in their affairs. A recent court decision had upheld federal authority over them and resolved certain issues arising out of a period of mixed state and federal jurisdiction. As the Indians quickly discovered, the decision had ironic consequences. Arguing that the Eastern Cherokees were noncitizen wards of the United States, state officials in 1900 denied them the right to vote—a privilege which they had long enjoyed and which federal authorities had long held as an ultimate goal for Native Americans. Afterward, though certain features of mixed jurisdiction continued, the U.S. government became a more intrusive force in Cherokee life.

In the following pages I shall develop two main arguments. First, the Eastern Band endured a precarious and anomalous legal status vis-à-vis their white neighbors, the state of North Carolina, and the federal government. This uncertainty posed a constant threat both to their homeland and their psychological well-being. And second, these people were somehow able to retain their identity as Cherokees throughout their travail. This is not to say they did not change. It is unfortunate that even today many whites seem to believe, at least implicitly, that "real" Indians are not subject to the historical process of change over time. According to their curious logic, the Native American who does adjust to circumstances is somehow less an Indian. I hope to show the Cherokee capacity to adapt to various exigencies and still retain an Indian identity.

Historians have long acknowledged the difficulty and even presumptuousness of writing Indian history, for the evidence upon which we rely is mostly written by whites. We all realize, moreover, that we inescapably reflect in various ways our own society and cultural biases. None of us, even with the most sophisticated background in anthropology and psychology, can ever expect to reflect adequately the views or aspirations of nineteenth-century Indians. Yet as historians we are all bound by the injunction of Francis Jennings "to make a special effort of imagination to see things as Indians might."[2] Of necessity I have devoted considerable attention to the roles of certain whites like William Thomas and to the policies of state and federal governments, but I have tried to remember Jennings's plea and return, ultimately, to the Cherokees. And to understand them.

A few words of warning are in order. Many Indians had varied spellings of their Cherokee names as well as English equivalents. Thus Enola was also known as Inoli or Black Fox. In such cases I have usually chosen the name that most frequently appeared in the documents of the time, whether it was the Cherokee or English variant. For an important individual I have indicated at an appropriate place in the text any common variation of name. For geographic place names, I have used the modern versions. For example, the old Cherokee settlement of Cheoih (or Buffalo Town) appears as Cheoah in this narrative.

Another potential problem derives from the frequent redrawing of county boundaries in western North Carolina during the nineteenth century. In 1838, for instance, the Quallatown Cherokees lived in Haywood County, but during the next thirty-five years, without ever having moved, many of those same Indians successively became residents of Jackson and Swain counties. Similar confusion exists over the creation or diminution of Macon, Cherokee, and Graham counties. In most cases I do not refer to such political changes and simply use the county names in effect at the time of discussion.

At various places I employ the term "acculturation," well realizing that it can have several definitions and, in some quarters, signifies a mutual exchange of traits and values among peoples of different cultures. I have chosen to use it in a more restricted sense, defining it as the acquisition by Cherokees of certain attitudes, skills, and behavior that typified whites of the day; in other words, it signifies the changes among Indians that made them, in the eyes of whites, more "civilized." It is also with some trepidation that I employ the terms "fullblood," "mixed-blood," and even "Indian." Nonetheless, they are terms readily understood by the reader and serve as a useful form of shorthand in a text as lengthy as this. I hereby disavow any intention of using them in a pejorative sense. To avoid undue monotony, I often employ "Eastern Cherokees" or "Cherokees East" to refer to members of the Eastern Band (and sometimes to Indians living in Georgia, Tennessee, and Alabama). When referring to those who moved west, I rely on "Cherokee Nation." If there is any doubt, the reader should assume I am discussing members of the Band.

In a project such as this, one incurs a number of debts that can never be repaid. The many archivists and librarians who served me were unfailingly courteous, helpful, and efficient, but I offer special thanks to Mattie Russell of Duke University, Robert Fowler of the National Archives, and Gayle Peters of the Federal Records Center at East Point, Georgia. Duane King, a good friend and Executive Director of the Cherokee National Historical Society, has assisted me on many occasions. In addition, I express my appreciation to the following individuals and organizations: Marion Smith, of the Andrew Johnson Project, who called my attention to a number of Civil War–era newspaper articles; Deborah Denton, my assistant for spring quarter 1982; Debbie Pierce, who cheerfully and efficiently typed this manuscript in its various drafts; Bruce Beckman, of the University of Tennessee Cartography Shop; Barbara Reitt, my editor; the American Philosophical Society, for a grant from the Penrose Fund; the University of Tennessee, Knoxville, for a summer research grant; the Southern Historical Association and the North Carolina Division of Archives and History, for permission to use portions of my published articles; and the National Archives for its microfilming program, without which this book would not have been written.

A number of friends and colleagues have read and commented on chapters of this book or have helped in other ways, including Susan Becker, Sarah Blanshei, Ralph Haskins, Charles Johnson, Milton Klein, and Theda Perdue. Ronald Satz and E. Stanly Godbold, Jr., carefully reviewed the entire manuscript and offered perceptive, constructive advice. Any shortcomings in the finished product, of course, are my responsibility alone. And last, I wish to thank Donna, Brian, Susan, and Michael Finger for their long-suffering patience while I have had Cherokees on my mind.

THE EASTERN BAND OF CHEROKEES 1819–1900

1

ORIGINS

No one knows how or when they settled in the southern Appalachians or even why they are called Cherokee. According to one legend, they were driven out of the North by an Indian coalition that included their distant kinsmen, the Iroquois. Similarities in the Cherokee and Iroquois languages and the mutual hatred of those peoples lend plausibility to this story. But any such exodus must have occurred in the distant past, for archaeological evidence suggests that the Cherokees' ancestors occupied the Southeast at least a millennium ago. And when they first appear in the historic record they were already ensconced in their mountain valleys, haughtily calling themselves the "principal people" and warring upon their neighbors.[1]

There were three general divisions among the Cherokees: the Lower Towns along the upper Savannah River in South Carolina; the Middle Towns occupying the upper Little Tennessee River and its tributaries in western North Carolina; and the Upper—or Overhill—Towns in eastern Tennessee and extreme western North Carolina.[2] Some scholars divide the Middle Towns into a fourth division, the so-called Out Towns that lay to the north and east of the others. Nestled beneath the towering Great Smoky Mountains and the Balsam Range, these remote villages were a Cherokee backwater. Yet one of them, Kituwha near present-day Bryson City, North Carolina, was apparently the "mother town" of all three divisions. As progenitors of their people, the Out Towns would be a powerful force in preserving the Cherokee identity and homeland.[3]

The sites and natural phenomena of the southern Appalachians nourished a corpus of legend and lore that helped shape a tribal identity rooted in time, place, and myth. The misty mountain passes and deep pools of streams, for example, were favorite abodes of the fearsome *utkena*, a snakelike monster with horns. Even to look upon one meant death. The forests were home to the bear, an animal that once had been human and for whom the Cherokees felt a special affection. And beneath the Nikwasi Mound in present-day Franklin, North Carolina, lived the Nunnehi, a friendly spirit people who once helped the Cherokees rout a powerful invader.[4] These and a host of other sites and legends afforded the tribe a stable link with the past.

At the height of their power the Cherokees claimed an area far exceeding their homeland—about 40,000 square miles encompassing portions of the Carolinas, Georgia, Tennessee, Kentucky, Alabama, and the Virginias. With perhaps 20,000–25,000 people at the time of contact, they were both a formidable potential enemy and a tempting trading partner. Hernando de Soto and other Spanish adventurers paid only brief visits in the mid-sixteenth century, but in 1673 the Cherokees made more enduring contact with the English. After that, traders from the southern colonies, especially South Carolina, made the long overland journey from tidewater with pack trains of goods to exchange for Indian slaves and deerskins.[5]

Trade brought significant change. The Cherokees quickly discarded the bow and arrow for firearms, incorporated white fabrics and fashions into traditional attire, and adopted the metal hoe and hatchet in place of ancient implements. Gradually, perhaps imperceptibly to themselves, they lost their self-sufficiency. The trade goods provided an incentive to collect more Indian slaves and deerskins, making the individual warrior, whether he realized it or not, an incipient capitalist. Indian warfare, traditionally circumscribed by a sense of honor and limitation, became more mercenary, deadly, and extensive. Southeastern tribes—the Cherokees, Creeks, Choctaws, Chickasaws, and smaller groups—found themselves entangled in a web of intrigue and rivalry spun in far-off England, France, and Spain. And yet the cultural exchange was not one-sided, the Indians no mere objects of European manipulation. Some southern chiefs were renowned for their diplomatic skills, and white negotiators had to be adaptable and wary when dealing with them.[6]

Each Cherokee town was an autonomous unit, its inhabitants striving for consensus when discussing major issues. There were no leaders in the European sense, no king or prince who wielded coercive authority over others. At most, a local chief led by persuasion and example. Such an atomized society was unfathomable to Europeans accustomed to more centralized authority. Sir Alexander

Cuming, a remarkable English eccentric, boldly addressed this problem in 1730 by traveling to the Cherokee country and proclaiming a single chief, Moytoy, as first chief and "king" of his people. No doubt impressed by such audacity, the Cherokees pledged their allegiance to Great Britain. To legitimize this impromptu alliance, Cuming even escorted a delegation of natives to England for an audience with King George II. Afterward the British usually recognized one principal chief and town, but most Cherokees continued to manifest an exasperating individualism and, in European eyes, near anarchy.[7]

Most incomprehensible of all to non-Indians was the Cherokee family system. Kinship, as defined by membership in one of seven clans, was the most pervasive feature of tribal life and cut across community lines. Intermarriage within a clan was forbidden. Clan status was inherited through the mother, making the maternal influence and that of her relatives paramount. A father might love his children and provide for their care, but he had no official relationship to them because they were of a different clan. His wife owned both the home and planting fields.[8] To the wonderment of Europeans, women also enjoyed considerable sexual freedom and a modicum of political and military influence, leading James Adair, a South Carolina trader, to denounce the men for being ruled by a "petticoat-government."[9]

To the extent that there was legal coercive power among the Cherokees, it resided within the clan in the form of blood revenge. A clan was obligated to repay in equal measure the murder of one of its own and was also responsible for its members' actions. Revenge for an injustice was a privileged action and not subject to further retribution. The clan system thus embodied restraints that precluded an endless chain of violence. To be without a clan, as was the case of some outsiders living among the Cherokees, was to be without identity as a human being. Such an individual could in theory be murdered with impunity, for there was no one to avenge his death. Clan membership also offered hospitality and sanctuary for a member in whatever Cherokee village he visited, even if he otherwise happened to be a stranger.[10]

Usually the Cherokees supported the English during the colonial wars, but occasionally they turned on their trading partners. Late in the French and Indian War they deserted the British cause, forced the surrender of Fort Loudoun near the Overhill town of Chota, and then massacred some of its garrison. The British retaliated by destroying a number of Cherokee villages.[11] This aberration in Cherokee-English comity had passed by the time of the American Revolution, and the colonists' insatiable land hunger made the Indians enthusiastic allies of the Crown. At almost the same moment the colonies declared their independence, the Cherokees launched widespread attacks on frontier settlements. Though colonial militia units quickly crushed them, intermittent raids against settlers continued for more than a decade after the Revolution. In the meantime, Cherokee villages were destroyed, rebuilt, and moved a number of times according to the exigencies of Indian-white relations. Abandoning almost all of South Carolina, the tribe increasingly edged toward the south and west, into southeastern Tennessee and northern Alabama and Georgia.[12]

The changes among the North Carolina Cherokees, especially the Out Towns, were less profound because they inhabited a region that was remote, mountainous, and uninviting to most whites. Had they lived farther east, there is little doubt they would have suffered the same fate as the Tuscaroras, who were decimated in wars with land-hungry whites and their Indian allies (including the Cherokees). It was therefore no great sacrifice when North Carolina promised in 1783 that the Cherokees could continue to hold the area they already occupied in the state. This did not negate the possibility, of course, that the Indians might cede portions of those lands in treaties negotiated with the new U.S. government.[13]

Historically the United States has had two objectives in regard to the Indians: first, to "civilize" them, and second, to acquire their lands in order to accommodate white speculators and settlers. In the late eighteenth and early nineteenth centuries these twin threads of policy were interwoven in curious ways, with the latter invariably dominating.[14] After all, a basic fact of life for Americans during that period was national expansion, an impulse so insistent that no tribe could possibly withstand it. The Indians were forced to give way, a fate some accepted passively while others fiercely resisted.

The definition and reduction of Cherokee lands began during the colonial period and continued under the aegis of the U.S. government. The first federal treaty with the Cherokees was at Hopewell, South Carolina, in 1785, followed by a number of others during the next few decades, nearly every one reducing the tribal homeland a bit more. Indian cessions were usually justified by the convenient logic of civilization: if the Indians gave up the "chase" and settled down to farming they would require a smaller land base, leaving the surplus for the just needs of an expanding white population. This argument ignored the fact that eastern Indians were not nomadic hunters but practitioners of a diversified economy of farming, hunting, fishing, and gathering.[15]

"Civilization" and land-grabbing, then, were inextricably bound together in policymaking. This is not to suggest that federal officials were always duplicitous or hypocritical, but, like most humans, they tended to justify and rationalize their material desires. The justification began in the 1790s with an ambitious federal program to educate, Christianize, and remold the Indian into a redskinned Jeffersonian yeoman. If such objectives seem ethnocentric to a twentieth-century observer, most thoughtful Americans of the time believed they were in the Indians' best interests. Few whites would concede that indigenous native cultures had any merit. The Indians would fully realize their human potential only when they had been assimilated into the dominant white society.[16]

But white leaders were often disappointed by the tenacity of aboriginal culture. Thomas Jefferson, that incorrigible optimist in matters regarding the human prospect, originally believed the Indians could rapidly change just as the American environment was evolving from pristine wilderness to a more civilized, pastoral ideal. Yet as president he implicitly acknowledged the failure of his policy by suggesting that white society could not patiently await such change, that in the meantime the eastern tribes should leave their homelands and move west of the Mississippi River. His interest in acquiring the Louisiana country partly reflected a desire to find a new homeland for those tribes.[17]

When traditionalist Indians went to war against the United States, as a portion of the Creeks did in 1813, their resistance simply served as further justification for expropriation. Andrew Jackson taught the Creeks the meaning of "civilized" warfare by killing hundreds and destroying their towns and crops. It is a supreme irony that at the climactic Battle of Horseshoe Bend in March 1814, he had as his staunchest allies a detachment of Cherokee warriors. They served him well and later boasted that he could not have defeated the Creeks without their support. But the general was not inclined to be magnanimous to any Indian, friend or foe. He forced both hostile and friendly Creeks to cede an enormous area to the United States and eventually, when the time was propitious, made similar demands upon his erstwhile Cherokee allies. Junaluska, a renowned warrior from North Carolina, later bitterly declared that had he

7

known Jackson's intentions he would have killed him at Horseshoe Bend.[18]

From the administration of James Monroe through the Jacksonian era, removal was increasingly incorporated into the warp and woof of federal policy. Civilizing the Indians was still an objective, but it would obviously take time and was often hindered by the influence of unscrupulous whites. Therefore, the logic went, the government should transfer the Indians beyond the Mississippi where, under the tutelage of ministers and teachers, the tribes could absorb the ways of civilization without contamination by unsavory whites—and without holding up the course of empire.[19] The Office of Indian Affairs, ironically located within the Department of War, was committed to the idea of creating Indian versions of the Puritans' godly City on a Hill, model societies blossoming in the virgin soil of the West. To put it less kindly, the West would be the laboratory in which Dr. Frankenstein transplanted the values and precepts of white society into the corpse of aboriginal custom.

But the Cherokees were another matter. They did not require a fresh environment to demonstrate their cultural adaptability. By the 1820s many had abandoned their towns and were living as nuclear families in log cabins similar to those of their white neighbors. They tended their own small farms, though the land still belonged to the tribe, and were probably as proficient in agriculture as most southern whites. Some mixed-bloods developed entrepreneurial skills and a capitalist outlook, owning black slaves, farming hundreds of acres for a market economy, and living in large frame or brick houses. A few owned mills, stores, tanneries, and ferries. Protestant missionaries established schools among them and converted many to Christianity. Sequoyah's invention of an easy-to-learn syllabary brought a rapid increase in literacy, and the highly acculturated Elias Boudinot was an articulate spokesman for progress as editor of the tribal newspaper, the *Cherokee Phoenix*.[20]

By 1827 the Cherokees had established their own nation modeled on that of the United States, complete with a constitution, courts, and system of representation. They had a Principal Chief, John Ross, and a capital at New Echota, Georgia. Ross, analogous to a president, was determined to enforce a tribal law against further sale of their lands. White Georgians were outraged, claiming the tribal government was an unconstitutional infringement on the state's sovereign prerogatives and, far from exemplifying Indian progress,

8

was simply the device of a few mixed-bloods to manipulate and abuse their traditionalist kinsmen.[21]

Cherokee "progress" supplemented Cherokee treaty rights as an argument against enforced removal, while denying their acculturation was a weapon in the arsenal of dispossession. Eventually, those who disputed their progress won both the political battle and the land, but Cherokee supporters found solace by winning the war of words. During the next 150 years historians and popular writers alike conjured up a compelling stereotype—the "civilized" Cherokee—and, having created it, could hardly challenge its validity. Today, however, one might safely question the extent of tribal civilization; indeed, beneath the upper socioeconomic level was a surprisingly durable stratum of traditionalism, especially in North Carolina.[22] But what usually impresses Americans is change rather than continuity; it has always been so for a society whose national ideology, such as it is, embodies not tradition but constant transmutation and progress.

The fact that many Cherokees did acquire the material possessions and skills esteemed by white society does not necessarily reflect a fundamental shift of values. As two scholars have noted, such outward changes do not mean "that the Cherokees were assimilationist or decultured. In many respects they were strongly resistant to deculturation—as their determined opposition to removal indicated. What was taken by contemporary white observers as 'civilization' was simply the acquisition of sufficient skills for economic survival and for political self-government—part of a conscious strategy to resist removal and maintain autonomy."[23] Principal Chief Ross, for example, was only one-eighth Cherokee and possessed all the trappings of "civilized" life, but he was as steadfast as any fullblood traditionalist in resisting dispossession and removal. What was perceived as civilization, then, did not necessarily signify loss of Cherokee identity or values. And whites of the day would have denied that the Indians were civilized precisely to the extent they retained such values.

There were several Cherokee paradoxes during this period. One was the way white sympathizers emphasized the remarkable "civilizing" that had occurred, even though traditionalism remained a potent force. A second was that, having accepted Cherokee progress as an article of faith, many whites were less than pleased by such advancement. Since the early colonial period, the "savage

Indian" stereotype had been highly useful as justification for dispos-session.[24] Now Indian policymakers were confronted with the need of finding a rationale for dispossessing "civilized" people.] This uncomfortable situation explains why some whites found Cherokee "progress" infuriating, perhaps without understanding why.

The Cherokees were, at the same time, too logical and too naive in believing their gestures toward acculturation would protect their lands. The pressures for land cessions and removal continued to mount even while Presbyterian ministers beamed at Cherokee chil-dren singing Christian hymns. [And, in truth, a sizable minority of the tribe was willing to move, particularly those who preferred a place where whites were less intrusive and the hunting was better.] [In this situation one sees the flexibility of American policymaking: at the same time the government emphasized civilization by saying removal would promote that end, officials were assuring Indian conservatives that emigration west would allow them to continue their old ways. Federal agents unashamedly used whatever argu-ment would most effectively promote removal. By the 1820s several thousand Cherokees—later called Old Settlers—had voluntarily located in present-day Arkansas and Oklahoma.[25]

The Cherokee treaty of 1819 supplemented one of 1817 and provided for a land cession that diminished the tribal domain to a block encompassing western North Carolina, northern Georgia, southeastern Tennessee, and northeastern Alabama. This cession was compensation for a large area the United States had made available to those Cherokees who wished to live in the West. The government agreed to pay for all improvements on the surrendered property and even promised that a Cherokee head of family could remain in the ceded area by applying for a 640-acre reservation and becoming a citizen of the United States.[26]

Following the treaty, most of the affected Indians relocated in what remained of tribal lands. But in North Carolina at least forty-nine Cherokee heads of families registered with federal officials and had their private reservations surveyed.[27] In this fashion such Cherokees as Euchella and Yonaguska, conservative members of the Middle and Out Towns, retained their lands along the tumbling watercourses flanking the Great Smoky Mountains—the Little Tennessee, Tuckasegee, Oconaluftee, and their tributaries. Since the boundary of the diminished tribal domain was nearby, they could enjoy frequent contact with their relatives who were still part of the Cherokee Nation.[28]

10

North Carolina was so hasty in taking possession of the ceded lands that eager officials even sold some of the reservations which the federal government had guaranteed to individual Indians. There was no malice in this, simply a traditional Anglo-American desire to acquire new lands. The resulting chaos and acrimony involving conflicting claims led to an 1824 decision by the state supreme court in *Euchella v. Welsh*, in which the court firmly upheld the validity of the federal treaty and Indian titles to reservations. Having acknowledged its error, the state decided to rectify it by buying the land from the Cherokee claimants and allowing them to settle elsewhere in the area. In August 1824 state commissioners negotiated terms for buying most of these Cherokee reservations, a process that was completed over the next several years. Eventually the state was reimbursed by the federal government.[29]

Euchella was among the sellers and moved back to the tribal lands, obtaining a small farm along the Nantahala River. Yonaguska (Drowning Bear) sold his tract on the Tuckasegee but, along with most of the former reservees, remained apart from the tribe and settled near the junction of Soco Creek and the Oconaluftee, at a site later called Quallatown. A tall, dignified man renowned for his oratorical eloquence and occasional alcoholic binges, he served as chief of the reservees for the next fifteen years. These people, known as the Oconaluftee or Lufty or Qualla Indians, were the nucleus of what became the Eastern Band of Cherokees.[30]

The Qualla Indians lived quietly, abided by the laws of North Carolina, and received no annuities from either the federal government or the Cherokees. Despite claiming to be citizens by virtue of the 1817 and 1819 treaties, they never attempted to exercise any of the normal rights of citizenship and wanted only to be left alone. At first they farmed very little, contenting themselves with trading some cattle and sheep to whites and selling ginseng at Felix Walker's Soco Creek store for ten cents a pound.[31] Yet their placid existence was not without troubles. Alcohol, the bane of Indians everywhere, was plentiful and Yonaguska's overindulgence set a poor example. And while there were no outward troubles with their few white neighbors, the Cherokees' ignorance of the law made them inviting targets. In 1829, claiming they had been "imposed on, cheated, and defrauded by some of the people of this country," they appointed John L. Dillard as attorney to protect their interests. This arrangement was merely temporary, however, for they soon came to rely on William Holland Thomas.[32]

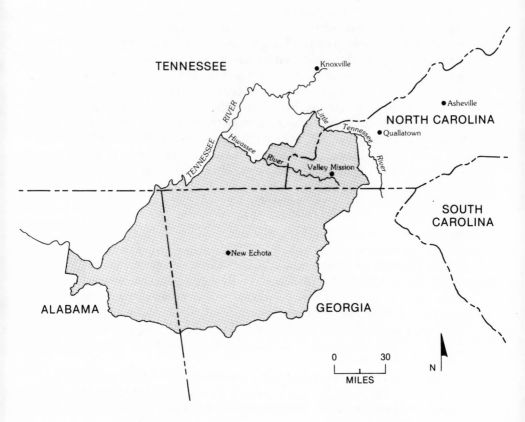

Map 1. Cherokee Nation, 1819–1838

William Thomas was without doubt the most important individual connected with the Eastern Band's history for forty years or
more. Born in 1805 near Waynesville, North Carolina, and raised
by his widowed mother, he was employed as a youth at Felix
Walker's store. Yonaguska took a liking to the waif, adopted him
into the band, and treated him as a son. Called Wil-Usdi (Little
Will), Thomas quickly became knowledgeable in every aspect of
Cherokee ways and formed a lifelong devotion to his adoptive
kinsmen. In 1831 he became their legal counsel as well as confidant.
Having spent much of his time poring over law books, he was as
well qualified as anyone to handle their affairs. By then he had
succeeded Walker as merchant to the Quallatown band, and before
long he owned several more stores in western North Carolina that
did business with other Cherokees.[33]

The mixed-blood Cherokee elites resided in Georgia, Tennessee,
and Alabama, as did most missionaries for the American Board of
Commissioners and other Protestant organizations. The North
Carolina Indians, both within and without the Cherokee Nation,
were almost forgotten stepchildren. They were predominantly
fullbloods, had less wealth, and were more traditional than their
brethren. As early as 1808 George Barber Davis characterized them
as "at least twenty years behind" other Cherokees, a view often
expressed in later years.[34] An effort to change this came in 1817,
when the Reverend Humphrey Posey, a Baptist, began preaching to
these "poor benighted" people. Three years later, at the urging of
tribal officials, he established a mission school on the north bank of
the Hiwassee River, squarely in the midst of the Valley Towns.
Before long he had constructed several buildings, enclosed eighty
acres as a mission farm, and started a school for about fifty Indian
children. Among those assisting him were the Reverend Evan Jones
and wife, who for many years would be stalwarts in missionary
activities among the Cherokees. In 1824 Jones became pastor of the
local church and soon assumed supervision of Baptist missionary
activities throughout the region.[35]

The mission farm, which had been thought necessary in order to
attract Cherokee interest, was gradually abandoned as the missionaries concentrated more and more on conversion. In 1823 John
Timson and his wife, of Peachtree District, became the first Cherokees to join the Valley Town church. Jones soon established several
outlying mission stations, where he frequently preached and attracted large crowds. Cherokee ministers assisted him, especially

Jesse Bushyhead, who had been baptized by an American Board minister and then started his own congregation at Amohee, where he became acquainted with the Valley Town mission. Soon ordained a Baptist, he worked at various mission posts in the area. By 1833, according to one church report, there were at least 250 Cherokee Baptists in western North Carolina. Nonetheless, the Valley Town mission remained a remote backwoods enterprise that made little headway with most of the traditionalist Indians. By the time of removal General John Wool could still describe the Cherokees there as the most backward and recalcitrant of their tribe—and the least disposed to emigrate west.[36]

The Qualla Indians were even farther removed from organized religion than the Valley Towns, though they possibly attended occasional frontier revivals or meetings of the Tuckasegee Baptist Association. Insofar as there was any missionary activity among them, it seems to have come from periodic visits by Methodist preachers. Methodism, after all, had a long history in the area, and the original circuit rider himself—Bishop Francis Asbury—had often criss-crossed the mountains between North Carolina and Tennessee.[37]

Despite their isolation, the Qualla Cherokees made some notable improvements in their lifestyle. Yonaguska finally became a teetotaler and, with Thomas's encouragement, organized a local temperance society. Thomas worked diligently to protect their interests and encouraged them to become more systematic farmers. Their neighbors, moreover, testified that they had shown significant progress since dissociating from the tribe—a disingenuous and self-serving compliment, for many whites viewed the Indians primarily as a convenient pool of cheap labor.[38]

→ This quiet isolation could not immunize the Quallatown people against the fear and uncertainty that spread like a cancer as whites, particularly those of Georgia, stridently demanded Cherokee removal to the West. When Georgia ceded her western claims to the federal government in 1802, she stipulated that the government do all in its power to convince the Creeks and Cherokees within her boundaries to give up their lands and leave. By the late 1820s many Georgians were incensed that the Indians still remained, and they adopted a bellicose policy. The discovery of gold in northern Georgia, the heartland of the Cherokee Nation, predictably reinforced demands for Indian eviction. The tribal capital was there, as was most of the population. Pointing to various federal treaties that guaranteed their lands, Principal Chief Ross denied that Georgia was sovereign over the Cherokees and could evict them. In rebuttal the Georgians claimed the Indians were mere tenants at will, occupying lands only on the sufferance of the state. The presumptuousness of the Cherokees in establishing their own nation within the state simply solidified the Georgians' determination to evict them.[39]

→ Confronted with Indian intransigence, the state resorted to coercion. It extended its authority over all Cherokee lands within its boundaries, refused to recognize the validity of tribal laws, courts, or claims, and distributed tribal lands to whites in a lottery. Defiant state officials in effect dared the federal government to intervene. But Andrew Jackson, who became president early in 1829, had no intention of opposing Georgia. He had always been firmly committed to removal and warned the various tribes that the central government had no right to interfere with what the states were doing. The Indians would either have to move, which was in their best interest, or come under the laws of the states in which they lived—the latter hardly an attractive alternative. By 1830 the president's message was very clear when, after a bitter fight in Congress, he secured passage of a general removal act that made it official policy to encourage Indian emigration to the West. It did not provide for the use of force, but Jackson intended to employ every measure short of actual violence to secure his ends.[40]

North Carolina was not as aggressive as Georgia or some other southern states, but it clearly favored a final cession of land by the Cherokees and their removal. In 1828 the General Assembly deplored continued Indian residency and informed Congress that "the red men are not within the pale of civilization; they are not under the restraints of morality, nor the influence of religion; and they are always disagreeable and dangerous neighbors to a civilized people. The proximity of those red men to our white population subjects the latter to depredations and annoyance, and is a source of perpetual and mutual irritation."[41] Despite such an unflattering opinion of them, the North Carolina Cherokees, assisted by the Reverend Jones, staunchly resisted federal efforts to enroll them for emigration.[42]

Meanwhile, Georgia's oppression reached almost unbearable levels and U.S. agents worked diligently to convince the Cherokees that removal made sense. Bribery, the suspension of annuity payments, and other forms of cajolery and intimidation were commonplace. While other tribes were capitulating one by one, the desperate Cherokees took their tormentors to court. Though they obtained a favorable Supreme Court decision in the landmark case of *Worcester v. Georgia*, Jackson had neither the power nor inclination to enforce it. The Cherokees must go. [43]

A prelude to removal was the 1835 tribal census authorized by the federal government. Before arrangements could be made for emigration, it was necessary to have accurate information regarding the Cherokee population, their distribution, the lands they occupied, their improvements, and other such matters. According to the census, 8,946 Cherokees lived in Georgia; 3,644 in North Carolina (including those in Quallatown); 2,528 in Tennessee; and 1,424 in Alabama—making a total of 16,542. The Indians owned 1,592 slaves, only 37 of whom lived in North Carolina. This and other data in the census confirm that the North Carolina Cherokees were significantly behind their kinsmen in material possessions and white skills. [44]

By the time of the census some Cherokee leaders had already decided the tribe could not survive in the midst of such hostility. A few even succumbed to the blandishments of white agents who offered attractive bribes. And so a small minority—including Elias Boudinot, Major and John Ridge, and a few others—signed the infamous Treaty of New Echota on December 29, 1835. By its terms the Cherokee Nation was to give up all its land in the Southeast for $5 million, a large tract of land in the West, and other concessions. The Indians would have to relocate beyond the Mississippi within two years of the ratification of the treaty. [45]

John Ross and the Cherokee majority used every conceivable ploy to prevent ratification. They lobbied incessantly with senators, and the North Carolina Cherokees, among others, pointed out that they had not been represented at New Echota. To no avail. After failing to convince the holdouts to reconsider, officials still contended that the pending treaty would be binding on all members of the Cherokee Nation. In contrast, the Quallatown residents were in a unique position because they had been living outside the Nation for about sixteen years. While they still held a proportionate interest in the lands of the Nation as their birthright, they were no longer subject to its authority. They claimed they had become citizens of North Carolina and did not have to leave. Even if authorities insisted they were still members of the Nation, the unratified treaty contained a loophole by which certain Cherokees could remain. According to Article 12,

> Those individuals and families of the Cherokee nation that are averse to a removal to the Cherokee country west of the Mississippi and are desirous to become citizens of the States where they reside and such as are qualified to take care of themselves and their property shall be entitled to receive their due portion of all the personal benefits accruing under this treaty for their claims, improvements and *per capita*; as soon as an appropriation is made for this treaty.
>
> Such heads of Cherokee families as are desirous to reside within the States of No. Carolina Tennessee and Alabama subject to the laws of the same; and who are qualified or calculated to become useful citizens shall be entitled, on the certificate of the commissioners to a preemption right to one hundred and sixty acres of land or one quarter section at the minimum Congress price. . . .[46]

A Cherokee could remain, then, if he was "qualified" and willing to come under state law. Jackson was confident few would wish to subject themselves to this, but to be certain he removed the provision allowing a preemption claim to those who stayed. Any Cherokees choosing to remain would have to acquire their own land and otherwise fend for themselves.[47]

In January 1836 William Thomas agreed to represent the people of Quallatown, Cheoah (Buffalo Town), and several smaller settlements at the conferences in Washington prior to ratification of the treaty. He was to inform federal authorities that these people intended to stay in North Carolina and was also to obtain recognition of their claims to a proportionate share of the treaty benefits. After collecting any money owed his clients, he was to keep a percentage as his compensation and then purchase land and other necessities for them. The resourceful Thomas won recognition of their rights both from government officials and the so-called treaty party of the Cherokee Nation, successfully concluding the first of what would become many treks to the capital in behalf of his Indian kinsmen and clients.[48]

After ratification of the treaty by the margin of a single vote on May 23, 1836, Benjamin F. Currey superintended the preparatory stages of removal, and a contingent of agents appraised the improvements which the Indians would surrender. William Welch,

Nimrod S. Jarrett, and Joseph W. McMillen performed this task in North Carolina. They were also to note the names of those Cherokees who wished to remain and become citizens of the state, after which officials would decide whether they were qualified to do so. Among those making such decisions was John Timson, the Christianized mixed-blood who had already been recognized as a permanent resident and freeholder of North Carolina.[49]

In the fall of 1836 Thomas assembled the Qualla Indians and again asked whether they desired to move west or remain in their homeland. Posting two men a few feet apart, he directed those who wished to stay to pass between them. Everyone did so. Obviously, they valued the advice of their beloved Yonaguska, who, with a prescience based on long experience, had argued against moving. If they did, he said, the government would soon want their new lands, too. There was no limit to white greed.[50]

The Cheoah Indians and others in western North Carolina were equally emphatic in expressing their intention to stay. Some later received certificates attesting to their qualifications to become citizens, but others did not. Perhaps the harassed authorities were too busy to issue them; or perhaps, being federal agents, they were simply reluctant to acknowledge the Cherokees' right to stay. Whatever the explanation, the situation offered obvious possibilities for misunderstanding and, on the part of the Indians, apprehension and fear.[51]

The Qualla Cherokees, at least, were confident they could avoid removal because of their peculiar legal position and recent recognition of their rights in Washington. Yet Thomas left nothing to chance, beginning an intensive campaign to persuade the state to sanction explicitly their continued residency in North Carolina. Through his influence, the Haywood County Court sent a memorial to Governor Edward B. Dudley, averring that the Qualla Indians were peaceful and industrious, making progress in civilization, and had already become citizens. The Indians themselves beseeched the state to extend its protection over them, noting that North Carolina had always treated them kindly. The General Assembly responded in January 1837 by passing an act which set up means to protect the Indians from fraud and which was to go into effect *after* the expected removal of most of the tribe. Only in this indirect, tacit fashion did the state acknowledge the right of Quallatown Indians to remain. And in no way did the state endorse their claim to citizenship. Despite this, sixty Qualla heads of families, representing 333 Indians, petitioned the federal commissioners to allow them "to continue" as citizens of North Carolina. Preliminary approval for them to remain was granted in September 1837, but the commissioners deferred final endorsement.[52] The Qualla Indians would have to endure uncertainty and anxiety as they watched the army round up their fellow Cherokees and deport them to the West.

2

RESISTING REMOVAL

After ratification of the Treaty of New Echota, federal officials and army officers began assessing the difficulty of enforcing it. To Brigadier General John Wool it was obvious that the vast majority of the Cherokee Nation opposed removal, none more so than the North Carolina members. And by the time Major General Winfield Scott arrived in the spring of 1838, there were rumors that the Indians were planning to fall back to the Great Smoky Mountains and wage guerrilla warfare against their white oppressors. The savage resistance of the Seminoles in Florida brought a sense of foreboding, and local militia units began organizing on the presumed threat of an Indian war.

In this atmosphere of incipient hysteria, the placid assurance of the Quallatown Indians that they were exempt from removal infuriated some of their white neighbors. Dr. M. Killian, a surgeon, complained to Governor Dudley that William Thomas's clients were poor, "debauched creatures" who still survived mainly by hunting. According to him, many of the Indians from the eastern portion of the Cherokee Nation had found refuge among them or had fled to the "interstices" of the mountains. Defenseless whites faced annihilation from "a number of baffled, and disappointed savages, driven from their homes through fear, and as they believe through fraud." Warming to his subject, he warned against "those merciless savages bursting forth in fury, from those huge, rough mountains, like a mighty torrent—rolling its rapid floods down those numerous rivulets, and overspreading that entire frontier in ruin and devastation, without leaving one weaping [sic] babe, to relate that fatal transaction." The florid rhetoric—if not the substance—was enough for the governor to demand a response from Thomas, who, along with a few other whites, reassured him about the true nature of the Indians.[3]

Though General Scott realized the Quallatown band had an

20

anomalous status, he believed they would be well advised to move west with their brethren. He even employed the Reverend Jesse Bushyhead to try to persuade them, but Yonaguska's people stubbornly rejected the minister's arguments. While Scott mulled over this situation, Thomas assured officers the Quallatown Indians would not provide refuge for fugitives from the Cherokee Nation. He was also buying the first of what would become thousands of acres of mountain land for his clients' future use. In the meantime they would have to tread softly in their moccasins and avoid controversy.[4]

[Scott's removal of the Cherokee Nation is one of the most familiar—and distressing—stories in the annals of Indian-white relations. Moving into the remotest corners of the Nation, soldiers rounded up thousands of Indians and temporarily incarcerated them in makeshift stockades before dispatching them westward over the infamous Trail of Tears. Many are the tales of Indian families accosted in their cabins and having just a moment to gather a few possessions before leaving forever.] As General Wool had predicted, those in North Carolina were hardest to evict, some slipping away into the mountains to avoid the soldiers.[5]

A few Cherokees did not bother to flee but openly defied the government. Hog Bite, a hermit of Cartoogechaye Creek who was supposedly ninety-seven years old, threatened removal agents with a gun nearly as ancient as himself. They wisely decided not to test his resolve, reasoning that he was too old to make the trip west and would soon die anyhow. (Hog Bite fooled them. More than a decade later he was still alive and vigorous.)[6] At the direction of federal authorities, other elderly Indians were also allowed to live out their final years undisturbed. But the rest of the Cherokees, except those living at Qualla or possessing the proper certificates, were expected to leave.

[William Thomas's desire to dissociate the Quallatown Indians from those who were being removed involved him and his charges in what has become the single most romantic tale of the Eastern Band's history, the saga of Tsali (known as "Charley" to whites of his day). Any student investigating the Band and their resistance to removal must deal with this now legendary figure and assess his actual role in the events. Accounts vary, but the most prevalent story, first related by the ethnologist James Mooney, can be quickly summarized. Tsali and his family were among the Cherokees rounded up by the army in preparation for their enforced removal. During their march to the holding camp, Tsali's wife was brutally mistreated by the soldiers. Enraged, Tsali killed one of his captors and escaped with his family into the mountains, where several hundred other Indians were already hiding. General Scott had already removed most of the Cherokee Nation, and the relatively few fugitives were occupying rugged terrain that was of little value. So, the story goes, he agreed to ignore most of the fugitives—in effect giving his tacit consent for them to remain in North Carolina—if they would turn in Tsali and his accomplices in murder. When informed of this, Tsali said he did not wish to have his own people track him down, and he surrendered voluntarily. As a final humiliation, the army required the other fugitive Cherokees to execute him, two of his sons, and a brother.[7]

From this often-told account the heroic Tsali emerges.[8] He sacrificed his own life so that his people, later to become the Eastern Band, could remain in their homeland. Today the hagiography of Tsali takes its most visible form in the romanticized outdoor pageant *Unto These Hills*, witnessed annually by thousands of tourists visiting the Qualla Boundary Reservation and the town of Cherokee, North Carolina. The pageant purports to depict the origins of the Eastern Band and devotes considerable attention to his heroic role.[9]

As is true with most hagiography, the facts are somewhat different. Tsali was an old, illiterate fullblood who lived with his family near the mouth of the Nantahala River at the time of the 1835 census. As a member of the Cherokee Nation, he was expected to leave with the rest. But he, his wife, and assorted relatives became fugitives as they sought to avoid the army's dragnet in the fall of 1838. This had been their only "crime." Enter now William Thomas. Believing that those Indians evading removal might jeopardize the right of the Quallatown band to remain, he assisted the army in its roundup and unwittingly became a central figure in the drama.[10]

On October 30, 1838, Second Lieutenant Andrew Jackson Smith, of the First U.S. Dragoons, was returning to Fort Cass, Tennessee, with a detachment of soldiers and sixteen Indian prisoners when he learned that Tsali's little band was camped nearby. Sending most of his force ahead with the prisoners, Smith and three enlisted men, accompanied by Thomas, located the fugitives' camp on a steep cliff near where the Tuckasegee joins the Little Tennessee. There were eight Indians in camp, all of whom surrendered "with-

22

out difficulty or resistance." But it was Smith's understanding that twenty belonged to the group. Hoping the remainder would come in and surrender, he kept the Indians under guard until the total number of captives had risen to twelve—five men, including Tsali, and seven women and children.[11]

On the morning of November 1, Smith set out with his three enlisted men and twelve prisoners, expecting to join the rest of his command before nightfall. For some unexplained reason, Thomas did not accompany them. The day passed uneventfully, but that evening Smith suspected there might be trouble and warned his men to be on guard. Soon afterward an Indian suddenly produced a hidden axe and buried it in the forehead of a soldier. In the next few confused moments the Cherokees killed a second soldier, wounded the third, and would have dispatched Smith if his horse had not become frightened and run away. After taking various articles from their victims, the Indians fled into the mountains.[12]

Thomas rejoined Smith the evening of the murders and then accompanied him to Fort Cass, where the officer wrote his official report to his immediate superior, Lieutenant C.H. Larned. This document was dated November 5, as was Larned's report to General Scott at his headquarters. By this time word of the incident had already spread like wildfire. On November 4 John Ross, preparing to lead the final detachment of his people west, sent his condolences to Scott, adding that the murders were an "individual" occurrence for which the Cherokee Nation could not be held responsible. He hoped those guilty would be captured and punished. And that same day Colonel William S. Foster, commander of the Fourth Infantry Regiment, was busily making preparations on Scott's orders to pursue the slayers. On November 6, having received the official reports of Smith and Larned, Scott informed the War Department of the recent events and summoned both Thomas and Foster to a conference. Thomas's expertise in Indian matters would make him most useful on Foster's punitive expedition.[13]

Scott's succinct orders to Foster, dated November 7, specified three main objectives: (1) "The Individuals guilty of this unprovoked outrage must be shot down"; (2) the white families living in the area must be protected; and (3) Foster must "collect all, or as many as practicable, of the fugitives (other than the murderers) for emigration." Scott was careful, however, to distinguish between Thomas's Oconaluftee Indians and the fugitives. The former were "not to be considered fugitives, or to be interrupted, if they continue, as heretofore, peaceable & orderly," while the latter "can now only be considered as so many outlaws."[14]

Scott reported to the War Department that most of the Cherokees were indignant over the murders and that it would be easy to obtain the services of many warriors in apprehending the killers. "I shall, however, only accept the services of a few runners . . . deeming it against the honor of the United States to employ, in hostilities, one part of a tribe against another." On the other hand, he had no qualms about using Thomas and his Indian wards: "Col. Foster will also have the aid, as runners, guides, and interpreters, of some of Mr. Thomas's Oconeelufty Indians, as well as the personal services of Mr. Thomas himself, who takes a lively interest in the success of the expedition."[15]

Thomas refused Scott's offer of liberal compensation by saying he did not want anyone to question his motives. After setting out with Foster and the troops, he soon moved ahead to enlist the aid of his Oconaluftee friends. Upon arriving at Quallatown, he dispatched some warriors to locate Euchella (Oochella or Utsala), the same Cherokee who had successfully defended his reservation in the state supreme court fifteen years before. Though he had since sold his property and moved within the Cherokee Nation, he still claimed to be a citizen of North Carolina. Not trusting the soldiers to adhere to legalities, he had fled to the mountains. Now he was a fugitive, leading a ragged, starving handful of people. His wife and son had recently died of hunger while in hiding, and the old warrior was understandably bitter toward the whites. Yet he could be of immeasurable assistance in finding his former neighbor and friend, Tsali. Thomas conveyed to Euchella the prospect of remaining in North Carolina with the Qualla band if he and his followers would aid in capturing the murderers. After considering the proposition a while, Euchella arrived in Quallatown on November 12, ready to lead his men in pursuit of Tsali. The Oconaluftee provided an additional force under the command of Flying Squirrel, bringing the total number of Indians engaged in the manhunt to about sixty.[16]

The most important information concerning the pursuit of Tsali is included in several letters and enclosures sent by Foster to Scott. The first, dated November 11, 1838, was from a farm on the Little Tennessee River, eighty miles from Fort Cass. Foster had nine companies of the Fourth Infantry with him, while the tenth company, a mounted unit under Lieutenant Larned, was well in advance. Foster described the difficult country and then noted the fear among white inhabitants of more hostilities. His second letter, dated November 15, was written at "Camp Scott" on the Little Tennessee in Macon County. He said that Lieutenant Larned and William Thomas, with the mounted company, had left for the Oconaluftee River "in pursuit of old Charley and his sons." Captain George A. McCall had taken a company of men and two Indian guides to the mouth of Deep Creek (the site of present-day Bryson City) and was following it into the mountains to its source; from that point he would cut eastward and link up with Larned, who was working his way westward from the Oconaluftee and its branches. Other officers, each with competent guides, were scouring nearby areas.[17]

Foster informed Scott that he had already accomplished one of his assignments—namely, to protect and reassure the "poor and ignorant population" of the area. A second order, to assemble the fugitives other than the murderers, would also be easy to achieve inasmuch as they numbered fewer than one hundred and were starving. But the primary goal, to capture and punish the murderers, "is from the smallness of their numbers & the nature of the country yet doubtful." Foster assured Scott, however, that his men and allies were on the trail of the culprits, "and these mountains can never again be a place of refuge to them." He did not mention that his allies included Euchella's band and the Oconaluftee Indians, who had been hunting Tsali for several days.[18]

On November 19 Foster announced to Scott "that I have *captured* (through the exertions of Mr. Thomas, the O. co ne lufty Indians, and Euchella's band, headed by himself) two of the murderers." They were Tsali's oldest son, Nantayalee Jake, and Nantayalee (or Big) George, who, according to Foster, "were the principal actors in the murder." Also taken prisoner were Tsali's wife and the wife and little daughter of George. Euchella's men and the Oconaluftee, by then numbering about forty, were aiding the mounted company "in close pursuit" of the other fugitives. Of the three men still uncaptured, Foster said, only one, Lowen, "was active in the murder." Thus, Foster's informants indicated that at most Tsali had played only a minor role in the killings.[19]

Just five days later, on November 24, Foster triumphantly notified Scott that his mission was finished. Of the twelve Indians held as prisoners by Lieutenant Smith at the time of the murders, all but Tsali had been captured. Three adult males "were punished yesterday morning by the Cherokees themselves in the presence of the 4th Regt. of Infantry." Only in this indirect manner did Foster acknowledge the executions that had taken place. With his Indian allies, he had tried the captives in military fashion. William Thomas later said the murderers still had the caps and other items taken from the dead soldiers.[20] Foster and his Indian allies agreed that three of the prisoners deserved death. Six Cherokee executioners were selected, two to fire at each of the condemned men; one was to aim at the head and the other at the heart. After Foster blindfolded the prisoners, they were shot and buried near the graves of the two soldiers they had slain.[21] Foster said he spared Tsali's teenaged son, Washington (Wasituna), because of his youth.[22]

According to Thomas, the Indians believed it almost an obligation to perform the executions themselves. Euchella, he said, told the doomed men "they must die for their offense, as the ancient custom existing between the whites and Cherokees required life for life. They were then, as in the practice of the Cherokees, shot by his warriors." On the other hand, it is possible Euchella and the other Cherokees viewed the executions not as an "ancient custom" but simply as an unpleasant necessity. Regardless of what the army actually required of them, they perhaps believed they had to perform the task in order to retain Colonel Foster's favor.[23]

In his letter to Scott of November 24, Foster included a strong plea that Euchella and his band be allowed to remain in North Carolina. He enclosed a petition signed by thirty-one white residents of the area who testified that Euchella's band was "a well disposed, peaceable, inoffensive, body of people, mostly women and children principally unarmed & few in number" who had been "very useful to us." They asked that the band be permitted to remain until the federal government could decide on the matter of their final residence. The same day he wrote to Scott, Foster issued a proclamation that allowed Euchella and his group to stay in North Carolina "as associates and Brothers" of the Oconaluftee Indians until the government decided otherwise.[24]

Following the executions, Foster gathered Euchella and his warriors together and told them that removal had officially ended and they should notify any Indians still in hiding to join their brothers at Quallatown. As runners carried the happy news throughout the mountains, little knots of Cherokees materialized like apparitions in the cold mist, taking the trails to Quallatown. There were enough of them to challenge the colonel's blithe assumption that only a few remained.[25]

It was logical for Foster to view his mission as completed, believing as he did that the uncaptured Tsali was not a principal figure. And, in any case, the officer had so much confidence in the Cherokees that he was willing to leave the lonely old man to their justice. The Fourth Infantry left the mountains on November 24, and later that same day Wachucha and a few others of Euchella's band captured Tsali. Euchella soon joined them, and at noon on the following day they executed Tsali in the same way as the others. There is nothing to suggest that he had surrendered voluntarily. Thus, as Thomas noted, the Cherokees themselves had accomplished in a few days what might have taken the army "months, and probably years" to conclude.[26]

In his final letter to Scott, that of December 3, Foster reported from Tennessee on the capture and execution of Tsali. He made a special point of commending Yonaguska for his assistance and again requested that Euchella's band be allowed to remain with Thomas and the Qualla Indians. Scott believed Foster had handled his mission with his usual "intelligence, judgment & success" and expressed neither surprise nor dismay over the colonel's actions regarding Euchella. In January 1839 the commissioners for Cherokee removal officially agreed to permit Euchella's band to stay with the Quallatown people.[27]

Within the next few years the legend of a heroic Tsali began to blossom. In 1843 Jonas Jenkins, a white man, testified that he had been an eyewitness to the Indian's execution. As Jenkins recalled it, the unfortunate man had asked Euchella to look after his surviving family members and had then faced his executioners with calm, dignified courage. This sober, matter-of-fact account has the ring of truth and was apparently the first small step in the emergence of the heroic Tsali. It may have been the inspiration for the 1849 account of Charles Lanman, a Whig journalist who portrayed Tsali making an impassioned speech before his execution in which he expressed his love for his homeland and family and rebuked Euchella. Although this smacks of the "noble savage" literary genre, Lanman had been a recent guest of Thomas and had presumably heard of Tsali from him—and perhaps from Jenkins and Tsali's son. It may be that Thomas thought a little embellishment of the episode would dramatize the love of the Cherokees for their homeland. And half a century later James Mooney added pathos to drama by describing

Tsali's supposed "sacrifice." Until recently the reassuring image of a Cherokee martyr has been unquestioned.[28]

It is now necessary to view the Tsali incident in a somewhat different light from that of the heroic legend. First, there is no documentary evidence to support the charge that soldiers mistreated Tsali and his band. This does not mean such cruelty did not occur—merely that a reasonable doubt exists as to the army's culpability in the drama. Furthermore, if one is to believe Colonel Foster and his informants, the younger male Indians rather than Tsali were the principal actors in the murders. As for Thomas, it is obvious he was an important participant in the events, but there is no evidence to support Mooney's tale of his visiting Tsali's lair after the murders and personally convincing the Indian to surrender.[29] The documentary accounts, moreover, make it clear that Tsali did not surrender at all but was tracked down by other Cherokees, apprehended, and executed by them. Thus, there was no noble sacrifice. And last, the capture and execution of Tsali little affected the right of the Qualla Cherokees to remain in North Carolina. They already had at least tacit permission to stay. Only Euchella's small band directly benefited from the episode.[30]

Finally, although Tsali does not measure up to his legend, he may at least be viewed as heroic insofar as he resisted enforcement of an unjust, arbitrary policy—Cherokee removal. Unfortunately, we have no way of knowing what his thoughts or motives were. But quite apart from what he actually did or his reasons for doing it, he provides a legitimate symbol for the Eastern Band of Cherokees, affirming their traditional attachment to their homeland. As long as his legend has meaning to his people it will endure.

By the end of 1838 the majority of Cherokees were already in the West. John Ross and other tribal leaders had acquiesced in their inevitable departure, taking with them their bitter hostility toward the "treaty party." As they resurrected the Cherokee Nation in present-day Oklahoma, they quickly settled old scores, resorting to intrigue and even murder against those who had betrayed them. The vituperation and factionalism would continue for years after removal, complicating federal relations with the tribe.[31]

In the meantime, those Cherokees who had avoided removal were dismissed by the economy-minded War Department as not worth the trouble and expense to remove (perhaps the appalling costs of the Seminole War served as an object lesson). If North Carolina did not object, they could stay, subject to her laws.[32] Approximately

700 Cherokees resided in and around Quallatown, consisting of the original inhabitants and refugees from other settlements. Most of the latter had lost their land, improvements, and crops, which federal agents had sold at fire-sale rates. During the harsh winter of 1838–1839 they had even been reduced to scavenging for food. Another 400 North Carolina Cherokees were scattered along the Cheoah, Valley, and Hiwassee rivers, making a total of about 1,100 in the state.[33] Following the Treaty of New Echota, the state disposed of the former Indian lands to white farmers and speculators. Although a few Cherokees retained their own property, the majority were unacculturated fullbloods who were forced onto less desirable lands owned by friendly whites or the state.[34]

Another 300 or so Cherokees East (as they were sometimes called) resided in nearby areas of Georgia, Tennessee, and Alabama. These included a number of mixed-bloods and whites who were Cherokees only by marriage. They often owned their own land, sometimes a few slaves, and in general were more acculturated than their North Carolina kinsmen. The total number of Cherokees remaining in the Southeast, then, was about 1,400.[35]

Now that most of the Indians had departed, the whites seemed little concerned about the Cherokee remnant that remained on the periphery of their day-to-day experience. The Indians were inoffensive and inconspicuous, and William Thomas was buying property on which they could live without disrupting white settlers. The occasional letter or petition to the governor advocating removal provoked little response. In November 1839 Governor Dudley forwarded one such petition to the secretary of war with a covering letter that was more an inquiry about removal than a request. Congressman James Graham, who represented western North Carolina, favored emigration of the Indians but was content to inquire periodically what the federal government planned to do about it. Commissioner of Indian Affairs T. Hartley Crawford replied that the Cherokees had a right under Article 12 to remain in the Southeast if they chose. In his annual report of 1839 he expressed a willingness to help them move west if they so desired, but he did not believe the government had an obligation to persuade them. By July 1841 Graham seemed resigned to the probability the Cherokees would remain in his district.[36]

Between 1839 and 1841 some of the Indians at least pondered rejoining the Cherokee Nation, but the intratribal factionalism and unhealthy climate of Indian Territory, along with a deep, abiding

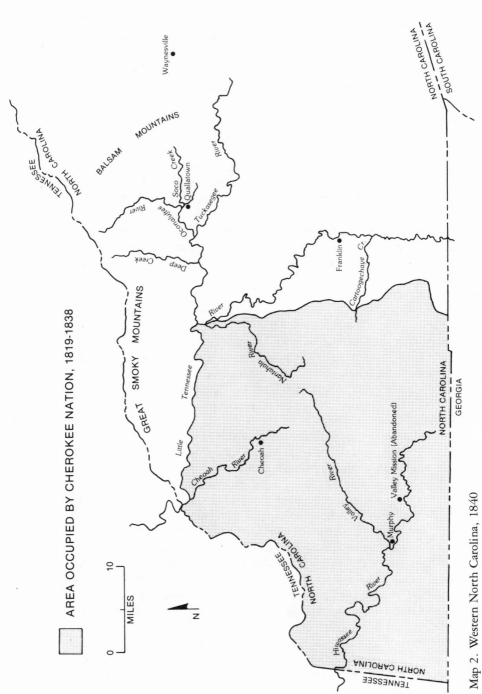

AREA OCCUPIED BY CHEROKEE NATION, 1819-1838

Map 2. Western North Carolina, 1840

love of their homeland, persuaded almost all to remain where they were. As Yonaguska lay dying in the spring of 1839, he was carried before his people and, in a dramatic whisper that reflected his oratorical brilliance, warned them never to forsake their mountains. It was his final injunction, a message that remained imprinted in the memories of those who heard him. They would never leave.[37]

Flying Squirrel later claimed to have succeeded Yonaguska in 1839, but it is clear that Thomas was the de facto chief of the Quallatown Cherokees. He directed them in many aspects of their daily lives and was frequently in Washington representing their financial claims against the government. These were based on various treaty provisions and involved per capita payments, spoliations, individual allotments, preemption rights, and loss of improvements. John Ross and other tribal officials argued similar claims for the majority who had emigrated. Thomas's persistence was rewarded in July 1840 when the Indian Office appointed him to take a census of the Cherokees remaining east of the Mississippi River and to serve as disbursing agent to pay part of the money due them.[38]

Many claims remained unsettled, however, and the legal tangle was extraordinarily complex. As it turned out, this situation provided a catalyst for renewed federal efforts to remove the Cherokees from the Southeast. By September 1841 both the Cherokee Nation and the Indian Office preferred to settle all remaining claims at the same time in the traditional way, by negotiating a new treaty. But this was impossible as long as some claimants lived apart from the Cherokee Nation as supposed citizens of the states. The obvious solution was for all Cherokees to come together in the West as members of the Nation and then conclude a new treaty.[39]

Late in September, Acting Secretary of War Albert M. Lea discussed the matter with Thomas C. Hindman, an Alabamian with close connections to the Ross family. Hindman suggested that Lea dispatch a special agent to North Carolina to explain to the Cherokees why it was in their best interests to rejoin the Nation. As long as they claimed state citizenship they could not enjoy the guardianship and protection of the federal government. If they moved west, they would enjoy equal rights with their Cherokee brothers and have a chance to prosper. Their claims against the United States would be included in the new treaty then being considered between the Nation and the government. Hindman suggested sending a delegation of two or three Cherokees from the

East to assess the situation in the Nation, confident they would return favoring such a move.[40]

Hindman also told Lea that as long as the Cherokees remained in North Carolina they would lack even a shadow of title to the poor lands they occupied. According to him, "designing" whites had used the Cherokees' money ostensibly to purchase lands in the Indians' behalf, while actually retaining title in their own names. This was a thinly veiled attack on William Thomas, who had already bought more than 50,000 acres in scattered tracts as a kind of restored homeland for his Indian clients. Hindman said that Thomas's influence was blinding the Indians to their own interests, and he implied the merchant had been dishonest in serving as disbursing agent. Therefore, Hindman told Lea, the special Cherokee agent should not only encourage removal but also replace Thomas, collect his accounts and unspent monies, and investigate any charges of misconduct against him.[41]

Hindman's insinuation about Thomas found a ready audience in the Indian Office, where Commissioner Crawford was already exasperated by Thomas's failure, after repeated warnings, to send his accounts and census. Consequently, on September 29 the office appointed Hindman special agent to replace Thomas as disbursing agent. More important, he was to collect information relating to the remaining claims of the Cherokees East, encourage those people to migrate west, and promise that "the government will take immediate measures for their removal if they desire it."[42]

Hindman was armed with a message from President Tyler to the Cherokees, explaining the agent's mission and informing them that their "continuing as residents of a state, necessarily embarrasses, if indeed it does not render ineffectual" the president's desire to extend his "paternal care and protection" over them. Counseling them "as a father, who would discountenance even the appearance of compulsion," he advised them to consider joining their brethren in the West. If they wished, they could send a small delegation to the Cherokee Nation to report back on the desirability of such a move.[43]

Thomas was dismayed by his dismissal and even more so by Hindman's appointment, though in a letter to the Indian Office he said, "I have no objections to his investigating what I have done." But he suggested that Hindman and the Ross family were conspiring against him because he had opposed some allegedly fraudulent claims they had submitted to the government. And he could not resist a melodramatic reference to the murders in the Cherokee

Nation by implying that the hands of Ross and his supporters were dripping with blood and that, just possibly, he might be the next victim.[44]

On December 5, Hindman arrived at his base of operations in Murphy, North Carolina. By then the magnitude of his task had become apparent, and he was no longer so sanguine. He wrote the Office that he would try to finish his mission as soon as possible, but the natural disposition of the Indians was to act slowly. They were scattered over miles of mountainous country, were under the influence of unscrupulous whites, and had a natural aversion to removal that required time to overcome. Perhaps he was aware that less than two months before, 618 North Carolina Cherokees, upset by news of his appointment, had sent a memorial to President Tyler opposing removal and expressing their distrust of both Ross and Hindman. In any case, the agent was obviously sensitive to the Office's concern for promptness and economy.[45]

Hindman's first efforts proved fruitless. After hiring as interpreter John Timson, the prominent mixed-blood freeholder, he visited the Cherokee community at Valley River, not far from Murphy. On December 15 he met with about forty-five of these Indians at the home of John Welch, another mixed-blood, and found them adamantly opposed to emigration. When the agent requested an opportunity to address the entire community before the Indians made their decision, the group said such a meeting was unnecessary. No one wanted to move west, and sending a delegation would serve no purpose. Hindman attributed this rebuff to the influence of Mrs. Welch, a white woman supposedly in collusion with Thomas.[46]

Two days later Hindman met with Thomas, and though they remained civil with one another, the agent was still suspicious of Thomas and his motives. Nonetheless, he found it necessary to seek his assistance in arranging councils at the other Indian communities. For the rest of December and well into January 1842, Thomas obligingly accompanied the agent through the snows and cold rains as he visited various Cherokee towns. He probably did this to retain such favor as he still possessed within the Indian Office, where he had a number of claims under review. Hindman believed that Thomas's only real service occurred when he helped locate a number of Indians who had fled to the mountains in a deep snow. But the agent claimed they had done so only because Thomas had told them Hindman intended to round them up and send the whole group west. Mostly, the agent charged, Thomas used his influence indirectly "and I might say almost directly against the wishes of the Govt." He suggested the merchant wanted the Indians to stay because they owed him a large amount of money for the poor, mountainous land he had acquired in their behalf.[47]

The council at Quallatown typified Hindman's futile efforts. About 150 chiefs and warriors listened attentively as he explained the advantages of removal and assured them his purpose was not to turn them against Thomas, who, he was certain, was an honest man (obviously, the agent felt it unwise to express his true feelings). But what would become of them when Thomas died? They would have no one to look after their interests. It was only logical for them to send a delegation to the Cherokee Nation to assess the situation there. After deliberating a short time, the Indians declined the offer; they would remain where they were.[48]

Despite this unequivocal rejection, Hindman expressed some optimism in his report to the Indian Office. Although he planned to return home, he thought it would be worthwhile for Timson to pay periodic visits to the Cherokee communities to encourage removal. By such efforts, Hindman believed, some 200 to 300 Indians might be ready to emigrate by fall. Yet he in effect conceded his failure by suggesting that the Indian Office cease further payment of claims until the Cherokees emigrated, a proposal that clearly conflicted with the president's disavowal of any hint of coercion. And even in the face of Cherokee refusal to send a delegation, he again recommended the government organize such a visit.[49]

The Indian Office, however, no longer favored sending a delegation west or even encouraging Cherokee removal. Hindman's own reports made it apparent the Indians did not want to emigrate, and organizing a delegation or keeping Timson in the field seemed unlikely to improve the situation. Besides, it would be expensive, and the Office—indeed, the entire Tyler administration— was preoccupied with economy. On February 1, Commissioner Crawford notified the agent that his and Timson's employment had been terminated. Albert Lea regarded Hindman's failure as evidence of the Indians' unwillingness to believe the government's promises and professions of goodwill, for which he conceded they had ample justification in past experience.[50]

During the next few months several new developments persuaded the Indian Office to revise its Cherokee policy once again. In May, Timson assured Congressman Graham that many North Carolina

Cherokees had finally confronted reality and now wished to move west. He advocated opening an office in Cherokee County to enroll them for emigration and to assist in paying their debts before leaving.[51] Meanwhile, many people, including the Cherokees East, their creditors, Congressman Graham, and other legislators, were pressuring the Indian Office to organize a new board of commissioners to adjudicate the multitude of claims arising from the Treaty of New Echota. This, the second such board, was necessary as long as the Cherokees East claimed to be citizens. The 1835 treaty was the last one affecting them, and new treaties could not be negotiated with supposed citizens.[52]

Another possible stimulus to Indian Office action was the increasing interest of Congress in Cherokee matters. There had been widespread allegations about corruption and mismanagement during the 1838 removal, and legislators were determined to learn the financial details. The congressional resolutions calling for complete information about the expenditures and alleged fraud may well have reminded Indian Office officials that the original goal of Cherokee emigration remained unfulfilled.[53]

What emerged, then, in the summer of 1842 was a new approach by the Indian Office to its Cherokee business. The president would appoint a new board of commissioners, which would examine the claims of the Cherokees East, and the Office would again encourage those Indians to emigrate west. If reports were correct, there was growing interest among them for such a move. The processing of their claims would restore faith in the intentions and promises of the government. Removing them peaceably and on honorable terms would also meet with the approbation of many white citizens and their representatives in Congress. The board of commissioners would then attend to the claims of the Cherokee Nation, or, if necessary, the Indian Office could negotiate a new treaty. A major concern in all these undertakings was to maintain strict economy so as to avoid further trouble from an inquisitive Congress.

It seems more than mere coincidence that on July 9, the day the House passed a resolution asking for information about the costs of the 1838 removal, Secretary of War John C. Spencer told Ross and his visiting delgation that it was desirable the Cherokees East join the Cherokee Nation "as soon as circumstances may permit." When Spencer sought assurance that the Nation would accept their brethren on equitable terms, the delegation promised that the Cherokees

East would be welcomed "with much joy & satisfaction" and would have "the same rights and immunities" as other members of the Nation.[54]

By late summer a new board of commissioners had been organized and James Robinson, a merchant from Franklin, North Carolina, appointed special agent to persuade the Cherokees East to emigrate. His assistant was to be the ubiquitous and faithful John Timson. Robinson's instructions from the Indian Office went well beyond those issued to Hindman, providing for enrollment and specifying the manner in which emigration was to take place. After enrolling, the Cherokees were to undertake removal on their own, preferably in groups of from fifty to one hundred. Observing the terms of the 1835 treaty, the government would pay each individual a total of $53.33, of which $20 was to cover the cost of transportation and $33.33 the cost of subsistence for one year in the West. But Commissioner Crawford carefully prescribed the manner of payment. He would not allow commutation—that is, payment in advance to the Indian. The first third of the $20 for transportation would be paid only when the emigrant was "fairly under way," the second third when he or she had crossed the Mississippi River, and the rest upon arrival in the Cherokee Nation. The emigrant would receive none of the subsistence payment until he had actually settled in the West. In this way the government hoped to ensure that the Indians would actually move, at minimum cost and inconvenience to the United States.[55]

Meanwhile other Cherokees besides John Timson were professing strong interest in making the move. Without doubt, the most articulate was William Rogers of Forsyth County, Georgia. At first he had been suspicious of the new removal policy, fearing it had been concocted by Ross simply to enrich himself and force negotiation of a new treaty. Now, with the assurances of the Cherokee Nation, he had come to support removal on the grounds that his people would no longer have to eat crumbs from the white man's table. In the face of such pervasive prejudice against them, their own self-esteem dictated their removal. William Thomas was a good man, Rogers admitted, but someday he would die and those Indians who had been dependent on him would be helpless, left without title to the lands Thomas controlled in their behalf.[56]

Rogers and the other acculturated Cherokees, those of mixed blood or Cherokees by marriage, were not hesitant about specifying the conditions of their removal. Those who owned land wanted assurance of a fair price, a promise not easily secured during the hard times that still lingered after the panic of 1837. Others demanded payment of their claims by the new board of commissioners before emigrating. Still others insisted on commutation of their transportation and subsistence, and a few were so bold as to ask for more than $53.33. But Commissioner Crawford viewed such demands as attempts to take advantage of the government and rejected them.[57]

While Robinson and Timson worked at enrollment, the state of North Carolina took belated action on the Cherokees. On December 31, 1842, the General Assembly agreed to establish a joint select committee on Indian removal, which soon received petitions and memorials from whites and Indians alike. A petition from some citizens of Haywood County was quite sympathetic toward the Cherokees, conceding they had made considerable progress, asking that justice be done to them in their claims, and suggesting that after the elderly Indians had died the rest would wish to emigrate.[58] This moderate view had earlier been summarized by a visitor to Haywood County who, after noting that "the best understanding exists" between the whites and Indians, said that a treaty to "provide for the removal of the Cherokees West in a friendly way at some future day as they may desire to go, after the old & infirm are no more, would give Satisfaction Generally."[59] A memorial from Cherokee County was likewise moderate, noting that emigration was in the Indians' own interest and that, if they remained, they should assume some of the less attractive responsibilities of the citizenship they claimed, such as working on public roads.[60]

In a memorial addressed to the "Chiefs" of North Carolina, the Cherokees of Quallatown affirmed their intention of remaining under the protection of a state that historically had been kind to them. They claimed they had made significant advances in the mechanical arts, Christianity, temperance, and other aspects of "civilized" life. They were willing to assume all burdens of citizenship, including working on the public roads, and they emphasized their patriotism by pointing out that their people had helped Andrew Jackson achieve victory over the Creeks at the Battle of Horseshoe Bend.[61]

Late in January 1843 the joint select committee expressed a fear that western North Carolina might become a haven both for Indians with a legal right to live there (like those at Quallatown) and also for the "refuse" of the Cherokee Nation, who were supposedly drifting back from the West. In the opinion of the committee, "The mixing of these people with our white population must have a demoralizing influence which ought to be resisted by all the means within our power." It proposed a resolution asking the president to do all he could to remove the Cherokees from the state in conformity with the Treaty of New Echota. Though the House of Commons passed the resolution, the Senate tabled it after the second reading. Clearly, the state of North Carolina did not consider removal a momentous issue.[62]

Robinson had been unable to accomplish much in the way of enrolling Indians by the time he died in June 1843 from a fever. Timson continued on his own, despite opposition from Thomas and others, until Robinson's successor, James W. Deaderick, arrived in August. A Tennessean and minor functionary in the Indian Office, Deaderick immediately succumbed to the same unwarranted optimism that had infected his predecessors, believing that removal would not prove difficult. According to the preliminary rolls he sent the Indian Office, between 300 and 400 Indians planned to move, and he predicted the number would soon double.[63]

While Deaderick continued his efforts, critics were busy attacking the removal scheme. Among these was Felix Axley, a lawyer from Cherokee County who, like Thomas, represented a number of Indian claimants. In a letter to Commissioner Crawford he insisted that only a few mixed-bloods and "worthless" whites with Cherokee families were interested in moving; the true Indians would never do so willingly. Perhaps anticipating the responsiveness of an economy-minded bureaucrat, he called the whole program a waste of time and money. The same point was made by J.W. King, a clerk in one of William Thomas's stores, who expressed amazement at the government's costly and fruitless course. And a council of Valley River Cherokees, in a memorial sent to Congressman Thomas L. Clingman, denounced the expense of keeping enrolling agents at work when the Indians steadfastly refused to leave. They would not emigrate, they vowed, even if the government tried to blackmail them by refusing to pay their claims.[64]

Axley's letter prompted Commissioner Crawford to ask Deaderick for a more complete list of the Cherokees intending to emigrate, designating those who were actually whites with Indian spouses and any who had received their transportation and subsistence money in 1838. The latter would not be eligible for additional federal assistance. Deaderick's revised lists shocked Crawford. One showed that 320 Cherokees or Cherokee-related whites hoped even-

38

tually to emigrate, along with 140 slaves. But 33 of the 75 families had white heads of household, and most on the list lived in Georgia and Tennessee rather than the Cherokee heartland of western North Carolina. The other list indicated that fewer than 200 of these people, including slaves, were actually prepared to emigrate, assuming certain conditions were met. If nothing else, these figures proved Axley's contention that most prospective emigrants were not the "real," relatively unacculturated Cherokees.[65]

Though Deaderick continued to be sanguine, Crawford was disgusted that so little had been accomplished in over two years, and on January 31, 1844, he advised Secretary of War James M. Porter that it was not worth the expense to enroll Cherokees for removal. The state of North Carolina seemed unconcerned about the matter, and the recent memorial from the Valley River Cherokees had requested they not be annoyed any more by federal agents. According to Crawford, the Office of Indian Affairs had merely been trying to assist both North Carolina and the Cherokees by its emigration program. But if neither the state nor the Indians wanted removal, it was hardly worth the trouble. If any eligible Cherokees were seriously interested, they could move west on their own and be reimbursed by the government upon arrival in the Cherokee Nation. Porter agreed with Crawford's assessment, and on February 2 the commissioner notified both Deaderick and Timson that their services were "at once dispensed with."[66] The second Cherokee "removal" had folded like a second-rate road show. In the years immediately afterward, perhaps fifty or so of the more acculturated Cherokees moved to the West on their own, while probably as many moved back from the Cherokee Nation.[67]

The removal program of 1841–1844, like that of 1836–1838, sprang from an amalgam of governmental self-interest and altruism. Commissioner Crawford, an enlightened administrator, sincerely believed removal would benefit the Indians, a conviction no doubt shared by President Tyler and other officials.[68] Governmental self-interest, however, appears to have been a more salient feature than concern for the Indians. In 1841 both the Indian Office and the Cherokee Nation viewed removal as a means of facilitating a new treaty that would resolve the many issues between the two. It was a misconception, of course, that the Indians *wanted* to move or could be persuaded to do so, and in their resistance they were immeasurably aided by William Thomas, who was thoroughly familiar with the labyrinths of power in Washington. Another factor was the self-defeating parsimony of an administration that was unwilling to spend more than $2,500 on the entire three-year program.[69] The lack of strong support in North Carolina also affected the outcome. Tyler, a states'-rights advocate, would never have dreamed of trying to enforce such a policy in a state where it was not popular. Besides, even a nominal Whig like himself preferred an Indian policy that would favorably contrast with the aggressive, coercive program of the Jacksonian Democrats. And considering how doggedly the Cherokees had resisted the first removal program, it was almost a certainty they would bide their time patiently until the inevitable frustration and swirling political currents in Washington brought yet another respite from the pressure. But for many more years, whenever the Eastern Cherokees encountered problems—legal, financial, or social—federal officials would suggest their removal as the perfect "final solution."

3

AN ANOMALOUS STATUS

The Cherokees who remained in North Carolina after 1838 faced
the monumental task of preserving both themselves and their cultural identity. The only way they could do this, William Thomas
believed, was by gaining recognition as citizens. First and foremost,
citizenship would carry an undoubted right of permanent residency
in the state and prevent a future Trail of Tears. It would also allow
them time to adapt and, he hoped, to become assimilated into the
dominant society. In arguing for citizenship, Thomas improvised
by referring to various treaties and assorted legislation, making
unabashed appeals for sympathy and justice, and, when it suited
him, occasionally contradicting his previous positions. The
Cherokees willingly followed his lead right up to the Civil War but
never succeeded in obtaining a precise definition of their legal status
vis-à-vis either the state or federal government.[1]

From his first trip to Washington in 1836 up through the 1838
removal, Thomas singlemindedly defended the right of his adoptive
kinsmen to remain in North Carolina. According to his carefully
honed argument, the Quallatown Cherokees had become citizens
under the 1817 and 1819 treaties and therefore did not have to leave.
In addition, Article 12 of the Treaty of New Echota allowed some
Cherokees to remain as citizens (although its wording was ambiguous). Commissioner of Indian Affairs T. Hartley Crawford finally
acknowledged their right to stay, assuming by the sheer repetitive-
ness of Thomas's arguments that North Carolina had agreed both to
their residency and citizenship. In any case, those Indians were no
longer the responsibility of the federal government. The attempts
between 1841 and 1844 to induce them to move west reflected
expediency on the part of the government, rather than any sense of
obligation. North Carolina was more indirect in its approach to the
Cherokees. Its assent for them to stay, regardless of what Thomas
said to Crawford, was merely tacit, in the form of a law passed to

41

protect them from fraud after the tribal majority had left. And it steadfastly refused to confirm the Cherokees' claims to citizenship, though it usually did not bother to deny them, either.

Thomas's initial problem was to offset the long-standing view that the North Carolina Cherokees were the most backward and traditional of their tribe. Whatever merit such a view might have had in earlier years, he claimed, those Indians were now following the road to civilization and were completely deserving of citizenship. Their beloved late chief, Yonaguska, had successfully weaned them from alcohol and they were progressing nicely. As proof, Thomas frequently offered the testimony of white citizens. In 1842, for example, a number of petitioners from Haywood and Macon counties, almost certainly at the prodding of Thomas, claimed the Quallatown Indians were a temperate, industrious people following the road to civilization. Reiterating this view in a memorial to the legislature, the Indians also insisted they were patriotic citizens, willing to assume all the burdens of citizenship while asking for few of the benefits. On this and other occasions they made it clear they primarily wanted assurance they could remain in their homeland.[2]

As they struggled to gain recognition of their legal rights, the Cherokees were joined by nearly 100 Catawba Indians. Former enemies of the Cherokees, this once proud and warlike people had been reduced by smallpox and liquor to a pitiful remnant occupying a reservation along the Catawba River in South Carolina. There they lived in squalor, their lands leased out to white neighbors, their days spent in dissipation and idleness. When Yonaguska warned his people against the dangers of liquor, he had pointed to the Catawbas as a horrible example. The latter had a somewhat higher opinion of the Cherokees, having visited them and seen their relative prosperity.[3]

When some Catawbas expressed interest in living among the Cherokees, authorities in South Carolina saw an opportunity both to oblige the Indians and to rid the state of them. In a "treaty" of March 1840 the Catawbas agreed to cede their reservation to the state if more suitable lands could be obtained for them. State officials intended to spend up to $5,000 for property in Haywood County, North Carolina, where most of the Cherokees resided. Thomas enthusiastically supported this plan, noting that he and the Cherokees had plenty of land to sell. By this time most of the more ambitious and responsible Catawbas were already settling among their northern neighbors or, in some cases, renting land from whites in Haywood County.[4]

Before South Carolina officials purchased any property for the Catawbas, they wanted to know the sentiments of North Carolina's Governor J.M. Morehead. The response, in September 1841, was emphatically negative. With less than gentle sarcasm, Morehead said

> I am utterly opposed to this species of population being brought into our territories nor do I believe it would meet with the approbation of any department of our Government or of our Citizens. . . . The same motives which induce your State to get clear of such a population, induces us to keep clear of it so far as we can and the arguments, which would readily occur to you, why our Cherokees should not be sent to your state to reside among and amalgamate with your Catawbas are agreeable against your sending your Catawbas to our state. . . .[5]

Resignedly, the South Carolinians took steps to reestablish the old Catawba reservation, providing adequate safeguards for the white lessees. As far as South Carolina was concerned, the Catawbas living in North Carolina were doing so voluntarily and were entitled to none of the $5,000 mentioned in the 1840 treaty. Thomas was understandably disappointed by the loss of a possible sale. Nonetheless, most of the reputable Catawbas continued to reside among the Cherokees, while those remaining in South Carolina, according to their agent, were "individually and collectively taken the most lazy, dissipated, worthless people that can possibly exist." The Baptists and other denominations had attempted to civilize them but with little effect. The South Carolina Catawbas, he said, "remain almost as Savage now as they were 50 years ago."[6]

The Catawbas in North Carolina were more civilized but lacked the security of their southern brothers. With no land or funds of their own, they were mere tenants at will, guests who had overstayed their welcome. Their hosts found it difficult to overcome traditional animosities and were disappointed when the newcomers did not bring the expected financial benefits. There was an occasional intermarriage, but the major contribution the visitors made to Cherokee life was the introduction of a style of pottery-making that quickly became prevalent among tribal artisans. Otherwise, the Catawbas remained on the fringes of Cherokee society, and some drifted back to South Carolina.[7]

Certainly the Cherokees East had more pressing concerns than their ragtag Catawba neighbors. Besides the persistent problem of defining their legal status, there was the matter of their many claims against the U.S. government. Most perplexing of all were their demands for removal and susbistence funds. Under the Treaty of New Echota, each Cherokee was allowed $53.33 for transportation to the Indian country and subsistence there for one year. The Indian Office and Treasury Department refused to concede that the North Carolina Indians were entitled to this money. In the face of Thomas's irritating persistence in the matter, federal officials reiterated time and again a refrain that was soon embedded in the bureaucratic subconscious: the Eastern Cherokees could not claim the $53.33 if they did not actually move to the West. But the Cherokee response was no less logical: under the Treaty of New Echota they had been forced to give up their equitable interest in the tribal domain and, through the efforts of Thomas, acquire new property. The removal and subsistence money was part of the compensation for their common sacrifice; they deserved it regardless of whether they moved. In addition, both the treaty party and the government had agreed in 1836 that Thomas's clients were entitled to a proportionate share of treaty benefits.[8]

In 1840 the government agreed to pay part of the Cherokee claims (but not the removal and subsistence) and appointed Thomas to disburse the money to those east of the Mississippi. He used some of the funds to pay himself for debts the Indians had incurred at his stores and used another portion, along with his own money, to acquire more land in western North Carolina. These scattered units, amounting to more than 50,000 acres by 1842, were to be a restored Indian homeland, with title remaining in Thomas's name until he was repaid. The largest block of land, acquired on a piecemeal basis well into the 1850s, became known as the Qualla Boundary.[9]

Thomas concluded that the most satisfactory way to protect some of this newly acquired property was to organize the Quallatown people as a corporation and then convey the lands to the company, which he would control as chief executive officer. Since North Carolina had no general incorporation law, he took advantage of an 1836 law that allowed organization of corporations dedicated to the cultivation and manufacture of silk and sugar. In 1845, at his request, the General Assembly authorized the Cheoah and Quallatown residents to organize under the terms of that act. Quickly setting up a so-called Cherokee Company among the latter Indians, Thomas forwarded the articles of incorporation to Governor William A. Graham and asked him to proclaim the legal existence of the company. Though the intention was ostensibly to produce silk and sugar, the major purpose was quite different. The preamble contained a lengthy statement of the Indians' legal rights, and Thomas apparently hoped that approval of the corporation would in effect represent approval of his interpretation of the Cherokees' status. The bylaws dealt almost exclusively with the Indians' landholdings, conveying to the company the land Thomas had purchased in their behalf. Individuals could acquire their own property within this tract but could not sell it without approval of the tribal corporation. Thomas was to be president, and two other whites would hold the other executive positions. Such a system of protecting Indian land tenure would be similar in certain respects to what exists today under the aegis of the federal government.[10]

Governor Graham was not deceived and declined to proclaim formation of the company because it was patently unrelated to the production of silk and sugar. Thomas then modified its bylaws, and in June 1847 the governor officially proclaimed the existence of the Cherokee Company. Though the company did not produce any appreciable quantity of silk or sugar, Thomas later alleged it did in fact control the lands occupied by the Quallatown people. And many years later federal investigators found this company to be the owner of record of large tracts within the Qualla Boundary. But these transfers to the company no doubt exceeded the limited and specific purposes for which the company had been recognized. Everyone knew that Thomas was the true owner.[11]

Meanwhile, as Thomas prowled the halls of Washington defending the myriad claims of his clients, he enlisted the support of influential allies. Most prominent of these were two local attorneys, the old Democrat Duff Green and his son Benjamin. For a percentage of the claims they agreed to assist Thomas, and before long they became fast friends with the Carolinian. In the mid-1840s they were also heavily engaged in some speculative schemes in Texas and Mexico that aroused the interest of Thomas. For a while he pondered the possibility of a mass migration of the Eastern Cherokees to the Southwest if attractive terms for land were available. It is possible he saw an exodus as a means of obtaining the removal and subsistence money without bringing the Indians under the authority of the Cherokee Nation. His interest soon waned, but it reflected one aspect of the man that should be remembered: he was not opposed to removal per se for his Indian clients. Under certain circumstances, he admitted, it might even be to their advantage. But he did object to any program of emigration that even hinted of coercion; the Indians themselves must desire such a move. And as their lawyer who was entitled to a percentage of their claims, he of course wanted the government first to settle its obligations to his clients.[12]

During the 1840s several different boards of commissioners were appointed to investigate the various Cherokee claims under the Treaty of New Echota. Unfortunately, they were undermined by questionable instructions from the Indian Office, occasional drunkenness and bickering among officials, and constant sniping by unhappy Indians and their attorneys. In the midst of this juridical chaos, the number of agents and attorneys for the Eastern Cherokees swelled to include men like Felix Axley, Preston Starrett, and a mixed-blood, Johnson K. Rogers. Their lobbying in Washington irritated the Indian Office almost as much as Thomas's persistence.[13]

In 1846, as the United States prepared to negotiate a new treaty with the Cherokee Nation, Thomas impressed upon the congressional delegations of North Carolina and Tennessee that the interests of the Cherokees East required protection. It was largely through his efforts that President James K. Polk ordered the treaty commissioners to consider these Indians in their deliberations.[14] The treaty of August 1846 resolved some of the internal problems of the Cherokee Nation and provided a means for satisfying most of the claims, but Thomas and the Greens were most interested in Articles 9 and 10. Article 9 upheld the right of the Cherokees East to a proportionate share in the Cherokee per capita fund, and Article 10 stated, "It is expressly agreed that nothing in the foregoing treaty contained shall be so construed as in any manner to take away or abridge any rights or claims which the Cherokees now residing in States east of the Mississippi River had, or may have, under the treaty of 1835 and the supplement thereto."[15] In effect, Article 10 confirmed the agreement Thomas had negotiated on his first trip to Washington in 1836 and was also a tacit admission by the federal government that the Cherokees East would remain distinct from the Nation, at least for the time. In later years this treaty stipulation would become a cornerstone for claims the Eastern Band held against the United States and the Cherokee Nation.

Another triumph for Thomas's clients was a measure which the Greens managed to insert in the Indian Appropriations Act of July 29, 1848. It stipulated that those Cherokees who had been living in North Carolina when the Treaty of New Echota was ratified, and who had not removed West or received money for such a move, were entitled to $53.33 each for any future emigration to the Cherokee Nation. If an Indian wished to make the move, the secretary of war would use the money to accomplish that purpose; or, if an individual chose to remove himself, he would be reimbursed the $53.33 upon arrival in the Nation. In the meantime, he was to receive 6 percent annual interest on that sum, dating from the treaty's ratification. A census would be prepared of all qualified North Carolina Cherokees, and the secretary of treasury would use this to make the annual interest payments. The latter provision complicated matters by dividing responsibility for the Cherokees East—to the very limited extent that the United States accepted it—between the War and Treasury departments.[16] Adding to the confusion was the transfer in 1849 of the Indian Office to the newly created Department of Interior.

Thomas and his Indian clients continued to insist they were entitled to the entire $53.33, as well as interest, without being required to emigrate. But the act of July 29 was as much as the government would concede for the present. And, in truth, both the Greens and Thomas seemed satisfied to have obtained this much, expecting to receive 15 percent of the interest money. They collected $6,910 in fees on the basis of this legislation but soon discovered that both the Indian Office and some of their clients were reluctant to reward them for other services.[17]

One other feature of the July 29 act deserves attention—a clause appropriating $5,000 for removal to the West of those Catawbas living among the North Carolina Cherokees. It appears that Thomas supported this measure, but he still believed the Catawbas could live in the Carolina mountains without offense, suggesting they might even "keep out Robbers and runaway slaves." Besides, tribes in Indian Territory either refused to receive them or haggled at length over extending them an invitation. Finally, in the early 1850s, a few of the North Carolina Catawbas were adopted into the Choctaw Nation. Others, like prodigal children, returned to South

Carolina. By the time of the Civil War there were probably less than a dozen identifiable Catawbas still living among the Cherokees.[18]

The man appointed to take the Cherokee census under the 1848 act was John C. Mullay, a longtime clerk in the Indian Office with extensive experience in Cherokee-related matters. Since a parsimonious or forgetful Congress had not appropriated money to take the census, Mullay performed the task as part of his normal duties, receiving as extra compensation only his necessary expenses. He was willing enough to do this, for he believed the Carolina mountains would restore his failing health. As he prepared to leave in August, he received detailed instructions from Indian Commissioner William C. Medill. He was not to include on the census any Indian born after May 23, 1836 (when the Treaty of New Echota was ratified), nor any white who had intermarried with a Cherokee after that date. He was to include the living heirs of those who qualified but had died since 1836. Where there was uncertainty about an individual, he was to conduct a thorough investigation into the merits of the case.[19]

The only curative that the mountains offered Mullay was the rigor of traveling nearly 300 miles by horseback from one isolated Cherokee settlement to another. William Thomas, Felix Axley, and John Timson helped him obtain most of the names, but the Valley River Cherokees remained unapproachable. As their leader John Owl (Chinoque) explained, they feared that Mullay's mission was a prelude to their removal from North Carolina. No amount of cajolery could convince them to cooperate, a perfect reflection of the understandable suspicion that many Cherokees had of the federal government.[20]

Mullay and Thomas were both devout Democrats but, unlike the Carolinian, Mullay faced the prospect of losing his job because of political partisanship. As the 1848 elections approached, Zachary Taylor—"Old Rough and Ready" of Mexican War fame—loomed as a likely Whig victor in the race for the presidency. Low-ranking Democrats like Mullay were threatened with the very axe of spoilsmanship by which they had profited. This situation offered a unique opportunity for Thomas. Though he was a Democrat, he could boast of kinship through his father with Zachary Taylor, and he suggested that he might have enough influence with the prospective Whig president to save the clerk's job. In return, Mullay could assist Thomas. The latter would receive a percentage of the interest money due those Cherokees who were enrolled. It would obviously benefit himself if as many Indians as possible were listed, and it would also mean more money for western North Carolina's frontier economy. Mullay was consequently sensitive to Thomas's wishes and was able to discover a surprising number of qualified Cherokees. Upon his return to Washington he remained solicitous of the Carolinian's goodwill, reminding him of his assurances after the November elections confirmed Taylor's election. Painfully aware of the impropriety of such an act, he even agreed to add to the census some names Thomas had recently forwarded. In one letter, labeled *"(Strictly Confidential!)*)," he wrote that after Thomas had finished with it "I will expect you to burn it."[21]

The Mullay Roll was the most important of the many payment rolls the federal government made of the Eastern Cherokees because most of the subsequent ones were based on it.[22] As the Second Auditor's Office in the Treasury Department compared the roll with records of previous disbursements, the Cherokees began to realize they were finally going to receive some needed cash. John Owl and the other census holdouts along Valley River reconsidered their stubbornness and now beseeched the government to include them on the list. Other claimants also clamored for inclusion. The result was that in the summer of 1850 Mullay, still employed by the Indian Office, made another trip to North Carolina. As a modest concession to his physical ailments, he now traveled by buggy, pausing occasionally to get down and hobble about with a cane while conducting his investigations. Darkened by the relentless sun so that he fancied himself almost an Indian, he made enough adjustments so that his roll totaled 1,517 Cherokees.[23]

On his second trip Mullay noted that many Cherokees from Georgia and Tennessee had moved into North Carolina and that others had returned from the Cherokee Nation. None of these was eligible for inclusion on his roll. By far the most illustrious of the returnees was the redoubtable warrior Junaluska, now an old man determined that when he died his bones would mingle with those of his ancestors. To its credit, North Carolina's General Assembly recognized a truly distinguished "native son" by granting him citizenship and a tract of land in the mountains of Cherokee County.[24]

In contrast to Junaluska, ordinary Cherokees continued to endure an anomalous legal status. Thomas insisted they were entitled to all rights of citizenship, including voting, but he hastened to add that they did not choose to exercise the latter privilege because they wished to avoid the tumult of party factionalism. He had become quite active in politics and knew that if the Indians voted for him the howls from his political foes would reverberate all the way to Raleigh. He once suggested that a prominent Whig opponent refused to acknowledge Cherokee citizenship because he feared the Indians would follow Thomas's lead and vote Democratic. Thomas was shrewd enough to realize that attempting to exercise this supposed right could well be the undoing of the Cherokees. In addition, participation in white politics might have shattered the traditional spirit of harmony and consensus that prevailed among the Eastern Cherokees prior to the Civil War.[25]

Nor did the Cherokees attempt to exercise some of the other rights usually accompanying citizenship, like serving in the militia or sitting on juries in cases involving whites. It appears that Thomas was seeking a comfortable "half-way house" for the Indians between the status of white citizens and free blacks, from whom they dissociated themselves (at least on the public level). Indeed, the burgeoning racial paranoia following the Nat Turner uprising probably accounted in large part for white ambivalence toward the Indians. Their place in southern race relations was undefined. The Lumbees of southeastern North Carolina might be treated as blacks (or near blacks) because of their uncertain ancestry, but the Cherokees were defiantly, unquestionably, *Indians*. What should be done with them? Perhaps it was best not to define their status too precisely but to leave it ambiguous.[26]

Decisions by the North Carolina courts regarding Indian citizenship were also shifting and inconsistent. The 1824 case of *Euchella v. Welsh* was unusual in affirming landholding rights and even citizenship for a few Eastern Cherokees. More often, legislation and court decisions focused on free blacks and applied to the Cherokees only by implication. The revised state constitution of 1835 limited the rights of free blacks and was also used against the Lumbee Indians. But three years later the state supreme court, dealing again with blacks, held that all free persons born within the state were citizens. The lack of certain privileges for free blacks, like voting, did not signify lack of citizenship; white women and children, it noted, were citizens even though they could not vote. By implication, at least, the Eastern Cherokees might be considered citizens. Over the next two decades, however, southern courts increasingly perverted this view, finally coming to argue that the absence of certain rights for free blacks proved noncitizenship. This is why Governor Thomas Bragg concluded in 1855 that the Cherokees, with few exceptions, were not citizens because they did not "exercise the ordinary rights of citizens." Nor could they achieve such status unless the General Assembly awarded it, a view further implied by the fact that on occasion the legislature *had* conferred citizenship on *individual* Indians like Junaluska. But state officials were seldom so precise in their reasoning regarding Cherokees.[27]

About the only right whites were willing to concede the Indians was that of paying taxes on the lands they occupied. Meeting these obligations remained a persistent problem for Thomas and the Eastern Band, and the merchant's personal records contain occasional entries indicating the amounts owed by individual Indians and whether they had paid. His 1853 ledgers, for example, show that the males within the Quallatown settlements owed a nominal sum of about eighty cents each. Usually Thomas paid the taxes himself, expecting to be reimbursed when the Indians received their claims from the government. It was fortunate that local tax collectors were somewhat lax, for if they had pursued their work energetically many poor whites and Indians would have been unable to pay. In fact, an embarrassing number of whites still owed the state for lands they had purchased at inflated prices after the Treaty of New Echota; their indebtedness for the former Cherokee lands posed a perennial dilemma for the state legislature.[28]

While almost all North Carolina Cherokees endured an uncertain status, those living along the Cheoah River found themselves in an especially precarious position. What they desired was the comparative security enjoyed by their kinsmen on the Qualla Boundary: possession in common of a large, unified block of land. Earlier attempts to get the federal or state governments to provide this had failed, and in October 1850 they turned again to Thomas. He signed a contract promising to continue acquiring lands for them, as he had done since 1838, until they possessed a large reservation or "boundary" like that at Qualla. The money would come from part of their interest and claims payments.[29]

Of more immediate concern was the status of a few Cheoah Cherokees who, along with many whites, occupied state lands that had not been worth the expense of surveying and selling. These poor squatters paid no taxes at all. When the Cherokees attempted in 1851 to claim these lands under a recent preemption act, Governor David S. Reid was asked whether the law applied to them. Thomas insisted it did and persuaded the governor to ask for an opinion from the state attorney general, William Eaton, Jr. Eaton told Reid the

Cherokees could enjoy the benefits of the law, but the governor thought otherwise and instructed the state land agent not to issue certificates of ownership to Indians until the courts could decide. Once again, their anomalous status had thwarted Cherokee aspirations.[30]

By the spring of 1851 the federal government had decided to take yet another census, this one of all Cherokees residing in North Carolina, Georgia, Tennessee, and Alabama. It was a necessary prelude to paying the per capita sums guaranteed the Cherokees under the 1835 and 1846 treaties. Would-be census-takers scurried about soliciting support, but the secretary of interior finally selected David W. Siler of Macon County, North Carolina.[31] As he began his work in June, Siler became an unwilling party to a squabble within the Indian Office. Johnson Rogers—never a man noted for moderation in his verbal assaults on others—accused Siler and his interpreter, George W. Hayes, of being in collusion with Thomas; they were supposedly adding names of ineligibles to the rolls while ignoring the names of others who deserved inclusion. Siler's roll, submitted in October, listed 1,961 eligible Cherokees as well as information on many more about whom the Indian Office would decide. The final number adjudged eligible was 2,133. Almost immediately a number of Cherokees, would-be Cherokees, and Cherokee agents joined Rogers in protesting that Siler had omitted them or their clients.[32]

Once Siler submitted his roll, the Indian Office lost no time in preparing to disburse the per capita funds. In November 1851 Indian Commissioner Luke Lea furloughed Alfred Chapman from his regular duties within the Office to make nearly $198,000 in payments. Chapman's assistant was Johnson Rogers, an unfortunate choice. For almost a decade he had been a source of irritation in Cherokee affairs, acting as self-styled agent, flitting back and forth between North Carolina and Washington, processing Indian claims, denouncing the claims of others, and resorting to the kinds of vitriolic personal attacks that often invited duels in the antebellum South.[33]

In the early 1850s William Thomas was a favorite target of Rogers, representing, it seems, something of a threat to the latter's own sense of importance in Cherokee matters. He was especially vituperative in attacking the claims of Thomas and the Greens for 15 percent of the per capita money, claiming that Thomas had actually worked against the 1846 treaty while he, Rogers, had been primarily responsible for its passage and the consequent per capita. This was simply not true. As Representative Thomas L. Clingman noted, it was Thomas who had worked for the per capita; Rogers, in contrast, had done nothing and was a man without means, influence, or character. Rogers also charged that Thomas was attempting to delay payment of the per capita until the following spring or summer; this way he and his fellow "speculators" would be able to sell the Indians various goods at rates so extortionate that each Indian would owe them the entire amount.[34]

Clearly, the accusations of Rogers and the reluctance of some Indians to confirm their previous powers of attorney to Thomas threatened the fees that he and the Greens had so long anticipated. Their anxiety was not relieved when the U.S. Attorney General decided that any payments due the Indians could not be made to their agents but must go directly to the recipients. Then, as Luke Lea noted, the Indians could pay their agents if they wished. Thomas railed against this federal decision, insisting it violated the contract laws of North Carolina and was therefore, according to his logic, "a species of abolitionism."[35]

Meanwhile, the wily Rogers prepared to take advantage of his official position. As Chapman and he visited the Cherokee settlements, he delivered a little spiel to the assembled Indians. It was he, Rogers said, who had managed to extract their per capita money from a reluctant government. While compensation for this service was optional, he was deserving and the government had decided it was permissible for the Indians to reward an agent once they had received their money. Because Thomas was absent when Chapman made his initial disbursement at Quallatown, Rogers was able to persuade fifty-five residents to pay him a total of $1,193. It was especially humiliating to Thomas that this had occurred in his very backyard.[36]

No doubt it was the merchant who quickly helped the Indians compose a petition to President Millard Fillmore, claiming they had been duped by Rogers and requesting immediate repayment. When interrogated about the matter by Luke Lea, Chapman said he had been surprised by Rogers's action and had offered no encouragement for the scheme. Instead, he had assured the Indians that such payment to Rogers must be of their own volition. After a second incident, he had asked Rogers not to repeat his actions in the agent's presence in order to avoid the logical impression that the government was sanctioning his claim for compensation. Chapman emphasized that he had fully complied with his orders, paying directly to each Indian his or her share. What a Cherokee did with the money afterward had not been his concern.[37] For his part, Rogers denied that he had done anything wrong and accused Thomas of being the real swindler.[38]

Indian Commissioner Lea finally decided there was no evidence of fraud on the part of Rogers, but he admitted that he would never have appointed him an assistant had he known that Rogers intended to solicit money. This incident simply demonstrates how the Eastern Cherokees were susceptible to the wiles of outsiders. Johnson Rogers may have been part Indian, but he "thought white" and took advantage of the Cherokees' vulnerability. The Indian Office was negligent in not recognizing that Rogers, a Cherokee agent, had a conflict of interest in serving as Chapman's assistant.[39]

For a few years following this debacle, disappointed claimants hectored the Indian Office with demands for inclusion on the Siler Roll, while officials steadfastly insisted that the roll was final and payments had been completed. But nothing is ever final in a democracy, and in July 1854 Congress appropriated $5,000 to pay those Cherokees who had been left off the roll. Alfred Chapman made a second trip to North Carolina but was not happy wandering about the mountains tracking down Cherokee recipients, vowing, "Nothing under Heaven would ever induce me to come to this country again." Even after the new round of disbursements, there were some claimants who insisted they had been overlooked.[40]

While Indians and agents argued over per capita money, the government was sporadically paying interest on removal and subsistence as provided for in the act of 1848. And in this matter one encounters a conflict of interest involving William Thomas. In October 1851 the secretary of treasury appointed James W. Terrell to make the annual interest payments, offering a 5 percent commission as compensation. From then until the Civil War Terrell continued in this capacity, simultaneously serving as Thomas's associate and confidant. On occasion he paid money to Thomas that the latter insisted was owed him by Indians. Although this violated Terrell's instructions, a federal court later decided that he had acted without criminal intent. And it concluded that the Indians had indeed owed Thomas the money. Nonetheless, the Treasury Department should have taken precautions to avoid such a compromising situation. Had the Department of Interior made the interest payments it is possible this particular conflict of interest would never have occurred—though there is little in the history of the Indian Office to inspire confidence on this point.[41]

Thomas, of course, realized that it made more sense for the Treasury Department simply to pay the Cherokees the entire $53.33 for removal and subsistence than to continue meting out the interest. Indeed, this is something he and the Indians had advocated from the outset. Certainly the present situation was absurd— Terrell's periodic treks through the mountains, miniscule interest payments to scattered Indians who sometimes could not be located, and the proliferation of paperwork in an already cumbersome federal bureaucracy. It cost the government more to disburse the interest this way than it would to pay the entire amount at once.[42]

While it is perhaps too much to say that it was an idea whose time had come, there was growing sentiment in Washington for making a lump-sum payment. Most knowledgeable officials were willing to concede that the North Carolina Cherokees wanted to remain in their homeland and would never require actual removal and subsistence. Yet the Indians were entitled to the money. Before they could be paid, however, the government needed assurance that the state of North Carolina would not someday evict them. In January 1855 Congress accordingly passed a law providing for the payment of $53.33 to those on the Mullay Roll or to their legal heirs. There were only two conditions: that each Indian receiving the money give his assent to such a lump-sum payment, and that the secretary of interior first be satisfied "that the state of North Carolina has . . . by appropriate act agreed that said Cherokees may remain permanently in that state. . . ." Recognition of their citizenship was not required.[43]

Confronted with this federal request, North Carolina equivocated. There were two reasons, the first being the anomalous status of the Eastern Cherokees. The state tacitly conceded their right to remain but was unwilling to confirm this explicitly. When asked if the Indians were citizens (and therefore having an undoubted right to remain), Governor Bragg responded negatively. Yet he cited North Carolina's long-standing policy of letting them stay, without making any promise for the future. The state was not unsympathetic. In fact, the General Assembly had passed some legislation and resolutions that were quite favorable to the Cherokees. But the legislators still refused to recognize them as citizens or even to confirm, formally and forthrightly, their right of permanent residency. It was all very frustrating to Thomas, who continued to insist the Indians were entitled to both privileges.[44]

The second aspect of this equivocation was the understandable reluctance of the state in a period of growing sectionalism to accede to what seemed an unfair demand by the national government. Strong southern adherence during the tense 1850s to a states'-rights philosophy dictated that North Carolina very carefully review any request from Washington. The most that state officials would do was reiterate that no specific ordinance was required because previous legislation *implied* a right of residence for the Cherokees. And, besides, the issue did not properly concern North Carolina. As one resident expressed it, why should his state, which had not been a party to the treaties between the Cherokees and the federal government, be required to make a commitment before the Indians received what was rightfully theirs under the treaty? But such arguments were to no avail. The government continued to insist that the terms of the 1855 act had not been met, and not until after the Civil War was the impasse resolved.[45]

Besides his unflagging service in prosecuting Cherokee claims, Thomas also protected his clients' proportionate interest in the lands occupied by the Cherokee Nation. After all, according to his 1836 agreement with the treaty signatories, these lands belonged to the Eastern Cherokees as well as the Nation. As talk developed in the early 1850s of an impending sale of some Cherokee lands in the West, Thomas asked congressmen and the Indian Office to remember the rights of his people. Of particular concern were the so-called Neutral Lands, a tract of 800,000 acres adjoining the Nation in present-day Kansas. This was more land than the Cherokees needed, and many were interested in selling it to the federal government. The area could then become available for white settlement, a prospect even more likely when Congress organized Kansas Territory in 1854. By then, however, various Eastern Cherokees had already petitioned the government to prohibit a sale without first obtaining their consent.[46]

Though nothing was done about a sale at this time, Thomas and his clients manifested a continuing concern about the Neutral Lands. They did not necessarily oppose selling the tract, but they wanted assurance that they would receive their share of the proceeds. After the Civil War this would become the major irritant in relations between the Eastern Band and the Cherokee Nation. The

William Holland Thomas, 1858
(Source: *Nineteenth Annual Report,* Bureau of American Ethnology.)

latter contended that the western lands belonged exclusively to the Nation, and that any Cherokee who refused to reside within the Nation had voluntarily relinquished his right to the tribal domain.[47]

Meanwhile, Thomas was still having difficulty collecting all that the Indians owed him, attributing the trouble to the machinations of other agents, a sometimes duplicitous Indian Office, and a lack of responsibility on the part of some Cherokees. He was quickly sinking in a morass of personal indebtedness, mostly for the lands he had been buying for himself and the Indians. His energies were dangerously divided—frequent trips to Washington in behalf of the Cherokees, constant land transactions, lobbying for a railroad in western North Carolina, and, since 1848, continuous service as a Democratic state senator. By the mid-1850s he was clearly concerned about his financial plight and saw as his only salvation the compensation the Cherokees owed him. Those who disappointed him in this regard quickly earned an epithet that became his favorite in later years—"vagabond Indian." When he was not in Washington during this period, his young mixed-blood friend, James Taylor, usually was. Besides attending to the claims of various Indians he himself represented, Taylor often looked after Thomas's affairs as well. Also appearing in the Indian Office at this time was George Bushyhead, a mixed-blood from Cherokee County. After the Civil War, Bushyhead and Taylor would become two of the dominant political figures among the Eastern Band.[48]

In the meantime, as the impasse over the transportation and subsistence fund continued, a movement began once again to encourage removal of the Eastern Band. By 1856 both Congressman Clingman and James Taylor supported the idea, the latter declaring that many North Carolina Cherokees wished to move but were too poor to do so. They would obviously require the $53.33 before they could leave. The Cherokee Nation also supported a tribal consolidation, hoping to stifle further controversy regarding possible sale of the Neutral Lands. That Thomas was likewise involved in this plan is indicated by his periodic discussion of it and his recommendation of James Terrell as agent to enroll those who wished to move.[49]

As for actually superintending the move, Taylor supported Colonel John Hoke, a prominent citizen of Lincoln County, North Carolina. Hoke agreed to undertake the proposed removal for $53.33 per Indian—enough, he said, to accomplish the task and earn a profit as well. The new Indian commissioner, James W.

Denver, had served with Hoke in the Mexican War and was interested in the proposal. Hoke assured him that the Indians were the ignorant dupes of "designing whites" in North Carolina, and that their only hope for progress was to join their brothers in the West. For anyone familiar with the history of the Eastern Band, it was a depressingly familiar refrain. Precisely the same arguments for removal had been heard in the late 1830s and early 1840s.[50] Amid all this "philanthropic" concern, there was little evidence the Cherokees wanted to leave. The latest removal ploy was just another scheme concocted by white men and a few mixed-bloods.

Secretary of Interior Jacob Thompson was impressed enough with Hoke's arguments to direct Denver to begin arrangements under the 1848 act to remove those Indians who wished to go. A major obstacle, however, was his direction that only $20 of the $53.33 could go for actual transportation, while the remainder was for one year's subsistence in Indian Territory. This was in strict accordance with both the Treaty of New Echota and the 1848 act. Hoke, it is clear, had hoped to obtain waivers so that the entire $53.33 could be used for transportation and subsistence en route West. Thompson's edict reduced the likelihood of a profit and convinced Hoke and Taylor that removal could not take place unless Congress appropriated additional money.[51]

By the end of 1857 this latest halfhearted attempt at removal had fizzled out. Thomas no longer seemed interested and was again concentrating on convincing the government to make lump-sum payments to the Indians. The North Carolina congressional delegation also urged this, while insisting the state did not have to pass the legislation the federal government required. The state judiciary committee was willing to make some minor concessions on the Cherokees' status but refused to support an explicit guarantee of permanent residency, saying only that it was "not probable" North Carolina would violate her traditional support of Cherokee rights—whatever they might be. This particular confrontation between state and federal governments, though inconsequential compared with other disputes, exemplified the growing mistrust and suspicion that would soon bring secession and Civil War. And when war came, the legal status of the Cherokees became less an issue than was their physical survival.[52]

4

A TRADITIONAL WAY OF LIFE

If they gained recognition as citizens, the Cherokees would have an undoubted right to remain in North Carolina and would perhaps be able to preserve a society that in many respects appeared traditional and, from the white perspective, nonprogressive. But therein lay a paradox. In order to persuade state authorities to acknowledge their citizenship, they found it desirable to emphasize their acculturation and progress rather than their traditionalism. Thus, the period from removal to the Civil War was a time when traditionalism and progressivism existed in curious juxtaposition and tension.

Whites had long viewed the North Carolina Cherokees as among the most traditional and backward of their tribe. While others of their people had made significant advances in agriculture, the mechanical arts, education, and the white man's religion, the North Carolina Indians were less affected by these changes. A recent analysis of the tribal census of 1835 concludes that they had less interracial marriage, less wealth, fewer white skills, and were less likely to be able to read and write in either English or Cherokee. Their farms were smaller than those of their kinsmen in Alabama, Tennessee, and Georgia. And none of the forty-two "elite" Cherokee families lived within the state.[1]

On the other hand, these Indians were traditional or nonprogressive only in comparison with the acculturated members of their tribe. Compared with many other Indians or their own ancestors, they reflected considerable white influence. By the 1830s most were residing as nuclear families in log homes not unlike those of their poor white neighbors; almost all, like their white counterparts, practiced a primitive agriculture, supplemented by hunting, fishing, and gathering. The traditional matriarchal aspects of their society were gradually giving way to male dominance; the men, for example, were doing more of the farming while wives concentrated on household chores. A few Cherokees, moreover, had converted to a nominal kind of Christianity. In short, according to some of their neighbors, the Indians appeared to be following the white man's road and were fully deserving of citizenship.[2]

There was no disguising Cherokee poverty, however, for they and nearby whites were far removed from the romantic stereotype of the aristocratic, antebellum South. Instead of a stately white-columned mansion, a typical Cherokee home was a windowless log cabin about thirteen feet square, with dirt floor and a chimney made of sticks and clay. Instead of a commercial plantation agriculture, theirs was at best a subsistence farming without benefit of slave labor and modern implements. Instead of cotton, they mostly raised corn. The 1835 census showed that they occupied farms averaging only 9.67 acres in size and producing less per acre than those of other Cherokees. According to one assessment of this data, the small farms and low productivity reflect "the mountainous area, the poor soil, the lack of money to invest in slaves or ploughs, and . . . the general poverty of the Cherokees in this region. Possibly the isolation from white settlements, adherence to traditional ways of life, and deliberate resistance to change contributed to these differences."[3]

Despite some relocations after 1835, the North Carolina Indians continued this pattern of living on tiny cleared farms. As for their low agricultural productivity, one might question the assumption that it was partly due to poor soil. Most Cherokee farms were in river and creek valleys where the arable land, though limited in extent, was quite fertile. A more plausible explanation is the inefficiency of Cherokee agriculture, fossilized by a stubborn peasant resistance to change. The Indians made no pretense of scientific farming, and even after the Civil War knowledgeable visitors were appalled by their methods; they were usually quick to note, however, that poor whites of the area were no more proficient. Livestock consisted mostly of pigs, sheep, and cattle, the latter usually grazing on the upper slopes of mountains where the grasses remained nourishing the year around. There were also numerous small orchards of apple and peach trees, both of which grew well in that climate and required little attention.[4]

In truth, many Cherokees and whites exhibited a casual indifference to farming and showed more enthusiasm for hunting. (It was said that one could judge the economic status of a mountain white by the number of hunting dogs he owned. Those who were relatively affluent and industrious owned one, while their less successful neighbors each had nine or ten.) Hunting and fishing added variety to an otherwise monotonous diet, and the Indians retained their aboriginal skills in building fish traps, tracking game, and using the blowgun to kill birds. In 1844 alone, according to one curious statistic, the Quallatown Indians killed 540 deer, 78 bears, 18 wolves, and 2 panthers; the number of smaller mammals and birds killed must have totaled thousands. Whites roaming the mountains occasionally stumbled upon isolated Cherokee hunting camps, and Alum Cave, now a magnet for visitors to the Smoky Mountains, was supposedly discovered by the young Yonaguska when he was tracking a bear. So important were these mountains as hunting grounds, so central to Cherokee identity, that Thomas often alluded to them in his legal treatises.[5]

Many of the Indians purchased their necessities on credit at one of Thomas's stores, but the merchant was lucky if he ever received full compensation. His ledgers show that he "carried" a number of customers for months and even years. It was not that his clients were deadbeats, but rather that there was little money or employment in the region. Often reduced to accepting corn as payment, he occasionally considered running a cash business, only to conclude that this would end his merchandising completely. Sometimes the Indians took their business elsewhere, as in 1854, when they traded animal hides to Valley River merchants for groceries.[6]

Cherokee food and clothing reflected an Indian-white dichotomy. Standard fare included cornbread and corn cakes fried in bear grease, as well as beans, squashes, nuts, and game animals large and small. A traditional procedure was to boil beans until they were soft, mix them with corn or rye meal, and then bake them as bread. Hominy was another favorite. Their clothing represented a transitional phase between aboriginal attire and a fashion common to poor whites best described as "nondescript yeoman." The wives increasingly made the latter at home, but Cherokee eclecticism and fondness for color appeared in startling array on dress up occasions with calico dresses, turbans, shawls, bright handkerchiefs, feathers, "scarlet belts, and gaudy hunting shirts." (At such times whites often referred to the Indians' exotic appearance as "Turkish.") And moccasins were still the preferred footwear, for white fashions did not offer anything so comfortable and practical.[7]

Most of our information on the Eastern Cherokees concerns those living around Quallatown because they were the ones directly under the influence of Thomas, an inveterate gatherer of data about them.

Not surprisingly, he consistently emphasized their progress over their traditionalism. According to his 1845 report to the secretary of war, they enjoyed generally good health, had increased in number to 781, and were making rapid strides toward civilization. Though almost all depended on agriculture, a surprising number were skilled in mechanical and domestic arts as well; artisans made such things as barrels, ploughs, and gunstocks for whites and Indians alike.[8] A gunsmith named Squirrel (Salola) was almost a mechanical genius, and Thomas even deposited one of his rifles in the U.S. Patent Office. The proverbial frontier jack-of-all-trades, Squirrel could build most anything, whether a rifle, farm implement, or gristmill. He was always a prize exhibit for curious visitors, a shining example of what these Indians could accomplish.[9]

Many whites considered conversion to Christianity the *sine qua non* for civilizing the Indians. While the stubborn Yonaguska lived, however, the Quallatown Cherokees received little encouragement for adopting the white man's religion. The old chief thought Christian theology embodied some wonderful concepts but, like many Indians before him, noted that Christian doctrine frequently stood in stark contrast to white behavior. Such a religion, he thought, was probably not worth much and was certainly less satisfying than traditional Cherokee ritual and belief. By the time of his death in 1839, most of the converts among the North Carolina Cherokees lived along Valley River rather than at Quallatown.[10]

Thomas, however, worked diligently to steer his adoptive kinsmen along a godly path, exhorting them to convert and importing a number of Cherokee Bibles and hymnals from the tribe in the West. By the mid-1840s, he boasted, there were 103 in Quallatown who qualified as "Sabbath school teachers and scholars." White preachers paid periodic visits, and the Methodist Episcopal Church of the South established the Echota missionary church along Soco Creek. Soon there were several native preachers who served the congregation.[11] When Charles Lanman attended one of their services in 1848, he found that except for "many little eccentricities" their worship was familiar to white Christians. Most of the congregation of 150 were neatly dressed women whose deportment "was as circumspect and solemn as I have ever witnessed in any New England religious assembly. . . . Their form of worship was according to the Methodist custom, but in their singing there was a wild and plaintive sweetness which was very impressive. . . . They sung four hymns; three prayers were offered by several individuals, and two sermons or exhortations were delivered."[12] The first sermon lasted about thirty minutes and was delivered by a native preacher, Big Charley. According to Lanman,

> His manner was impressive, but not particularly eloquent. After he had taken his seat, and a hymn had been sung, a young man stepped into the rude pulpit, who has distinguished himself by his eloquence. His name is Tekin-neb, or the Garden of Eden. He spoke from the same text, and his remarks bore chiefly on the redemption by Christ. At the conclusion of his address he gave a sketch of his own religious experience, and concluded by a remarkably affecting appeal to his hearers. His voice, emphasis, and manner were those of a genuine orator, and his thoughts were poetical to an uncommon degree. In dwelling upon the marvellous love of the Saviour, and the great wickedness of the world, he was affected to tears, and when he concluded there was hardly a dry eye in the house.[13]

Thomas ended this display of Christian rectitude with a discourse on the virtues of temperance. The entire service had been conducted in Cherokee and translated for Lanman by his host, leaving one with the suspicion that Thomas had orchestrated parts of it in order to win favorable comment from his young guest.

That the Cherokees took advantage of the emotionally satisfying aspects of Christianity was shown by the way their camp meetings or revivals sometimes degenerated into a frenzy of dancing, shouting, and wild gesticulations. William Stringfield, a good friend of the Cherokees, conceded that they were "absolutely fiends" at such gatherings. Yet this was hardly surprising. The religion of the frontier was a quantum leap beyond that of urban America, and the kind of emotional outbursts he witnessed was also common at white camp meetings in the upper South. More conclusive evidence of the syncretic nature of Cherokee Christianity was the way a man could be a shaman one day, reciting traditional incantations, and a hellfire preacher the next. Enola (Black Fox), for example, was a prominent Sunday school teacher, Methodist preacher, and all-purpose conjurer. He approached religion and life much the way a good cook improvises in the kitchen, combining various ingredients into a satisfying whole.[14]

Whites also attached great importance to educating the Indians, and some believed that a basic eduction was necessary before the Indians could comprehend the subtleties of Christianity. In this area Cherokee progress was almost nonexistent, a fact most conclusively proven by their pervasive illiteracy. Thomas frequently boasted of their ability to read and write, but this was hyperbole meant to impress officials in Washington and Raleigh. No more than a handful of North Carolina Cherokees could speak English, and virtually every state or federal agent required interpreters when dealing with them. Even in regard to literacy in the Cherokee syllabary, Thomas made exaggerated claims. Probably the closest he came to accuracy on this matter was his 1845 estimate that only about one-fifth of the population could read and write. The true figure may have been even lower. The 1835 census indicates that only 14.7 percent of the North Carolina Cherokees could read their own language, while a mere 1.5 percent could read English.[15] Enola's facility at reading and writing Cherokee explains why he performed so many official duties among his people, religious and otherwise, and steadily became more prominent.

Thomas diligently sought to establish schools among the Indians, but the best he could do was obtain the services of an occasional itinerant teacher who might stay for a few months. In 1850 the Holston Conference of the Methodist Church took preliminary steps to establish a school at Quallatown but little came of it, despite Thomas's offer of a free building site. Desperate, he requested assistance from the Indian Civilization Fund, an annual federal appropriation that was divided among those Christian denominations working with Indians. Acting Indian Commissioner Charles E. Mix responded by referring to Thomas's earlier exaggerated reports of Cherokee progress. Such Indians obviously did not need assistance and, besides, the federal government could not aid supposed citizens of North Carolina. He noted that education was already being provided for the Cherokee Nation and would be available for any of the Eastern Band who chose to move there. Hoist with his own petard, Thomas vainly looked elsewhere for assistance. In the meantime, whatever education occurred was largely in the form of one Indian's informally instructing another in the use of the syllabary.[16]

Cherokee progress was more apparent in other areas, especially in their successful resistance to the degradation by liquor that befell many tribes. Temperance had not always been the norm, and before 1830 alcohol had spread its insidious tentacles among the Band. But one day, according to a story that varies in the retelling, Chief Yonaguska, who was something of a drunk, fell into a trance and appeared to die. In the midst of preparations for his funeral he suddenly awoke, saying he had visited the spirit world and had been told to correct the errant ways of his people. He became a reformed person, abhorring all alcohol, and requested his council to sign a formal pledge not to partake of any spirits. They did, and even agreed to establish a local temperance society. Any Quallatown Indian who drank was subject to a fine or whipping. Through such showmanship, contrived or not, Yonaguska had committed his people to a cause that they supported even after he died.[17] By 1845, Thomas declared, there was not a single drunkard and not more than eight who ever used alcohol of any kind—the main reason why, he averred, there had not been a murder or even a case of assault and battery among these Indians in the preceding few years.[18]

But this record of nonviolence did not remain intact. In 1850 a local Indian, Cunning Deer, fatally stabbed another Cherokee and then disappeared, despite Thomas's efforts to bring him to justice.[19] More shocking because of its cold-blooded nature was the murder of John Timson of Cherokee County. Stalwart John Timson—first Baptist convert of the Valley Town mission, a delegate to the Cherokee constitutional convention, and freeholder of North Carolina—had stood out among his people. During the 1840s he had faithfully served a series of federal agents in their dealings with the Indians. He had often expressed his intention to move west, and most of his family had already left for Indian Territory. On the night of August 31, 1856, several men, apparently intent on robbery, set his house afire and then shot him as he attempted to escape the flames. Two men were arrested and one, a mixed-blood, implicated a local white named Goldman Bryson as the instigator and chief perpetrator of the crime. The mixed-blood's testimony was not allowed, however, and Bryson's brother and sister testified that he had not been involved. Although Bryson was acquitted, one indignant citizen said that residents still viewed him as a murderer. A few years later Bryson became a feared Unionist marauder in Cherokee County, and the Cherokees were to enjoy a belated revenge.[20]

Petty crime also occurred among the Cherokees, as in the case of Tahquit, who was indicted by the Cherokee County Superior Court for stealing twelve silk handkerchiefs from Thomas and another man. Tahquit promptly fled to Tennessee. The solicitor of the Seventh Circuit Court described him as "a most notorious rascal" and asked the governor to approve a reward of one hundred dollars for his capture. Publicizing the reward would simply put him on guard, so the solicitor recommended informing only a few bounty hunters who would be able to apprehend the fugitive. The matter apparently ended when the governor declined the suggestion.[21] Occasional crimes such as Tahquit's, and the even less frequent intratribal violence, in no way diminished the common view that the Cherokees were among the most law-abiding people in western North Carolina.

The main concentration of Cherokees in North Carolina, of course, was at Quallatown. They were always among the most conservative of the Eastern Band, and it is typical of Thomas's pragmatism that he incorporated traditional Cherokee institutions into his program of modernity. In July 1839, after federal officials conceded the right of his clients to stay, Thomas instructed them to begin construction of a council house. Built in the traditional manner, it was a large, circular edifice of logs with a single bench to accommodate the town dignitaries. At this and similar structures in other Cherokee communities people gathered to discuss matters of importance. Chiefs—or headmen—exercised considerable influence but, as in earlier days, wielded no coercive powers. Thomas also divided the Quallatown Indians into three distinct settlements, each with the name of a Cherokee clan—Bird Town, Wolf Town, and Paint Town. Eventually there would be two more, Big Cove and Yellow Hill. These settlements, something like Cherokee towns of an earlier period, helped maintain cohesion and homogeneity even while Thomas, paradoxically, was attempting to bring about change. He no doubt viewed them as a means of maintaining Indian stability in a period of uncertainty. The Cherokees lacked authority from the state to govern themselves, but, on the other hand, North Carolina seemed largely indifferent about what they did in their own communities. Like white frontiersmen before and after them, they simply went ahead and created familiar institutions of self-government.[22]

The discrete groups of Indians residing on Qualla Boundary were in such close proximity that most whites simply referred to them as the Quallatown Cherokees. Most prominent were the elderly Euchella, chief of Wolf Town, and Flying Squirrel, chief of Paint Town. Both had figured prominently in the capture and execution of Tsali, and Euchella even enjoyed the status of minor celebrity among whites for his exploits. While the two provided leadership on the local level, they mostly deferred to Thomas in their dealings with state and federal governments, contenting themselves with signing the occasional petitions he forwarded to Raleigh and Washington. He was the man who could best protect their interests, and they knew it.[23]

The harmony ethic, the striving for consensus on all matters of importance, remained intact among the Eastern Cherokees. Prior to the Civil War, there was little of the factionalism and backstabbing that existed among their more acculturated kinsmen in the West. Their town councils represented a kind of consensual municipal government, and a white who attended one was amazed that 300 to 400 Indians could assemble without one argument or dispute. Whites could never do so well, he remarked.[24] The Indians did recognize differences of locality and even of dialect among themselves, but they revered their common tribal heritage and kinship.

At the time of the 1835 census an astounding 88.9 percent of the North Carolina Indians were classified as fullbloods,[25] a figure that gradually declined after the removal era. Racial intermarriage was most prevalent along Valley River, especially near Murphy, and some of the Cherokees there could not be distinguished in appearance from their white neighbors. A few Cherokees (like Squirrel) married Catawbas, while others mixed with slaves and free blacks. In fact, a slave of William Thomas served as a kind of magistrate among his people and solemnized several "marriages" with Cherokees. Apparently no one objected, though an Indian lost status within the tribe for mixing with blacks. When David Siler prepared his census in 1851, he was confronted with the problem of deciding whether to include the children of these unions. The Indian commissioner instructed him to record those of such parentage who were acknowledged as Cherokees by the Indians themselves.[26]

More significant was the intermarriage or cohabitation of Indians and whites. Some observers feared this might result in "savagery" prevailing over "civilization." Andrew Barnard, living near Valley River, complained in 1840 that young whites and Indians were slipping into nearby Georgia, where they could be married without difficulty. Returning to North Carolina, they quickly sank into a way of life so odious that Barnard would rather see his offspring "in the grave." The Indians seemed immune to civilization and even now, he said, they "are forming Settlements, building town houses, and Show every disposition to keep up their former manners and customs of councils, dances, ballplays, and other practices, which is disgusting to civilized Society and calculated to corrupt our youth, and produce distress and confusion among all good thinking people—"[27]

Thomas, in contrast, feared that those traditionalist Indians who still lived along Valley River would be degraded and dispossessed by whites. The merchant's early influence among them waned during the 1840s, and they received conflicting and sometimes bad advice from their other friends. Of particular concern was their proximity to unsavory white influences in and around Murphy, posing a threat both to their morals and their land. Both Thomas and Felix Axley believed that the only way these Indians could avoid complete destruction would be to consolidate with the Cherokees at Quallatown or Cheoah—or perhaps to emigrate west. Some of the Valley River Indians themselves recognized their precarious position and sought a grant of land where they could resist their piecemeal dispossession.[28]

The Quallatown settlements were the showcase Indian communities, the people on whom Thomas lavished his attentions and to whom he most proudly pointed. He made certain they never gave offense to their white neighbors, never presumed too much in the way of social intercourse, and stood readily available to work on public roads and perform other civic duties. The roads through their settlement, in fact, were described in 1845 as the best maintained in that part of the state (faint praise indeed).[29] In time, Quallatown became almost an obligatory stopover—a kind of Boys' Town for Indians—for the few white outsiders who ventured into that remote region. John Mullay visited when he compiled his payment roll in 1848 and, though shocked by "wild & grotesque" dances, was gratified to discover that they were "a moral & comparatively industrious people—sober & orderly to a marked degree—and although almost wholly ignorant of our language, (not a single full-blood & but few of the half-breeds speaking English) advancing encouragingly in the acquirement of a knowledge of agriculture, the ordinary mechanical branches, & in spinning, weaving & c. . . ."[30]

Another visitor was Charles Lanman, a Whig journalist who was still indignant over the inhumane removal policy of Democratic administrations. He spent part of May 1848 with Thomas, and his articles on the Eastern Cherokees appeared in 1849 as part of his book *Letters from the Alleghany Mountains*. He was charmed by Quallatown, depicting it as an idyllic and progressive settlement—indeed, a Jeffersonian Arcadia. From the careful arrangements made to accommodate him, however, one suspects that Quallatown was a Thomasonian Potemkin Village. Rather than seeing an impoverished people eking out a living from a sometimes harsh environment, the impressionable journalist perceived a bucolic society enjoying the fruits of a cooperative ethos.[31]

It was Lanman, too, who published the first widely read and popularized account of Tsali, a significant step toward the heroic figure that would emerge in full romantic attire in the writings of James Mooney. Somehow, Lanman was able to pay appropriate homage both to Tsali and his captor and executioner, Euchella. The former represented savage resistance to the cruelty of Jacksonian removal and stolid courage in the face of death; the latter personified the unyielding resolution necessary to perform a distasteful but necessary duty. Considering the fact that the "noble savage" stereotype was common in literature of the day, it is hardly surprising Lanman found appropriate candidates among the Eastern Cherokees.[32]

The 1850 census represented something of a triumph for Thomas because he was able to get the Quallatown Indians included in the Haywood County enumeration by insisting they were citizens. They were listed separately, however, and identified as "Indian." Having argued for inclusion of the Indians because they were supposedly citizens, the wily merchant then claimed that their appearance on the census rolls proved their citizenship, an argument officials did not dignify by disputing. In contrast, the Cherokees of Macon and Cherokee counties were not listed, though a few mixed-bloods were found among the names of whites.[33]

According to the census, 710 Cherokees lived in a total of 152 separate dwellings on the Qualla Boundary. They ranged from newborn infants to five individuals whose ages were listed as one hundred or more years, including a female who was purportedly 140. Although they claimed ownership of a large tract (through the Cherokee Company), only 1,440 acres were improved. Their chief produce was corn, supplemented by ample quantities of beans, Irish potatoes, sweet potatoes, and orchard fruits. Their livestock included 516 swine, 416 sheep, 105 cows, 45 oxen, 135 "other cattle," and 93 horses. Almost all of the Cherokee males farmed, but there were also a few blacksmiths, gunsmiths, and wheelwrights. Many of the women, moreover, were skilled in such domestic arts as sewing and weaving.[34]

The Siler Roll of 1851 provides a more systematic breakdown of the individuals inhabiting Quallatown, as well as those in other counties and states. In Paint Town, for example, Siler listed 86 family groups totaling 350 people. Wolf Town had 61 families with

266 people, and Bird Town had 72 family groups with 267 individuals for a total of 883 residing in and around Quallatown. This was a significant and unexplained increase over the number listed in the 1850 census. In Cherokee County Siler found 68 family units at Cheoah numbering 168 people, including the aged Junaluska and his family. The Valley River Cherokees numbered 21 families and 98 individuals. The 152 living in the environs of Murphy were listed separately and consisted mostly of mixed-bloods. These included many who were among the most persistent in their claims against the United States—people like the Hensons, Panthers, Rapers, and Starretts.[35]

In Macon County, Siler found 17 families with 56 individuals along Cartoogechaye Creek. One of them was the redoubtable Hog Bite, supposedly 110 years old, who had driven off removal agents thirteen years earlier. Still living as a hermit, he depended on one or two friends but was vigorous enough to kill a turkey or deer by himself when necessary. Moving outside the state, Siler located 87 alleged Cherokees in southeastern Tennessee, 50 more in Alabama, and 321 in Georgia. Two others, David Taylor and Johnson Rogers (Thomas's enemy), were residing in Washington. In addition, Siler included information on a large number of others who claimed to be Cherokees. The Indian Office added enough to his roll to bring it to 2,133.[36]

There was a rough equality among the North Carolina Cherokees, but some were more equal than others. As was true with other Indian tribes, the mixed-bloods usually possessed the most capital, land, and entrepreneurial skills. A few, like David Taylor and his son James, were familiar with the byzantine workings of Congress and could be seen trekking from office to office on Capitol Hill. Even among the fullbloods living in Quallatown, there were economic and social disparities. Leaders like Euchella and Flying Squirrel occupied more land than most other Cherokees and also listed some personal property for the census-taker. Before them, Yonaguska had enjoyed his own perquisites of rank, including two wives and a slave. The latter, a man called Cudjo, was treated as a member of the family and never had to worry about working too hard or being sold to chop cotton in Alabama. Yet, despite these gradations of wealth, none of the Eastern Cherokees possessed the property of any one of a number of prominent whites in western North Carolina.[37]

Though males increasingly dominated Cherokee households, at least in the eyes of whites, family and domestic arrangements retained some of their traditional character. Clan restrictions on marriage remained in effect, especially among fullbloods, and Thomas believed the prohibition against marrying within one's clan accounted for the absence of feeble-minded Cherokees. It is also clear that marriage often followed the old pattern of shifting domestic arrangements unencumbered by formal vows or record-keeping. Husbands and wives continued to drift apart and find new partners, and children designated by whites as "illegitimate" continued to be born. Thomas, devout Christian that he was, tried to show them the error of their ways but with little lasting effect. A wedding "in the white fashion" was still unusual enough for him to mention in his diary. A Quallatown council in 1859 finally set up a procedure for regularizing and recording marriages, but even after the Civil War, visitors found the Indians indifferent to white notions of marital propriety. If sexual freedom was an essential element in emancipating females, as some feminists claimed, then the Cherokee women had always been a step or two in advance of most white females. Furthermore, there is little evidence to suggest that the work of a Cherokee woman was any more demanding or exhausting than that of her white frontier counterpart.[38]

In most respects, however, the role of Cherokee women was probably becoming as circumscribed as that of white females. Thomas and the missionaries—indeed, the whole thrust of Western thought insofar as it intruded into Cherokee life—attempted to assure male dominance and limit females to the household. A white visitor to Quallatown noted some of the changes, and misinterpreted the traditional role of Cherokee women, when he boasted that "Their females are no longer treated as slaves, but as equals." They now had the debatable advantage of cooking, cleaning, spinning, and sewing while their husbands labored in the fields.[39] The growing ascendancy of white norms had undermined the traditional role of Cherokee women in other respects as well. Since the eighteenth century they had been losing their former political influence, as was true for women in certain other tribes.[40] On the other hand, there is no reason to assume that Cherokee females lacked the ability or will to influence men in ways that archival records cannot convey. There is simply no way traditional historical sources can reveal the complexity and richness of family relationships among Indians.

Probably the foremost problem for the Cherokees, other than defining their legal status and protecting their land, was their hardscrabble existence. In 1846 Thomas made a nominal effort to diversify their economy by attempting to teach them how to manufacture brooms, but this was of little help to the impoverished Indians. He had greater hopes for another project he envisioned about the same time: the cultivation and manufacture of silk. As early as colonial days, propagandists had viewed the South as ideal for growing mulberry trees and raising silk worms, and a silk industry had briefly flourished. During the 1830s, in the midst of another craze for silk culture, many people became convinced that the soil of the southern mountains would be ideal for such an enterprise, and a proliferation of "expert" literature fueled this euphoria. In response, North Carolina passed a law in 1836 providing for the incorporation of companies organized for the manufacture of silk and sugar.[41]

In 1845 Thomas asked the legislature to extend the provisions of the act to allow the Cherokees of Quallatown and Cheoah to participate. This was done, after which he organized the so-called Cherokee Company at Quallatown. His original preamble and bylaws make it obvious that he had objectives in mind other than simply producing silk, so the governor required a modification before officially proclaiming existence of the company in June 1847. Thomas then leased a large tract of land in Haywood County to the corporation for a 99-year period.[42] As suggested in the previous chapter, this was probably the primary purpose of the Cherokee Company, to serve as a holding company for the land Thomas had acquired for the Indians; ideally, it would be an umbrella organization protecting Indian land tenure and relieving Thomas of some of the personal legal liability. At the same time, however, he was genuinely hopeful that silk culture would succeed, and he imported a number of Chinese mulberry saplings to distribute among the Band. But a thriving silk industry proved to be chimerical, just another of Thomas's elusive dreams, and the Cherokee Company faded into obscurity.[43]

The Cherokee Company resembled in certain aspects the *gadugi,* a traditional Cherokee institution which has been defined as "a group of men who join together to form a company, with rules and officers, for continued economic and social reciprocity." The origins of the *gadugi* may be seen in such early communal activities as constructing public buildings and tilling community fields, and the institution evolved through the nineteenth and early twentieth centuries. Thomas's original bylaws describe a kind of cooperative endeavor that seems to fit within such a context, but it is not clear whether he was consciously seeking to meet contemporary Cherokee needs with a familiar institution.[44]

It is certain, however, that some traditional social activities remained intact. Though Lanman claimed the Cherokees had voluntarily abandoned "a goodly number of their more ridiculous games," they reveled in their hotly contested ballplay, which was similar to that of many other North American tribes. Probably it was a reflection of traditional religious values as well as a familiar, enjoyable form of competition. According to Lanman, the ballplay was conducted as in earlier days, with only a few exceptions: "In the first place, they are not allowed to wager their property on the games, as of old, unless it be some trifle in the way of a woollen belt or cotton handkerchief, and they are prohibited from choking each other, and breaking their heads and legs when excited, as was their habit in former times." He then described a contest that attracted a large and "picturesque" crowd of men, women, and children. The young male contestants had gone through an elaborate ritual and preparation the preceding evening. The next morning the opposing sides stayed out of view while the "game-director" prepared the field, a large level plain. After every stick and stone had been removed, two goals were set up about six hundred yards apart. Then, when everything was ready,

> a shrill whoop was given from one end of the plain, and immediately answered by the opposing party, when they all made their appearance, marching slowly to the centre, shouting and yelling as they passed along. Each party consisted of thirty splendidly formed young men, who were unincumbered [sic] by any clothing, save their common waistband [sic], and every individual carried in his hand a pair of ball sticks, made with a braided bag at one end. As the parties approached the centre, the ladyloves of the players ran out upon the plain and gave their favorite champions a variety of articles, such as belts and handkerchiefs, which they were willing to wager upon the valor of their future husbands.

The game director delivered a lengthy speech, then threw the ball high into the air to begin the contest. Starting at midfield, the teams would play until one had managed to get the ball beyond the other's goal twelve times. The equipment and rules, such as they were, would be familiar to a modern lacrosse player. Contestants carried the ball in the pouches of their sticks, and there was considerable body contact. In fact, the "game" assumed a primitive inten-

Sawanugi, a Cherokee Ballplayer, 1888
(Negative 1043-A, National Anthropological Archives, Smithsonian Institution.)

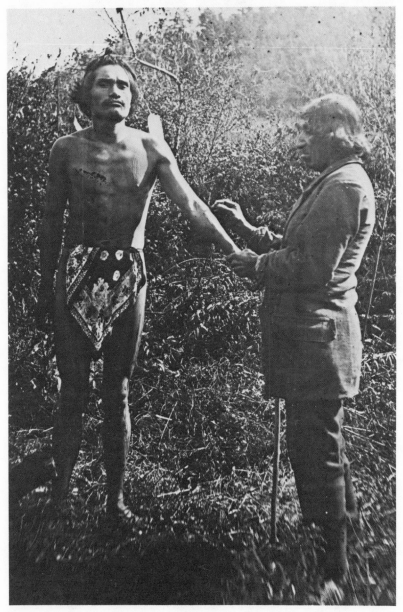

Scratching a Ballplayer. Scratching the contestants was a common ritual preceding the ballplay.
(Negative 1042, National Anthropological Archives, Smithsonian Institution.)

Cherokee Women and Children Watching the Ballplay, 1900. More than fifty years after Charles Lanman's visit, the ballplay was still a dressup occasion for spectators.
(Negative 1029-2, National Anthropological Archives, Smithsonian Institution.)

Cherokee Ballplayers in Action, 1900
(Negative 1038-16, National Anthropological Archives, Smithsonian Institution.)

Ballplayers Wrestling. The ballplay frequently included wrestling and other physical contact.
(Negative 1038-36, National Anthropological Archives, Smithsonian Institution.)

sity as niceties were forgotten. An amazed Lanman observed that a horde of participants

> would rush together in the most desperate and fearful manner, presenting, as they struggled for the ball, the appearance of a dozen gladiators, striving to overcome a monster serpent; and then again, as one man would secure the ball and start for the boundary line of his opponent, the races which ensued were very beautiful and exciting. Wrestling conflicts also occurred quite frequently, and it often seemed as if the players would break every bone in their bodies as they threw each other in the air, or dragged each other over the ground; and many of the leaps, which single individuals performed, were really superb. The exercise was of a character that would kill the majority of white men.

When the struggle finally ended after two hours, the participants rushed to the river for an icy bath. After they reappeared on the field in their normal attire, the chief who had held the stakes paid the victorious athletes.[45]

Not surprisingly, many whites eagerly flocked to watch such enthralling contests, and Thomas was shrewd enough to take advantage of this. For many years he scheduled the ballplay in conjunction with political speeches or rallies, guaranteeing large crowds for his own electioneering. The guests at these spectacles included such prominent men as Governor Charles Manly and the son of Senator John C. Calhoun of South Carolina.[46]

We have less information on other traditional games and rituals, perhaps because Thomas viewed them as anachronistic. But we do know that the Eastern Cherokees continued to celebrate the green corn ceremonies and dances that had always been an essential element of tribal life. There were also frequent speeches and festivities in the town houses. We know, too, that Enola continued to practice his curious blend of Methodism and conjuring while a young man named Swimmer (Ayunini) was learning and compiling traditional lore that would make him the Band's most influential traditionalist. Born about 1835, he spent the years preceding the Civil War at the knees of his elders and learned the Cherokee syllabary in order better to preserve the ancient mysteries.[47]

By the eve of the Civil War, little had changed among the North Carolina Cherokees. The 1860 census showed a significant increase in population at Quallatown to 1,063, but it was still overwhelmingly a primitive agricultural society, with only eleven males listing nonfarm occupations; five were blacksmiths, four ministers, one a mechanic, and one a school teacher (despite there being no school at the time). They still principally raised corn, along with potatoes, wheat, peas, and orchard fruits. They had about the same number of farm animals as in 1850, but now over half were swine. Just nine Cherokees owned real estate, indicating that most had not yet paid Thomas, and a few also claimed small personal estates.[48] Otherwise, their society was much the way it had been in 1838, and this appears to have been the case for most other North Carolina Cherokees as well.

Cherokee life, then, was a mixture of traditionalism and progressivism, with the former clearly prevailing despite Thomas's claims. Both he and Charles Lanman tended to see the Indians through rose-colored glasses, glossing over their obvious poverty in favor of depicting an idealized Jeffersonian stereotype—Thomas because he wanted to prove them worthy citizens, Lanman because he was naive. And yet, even though theirs was a "backwards" society, so was that of most of their white neighbors. There is little doubt, moreover, that most Indians preferred their lifestyle to any other. Lanman was probably correct when he said the Cherokees were "the happiest community that I have yet met with in this Southern country."[49] Certainly, they clung to their Indian identity with a tenacity that defied attempts to make them something else. That was the true measure of their traditionalism. They were *Cherokees*. Unfortunately, as Indians they were poorly prepared to cope with either the concept or reality of the American Civil War.

5

THE CIVIL WAR

Most white southerners could readily invoke one or more sociopolitical theorems to justify secession, but if the Eastern Cherokees comprehended the dissolution of the Union it must have seemed threatening to their interests. William Thomas, after all, had pressed their claims for many years in Washington and had continually emphasized the obligations of the United States to them. Now, having voted for North Carolina's secession as member of a special convention in May 1861, he was asking them to repudiate that federal connection. It is a measure of his persuasiveness that the chiefs, after admitting their bewilderment, declared themselves ready to defend North Carolina against any aggression by the United States. Thomas then organized about 200 Indians into a local defensive force called the Junaluska Zouaves, a tribute to the great warrior who had died just a few years before. A Raleigh newspaper, in noting this development, warned the "Northern barbarians, with A. Blinkun at their head, to guard their scalps" whenever they heard Cherokee war whoops. But for the present the Zouaves remained inactive as Thomas returned to his political responsibilities as state senator and member of the secession convention.[1]

Many whites in western North Carolina responded enthusiastically to the Confederacy's need for fighting men, organizing volunteer units in Haywood, Jackson, Cherokee, and other counties. G.T. Jarrett raised one such company and suggested that Thomas ask President Jefferson Davis about the propriety of incorporating some Cherokees into his outfit. The combined force would use the mountains of Kentucky as a base from which to harry federal troops before they could reach Cumberland Gap.[2]

A number of Cherokees appeared eager to join the volunteer forces. B.M. Edney was raising a regiment near Asheville and reported that 200 Indians were "begging" to enlist. George W.

Hayes, a former friend of Thomas turned political foe, had at least two Cherokees in his cavalry unit, but it was said he would as soon be caught in a voting booth with a free Negro as to associate with them—a mortal insult to Cherokees. Such treatment may have been part of a calculated policy to discourage them from volunteering.[3]

Thomas meanwhile devoted himself to his ongoing political work and made preparations for the November elections, when he hoped to win his race for the Confederate Congress. He did find time to engineer the introduction of a bill authorizing the governor to raise a battalion of Cherokees into Confederate service, and when it passed the senate he wrote President Davis that such a force was ready. Davis responded affirmatively, noting that the Cherokees might be useful defending the coastal and swampy regions of the state (a disease-ridden area that later claimed the lives of many Lumbee Indians who were conscripted to work there). But George Hayes helped defeat the bill in the house, apparently because he believed it would confer citizenship on the Indians. The exasperated Thomas complained to a friend that it seemed advisable to pass such a bill before the Cherokees enlisted because they had never served in the militia. And he once again argued that the Cherokees were *already* citizens of North Carolina by virtue of the treaties of 1817, 1819, and 1835.[4]

In any case, Davis's authorization was sufficient for Thomas to begin organizing a Cherokee battalion, which probably included the former Zouaves. He also suggested that troops from an existing regiment combine with local Indians and whites into a unit to be known as the North Carolina Highland Brigade or Legion. The state adjutant general was willing to muster the Indians into service, but Thomas proved difficult. He wanted the state first to recognize Cherokee citizenship and to arm and equip them. In the face of such preconditions, state officials decided against the muster.[5] This setback merely caused Thomas to redouble his efforts to create an Indian fighting force, especially after he lost his bid for a seat in Congress. He was also preparing defenses near Oconaluftee Gap in order to protect the route linking Quallatown and Sevier County, Tennessee. This latter action reflected his often expressed belief that the mountains were the key to southern defense, as well as his knowledge that East Tennessee was a region predominantly Unionist or "Tory" in sentiment.[6]

As part of his overall strategy, Thomas visited Richmond early in 1862 to promote his views on using the Cherokees as allies. The

Confederate Congress had already ratified a series of treaties with the Five Civilized Tribes of Indian Territory, promising them, among other things, a continuation of the annuities formerly paid by the United States. Thomas, who previously insisted on a clear separation between his clients and the Cherokee Nation, now claimed that the Cherokee treaty also applied to the North Carolina Indians and that they should receive their share of the annuities and interest. He persuaded James Terrell to provide a copy of the Mullay Roll to the Confederate commissioner of Indian affairs and to certify how much remained to be disbursed to the enrollees since the last payments of 1859. The Confederacy later agreed to pay the North Carolina Cherokees more than $19,000 in interest, but the exigencies of war apparently prevented it from doing so. Meanwhile the U.S. government suspended payments to all disloyal tribes, including the North Carolina Cherokees.[7]

Soon after his return from Richmond, Thomas agreed to turn over his Cherokee troops to the Confederate States and accept a commission as their commanding officer. In April 1862 Major George Washington Morgan, himself part-Cherokee, mustered Thomas and a detachment of Quallatown Indians into Confederate service as part of the North Carolina troops supplied to the central government; they were to serve for three years or the war's duration. Eventually this detachment was divided into two companies, each numbering more than 110 Indian privates and noncommissioned officers. Commissioned officers included whites, mixed-bloods, and fullbloods. Among the junior officers were James Taylor and John Ross, who were to assume great prominence among the Indians after the war. Enola and Swimmer served as sergeants.[8]

For Swimmer the war must have produced a sense of anticipation, a stirring of the old Cherokee juices so carefully distilled in him by his elders. Now in his mid-twenties, he was strong and lithe and imbued with the knowledge and lore of countless generations. He knew of the heroic deeds of Oconostota, Dragging Canoe, and Junaluska. And perhaps he had already begun compiling the sacred tribal rites in his private notebook, using the Cherokee syllabary to preserve the wisdom of the past. He and the other young males must have instinctively responded to the exhortations of Major Morgan to participate in the first Cherokee warfare since the Creek campaigns of 1813–1814. When Morgan told them the South had just won a great victory at Shiloh (a misrepresentation), they were quick to let their war whoops echo off the mountains. Delighted with the reaction, a Confederate officer called them "as fine a body of men as ever went into the service."[9]

One can only surmise that Swimmer took a leading role in the traditional rituals invoked at Quallatown as the Cherokees prepared for war. According to James Mooney, the war "brought out all the latent Indian in their nature. Before starting to the front every man consulted an oracle stone to learn whether or not he might hope to return in safety. The start was celebrated with a grand old-time war dance at the townhouse . . . and the same dance was repeated at frequent intervals thereafter, the Indians being 'painted and feathered in good old style.' "[10]

The first order of business was to proceed to Knoxville, where the Cherokees would be stationed. It was a leisurely and circuitous march, taking them through Franklin and Valleytown, North Carolina, and Madisonville and Sweetwater, Tennessee. The time was used to instruct the warriors in the rudiments of white tactics, and messengers were dispatched to Cheoah, Sand Town, and other Indian districts inviting able-bodied males to join the entourage. As the officers became more familiar with their Indian enlistees, they were pleasantly surprised. Not only did they seem more adept at drills than their white compatriots, but they were also the best behaved soldiers raised from the mountain districts. At Sweetwater the Indians went into temporary camp while Thomas and Morgan took a train to Knoxville to make preparations for their arrival. James Terrell, the unit's first lieutenant, assumed command in their absence. When arrangements were complete, the Indians made the short trip in railroad freight cars while Terrell rode by invitation in the passenger car.[11]

The Cherokees proved to be a major attraction in Knoxville. As they marched from the depot down Gay Street, the main thoroughfare, a jostling, growing crowd of townspeople vied for a closer look at the newcomers. The Indians stayed at nearby Camp Oconostota for about two weeks, during which time they received visits from the elites of Knoxville society and were the "wonder of all the city." The highlight of their stay occurred when they conducted Christian services in their own language at the First Presbyterian Church. Goggle-eyed whites filled every available pew, eager to witness the strange spectacle. The Indians had their Cherokee hymnals, and Unaguskie, their chaplain, led the service. A local editor described him as tall, slender, graceful, and eloquent, though having "little of the mannerism of the modern pulpit. His sermon seemed to be persuasive rather than denunciatory, advisory and parental rather than condemnatory and authoritative." The music struck the reporter as "less artistic" than in a white service; and of Unaguskie's theology, he said, "nothing can be known certainly." The whites sat through the entire proceedings, enrapt but not understanding a word of what was said.[12]

By the end of May, Thomas had set up permanent camp at Strawberry Plains, near Knoxville, and divided his Indian force into two companies. In apprising Governor Henry T. Clark of his efforts to complete an Indian battalion, he noted that his warriors had already proved their effectiveness by rescuing Confederate pickets in the Cumberland Mountains and harassing Union bushwhackers. In June about forty of them accompanied their leader to Chattanooga to observe the fighting there, and Thomas was lucky enough to capture an errant Yankee soldier from Michigan. Reporting the event to his wife, he wrote, "The Indians say as I took the first prisoner each of them must take one to be even with me."[13]

Except for such occasional forays, camping at Strawberry Plains was monotonous at best and miserable the rest of the time. Camp fever, measles, and other diseases were rampant, killing three Indians by late June and temporarily incapacitating others; another Cherokee died under the wheels of a train. An outbreak of mumps completely mystified the warriors, and, lacking a white physician, they relied upon the traditional charms and incantations of their own doctor, Oosawih. These seemed to work as well as any orthodox medical procedures, and before long the Indians were well acclimated to the rigors of bivouac. They enjoyed reasonably good health during the rest of the war.[14]

Like many Confederate troops, Thomas's men were at first poorly equipped. The Indians commonly had only small squirrel rifles, some bored to a wider diameter for larger bullets. Other standard equipment included percussion caps, powder, and bar lead to be melted down and molded into bullets. Many also had long, steel-tipped spears, similar to those issued other North Carolina troops at the beginning of the war. Such weapons were probably less effective than traditional bows and arrows, and were soon replaced with more modern weapons. Union army accounts by late 1863 make it appear the Indians were reasonably well armed.[15]

Thomas was successful enough in his recruiting efforts that by July 1862 his force of Indians and whites had reached battalion strength. By September he was commanding colonel of a regiment, later mistakenly referred to as the Sixty-ninth North Carolina Infantry Regiment. Companies A and B consisted of the original Indian recruits. The regiment was soon supplemented by additional infantry, cavalry, engineers, and light artillery, and the entire fighting force became known as Thomas's Legion of Indians and Highlanders—or, more simply, as the Thomas Legion. During its existence, and taking into account the many unit transfers, it totaled about 2,800 officers and men and included another two companies of Indians. Thus approximately 400 Cherokees served in the Legion at one time or another, representing most of the able-bodied men of the Band.[16]

The Legion was part of the Confederate Army's Department of East Tennessee, headquartered at Knoxville, and through most of 1863 was stationed at Strawberry Plains or Zollicoffer, in upper East Tennessee. Its units operated along the axis of the vital railroad linking Chattanooga, Knoxville, and Bristol; in addition, they ranged into western North Carolina and the Cumberland Mountains of Kentucky and Tennessee. On one occasion a Legion force also ventured into Georgia to arrest deserters, tories, and fugitive conscripts. Despite their seldom being more than a hundred miles from Quallatown, they might as well have been on the opposite side of the continent. Thomas complained in June 1863 that he had been home only four days during the previous fourteen months. And a warrior probably spoke for soldiers of all eras when he lamented that by the time he returned to his family his children would no longer recognize him.[17]

As it turned out, a serious military setback enabled some of the troops to enjoy Christmas of 1863 at home. A federal army under General Ambrose Burnside captured Knoxville in September, necessitating Thomas's retreat with a portion of his command to the North Carolina side of the mountains; from there he launched periodic sorties back into Tennessee. But his effectiveness was limited because he had under his immediate command only about 300 men, mostly Indians; the rest of the Legion, as well as a few Cherokees, remained in upper East Tennessee as part of General Alfred E. ("Mudwall") Jackson's force. Thomas's pleas that it be reunited under his command for the defense of North Carolina provoked no affirmative response in Richmond.[18]

The initial enthusiasm for the Confederacy quickly faded in western North Carolina. Fiercely independent mountain people came to resent the all-too-frequent visits of officers who requisitioned their crops and livestock to feed hungry troops. Even worse, the onerous Confederate conscription law convinced many that the wealthy slavocracy expected poor people to win the war with their blood; not surprisingly, men had few qualms about avoiding the draft or deserting at the first opportunity. It became dangerous for a conscription officer even to show his face in some quarters. Enforcement was almost impossible, and many men fled to join Union forces. With few slaves, and the able-bodied white men either hiding or in the army, many mountain families had insufficient manpower to operate the farms. Unseasonable frosts killed the few crops that did grow. Bushwhackers took advantage of the chaos by hiding out in the mountains and engaging in an orgy of pillaging, burning, and murdering. The country, poor to begin with, was devastated, a land of famine and fear. Soldiers serving loyally on the lines in Virginia were demoralized by plaintive letters from wives beseeching them to come home before their children starved. Soon, they joined the long line of deserters straggling back through the mountains.[19]

Cherokee women and children suffered along with other civilians. By the spring of 1863 they were unable to acquire such necessities as corn meal, flour, and salt. A year later they were even more desperate. In February 1864 Thomas pleaded for supplies from South Carolina to relieve the distress of his Indian troops and their families, who were "now in a starving condition." Such assistance, he feared, might come too late to prevent starvation among the Cherokees, which would obviously diminish the Legion's fighting effectiveness. In that case he would probably have to withdraw eastward across the Blue Ridge, leaving the western Carolinas open to Yankee incursions.[20] Colonel John B. Palmer, Thomas's immediate superior, thought the Indians' suffering might be alleviated if Thomas prepared a memorial describing their distress and forwarded it to Richmond. If anything, however, the Cherokees' plight worsened. Though they received some corn meal and flour from South Carolina, it did little more than whet appetites that had too long been deprived. Margaret Love, wife of a Legion officer, reported that some Indians were attempting to survive by eating weeds or gnawing on the bark of trees. A few even took the extraordinary step of moving out of their beloved homeland into Georgia and South Carolina, where conditions were not so bleak. During the remaining months of the war Thomas often bought on his own account what foodstuffs he could for distribution among the Indians, but his actions simply worsened his own financial situation. Unable to attend to business affairs because of his military responsibilities, he sank ever deeper into indebtedness.[21]

The Indians saw little of the combat romanticized by Civil War popularizers, and probably not more than a handful died in action. They mostly stood guard, rounded up conscripts, appropriated foodstuffs and livestock from unhappy farmers, and pursued deserters and bushwhackers—necessary and sometimes dangerous duty, but hardly glamorous. They were especially noteworthy for their skill as trackers and for their devotion to duty. One stalwart sentinel, to the amazement of his white officer, stood an uninterrupted fourteen-hour watch "in one of the fiercest and most terrible snow storms" in the region's history. When the occasion arose, moreover, the Cherokees fought with skill and courage in traditional Indian style; being rational men, however, they were reluctant to confront Yankee cannons, the "big guns on wheels."[22]

There were critics who believed that Thomas's own timidity limited the Legion's combat experience. Occasionally they expressed their sentiments in forceful language, but usually they were circumspect. As Burnside's army prepared to occupy Knoxville early in September 1863, a Confederate sympathizer reported that "a small party of federals approached within four miles" of Strawberry Plains and burned a bridge. Then, in her laconic words, "Col Thomas seeing the light and believing the 'Philistines' were soon to be upon him skidadled [*sic*] with his indians and one company of dismounted cavalry—I have heard nothing from that quarter since." There were rumors that the federals had captured him, but a Union cavalry commander who pursued the Legion complained that the Cherokees refused to stand and fight. This may have reflected a traditional Indian desire to avoid combat unless possessing a clear superiority in numbers, or, more likely, Thomas simply recognized that on this occasion discretion was the sensible course. Certainly, his small force could not have prevented Burnside's occupation of the area.[23]

At times, however, the Indians knew the acrid smell of battle. There were the predictable skirmishes, one of the best-chronicled of which occurred on December 10, 1863, when the Fifteenth Pennsylvania Volunteer Cavalry attacked a detachment of Cherokees camped along a ridge near Gatlinburg, Tennessee. Leading the charge was Colonel William Jackson Palmer, who was a general by war's end and later gained fame in the construction of western railroads. As the federal troops dismounted and advanced toward the camp, the Indians let out their war whoops and directed several volleys toward the enemy, wounding three. What followed was "a brisk fight from behind trees, rocks and fallen timber, in regular Indian fashion." Then the Cherokees retreated, abandoning their camp, some arms and provisions, about fifteen horses, and their corn cakes, still cooking over campfires. The famished Yankees wolfed down the cakes and pursued the Indians into the mountain forest, where, after more exchanges of gunfire, the Cherokees hid "as quickly and successfully as a flock of frightened partridges." Palmer captured one Indian but did not know the number of enemy casualties. He speculated that the Cherokees had planned to winter in the area, since they had constructed log huts and frame buildings and were living with their "squaws." Next day the Pennsylvanians and a detachment of Tennessee Unionists resumed pursuit of the Indians through the rugged terrain of what is now the Great Smoky Mountains National Park. But because Thomas had fortified the passes, the Yankees retired to the flatlands and savored their victory of the previous day.[24]

Regardless of how often the Cherokees actually fought, there soon emerged among Unionists the distressing stereotype of the savage, implacable warrior—a fearsome beast immune to the amenities of "civilized" warfare. Perhaps it is too much to expect that such stories would *not* circulate. Few people during wartime discriminate too carefully when it comes to dividing truth from fiction, and the "savage Indian" stereotype is an enduring one in American history.[25] Thomas A.R. Nelson, a Unionist Tennessee politician, compared the Cherokees to bloodhounds in their search for refugees and conscripts. "England, in her wars with America," he noted, "received and deserved the execration of the world for her barbarity in employing the Savages; and the Southern Confederacy will become equally odious."[26]

As stories about the Cherokees circulated, they were embellished in the retelling. From the predictable and rather mild complaint that the Indians were "doing the work of Treason, Hell and Secession," the characterizations became more personalized. An East Tennessee Unionist referred to them as the "wretched, ignorant, half-civilized offscouring of humanity," and "long-haired, greasy-looking savages who could not even speak a word of English, or understand a plea for mercy." A Yankee general said that Thomas's force "had become a terror" to Unionists by "the atrocities they were daily perpetrating." And Andrew Johnson, the Tennessee Unionist appointed by Lincoln as wartime governor of that state (the Yankee portion, at least), alluded to the Indians in the course of a lengthy speech to the Union League in New York City. Dramatizing the supposed horrors besetting southern Unionists, he remarked, "Women are now insulted, children murdered, fathers and sons chased and hunted in the woods by red Indians, who cut off their ears and show them as trophies."[27]

Daniel Ellis, a noted Union guide from East Tennessee, subscribed to the savage Indian stereotype in his memoirs, published in 1867. He said a company of "red savages" appeared in upper East Tennessee in the spring of 1863 to track down conscripts and Unionists. Many whites hiding out in the mountains, he claimed, "had the greatest dread" of the Indians. "There was not a day passed but some of the poor Union men were either killed or captured by these infernal Indians," although he admitted "they were not half so cruel as the white rebel soldiers." Having tempered his criticism of the Cherokees somewhat, he later returned to the stereotype by saying that he particularly "desired to kill some of them for the mischief they had done . . . when they were engaged in catching conscripts, murdering white men, plundering houses, and frightening women and children to death." Because of this, he was "in favor of killing all the Indians that might fall into our hands." And to further enforce the stereotype, an illustration in his memoirs shows an Indian scalping a Union soldier while another triumphantly holds aloft a bloody trophy. The caption reads, "Thomas's Rebel Indians Murdering Union Men."[28]

The sources disagree on whether the Cherokees actually committed atrocities. Thomas, of course, was proud of his Indian troops and viewed their participation in the war as honorable proof of their loyalty to the South. He had warned them against scalping, and Major William W. Stringfield, one of his officers, insisted that the Indians took scalps on only one occasion. That occurred at Baptist Gap in the Cumberland Mountains in September 1862. When Lieutenant Astoogatogeh, a grandson of Junaluska, was killed in a skirmish, his tribesmen were so enraged that they gave a blood-curdling war whoop, dashed forward, and, before they could be stopped, scalped several of the Yankee dead and wounded. The mortified Confederate officers apologized to their Union counterparts as best they could. Otherwise, Stringfield maintained, the Indians were "humane and generous" toward Yankees. Though a few occasionally got drunk or became involved in minor scrapes,

"Thomas's Rebel Indians Murdering Union Men." Unionists were quick to resort to the "savage Indian" stereotype when discussing their Cherokee foes. (Source: Daniel Ellis, *Thrilling Adventures of Daniel Ellis* [New York, 1867], p. 406.)

"their average behavior was better than that of the whites." In contrast, James Terrell claimed that not even Thomas could prevent them from scalping whenever they had the chance, and that by the end of the war they had a number of these grisly souvenirs.[29] This seems an exaggeration, since the Indians did not engage in many battles, and if they had scalped at will the memoirs of Union veterans would have been even more vitriolic in their denunciations.

It must be admitted, however, that Thomas and other southerners from time to time accepted and even cultivated the image of the warlike Indians. A Raleigh newspaper warned the Yanks to guard their hair, and a prominent white lady who visited the Cherokees in Knoxville asked them to bring back some scalps—much to the consternation of Thomas, who gently rebuked her. This stereotypical association of Indians, war whoops, and scalping appeared again in an otherwise flattering account published in an Asheville newspaper: "Their shrill war whoop makes one immediately clasp his hand on his head to see if his scalp is safe!"[30] That many found such images appealing is apparent in the report of a visitor to Zollicoffer who found the Indians yelling war whoops and engaging in their traditional ballplay for the amusement of a large crowd of whites. The Cherokees were "in their *original costumes*, and *barefooted* besides." It seems that Thomas was using his warriors as a kind of sideshow to impress his audience and drum up enlistees. Local people were not the only ones fascinated by the Indians; a newspaper as distant and influential as the Richmond *Enquirer* devoted attention to North Carolina's "aboriginal warriors."[31]

Thomas doubtless delighted in the image of invincible—if not savage—Cherokees and circulated stories of their prowess. And Unionists readily acknowledged that prowess, whether real or imaginary. A story circulated about a Union Army recruiter who, knowing the Indians were on his trail and that escape was "hopeless," surrendered to a white southerner to avoid being taken by the warriors. The *Knoxville Register* fairly chortled when it averred that Thomas and his "trusty and sagacious" allies would soon "root out" the traitors of East Tennessee. But Daniel Ellis insisted that Confederate officers did more than simply exalt Cherokee prowess; he charged them with actually goading the Indians into perpetrating cruel deeds.[32] That seems unlikely, in view of the character of Thomas and most of his fellow officers.

Though they lacked much combat experience, the Indians proved to be as effective as anyone in campaigning against tories and bushwhackers. For example, detachments of Cherokees cooperated with various army units in operations on both sides of the state line near Shelton Laurel, North Carolina, a site in Madison County that was notorious as a haven for desperadoes. A major atrocity occurred there early in 1863, when a Confederate officer executed without trial thirteen men and boys he suspected of being allied with the criminals. Fortunately for their reputation, the Cherokees were not involved in this episode.[33]

The fine line between bushwhacking and making legitimate war is exemplified by the case of Goldman Bryson, accused of murdering John Timson in 1856. Confederates viewed him as nothing more than a tory desperado whose gang terrorized Cherokee County. On the other hand, Bryson held the rank of captain in a Unionist outfit and was under orders to recruit men for federal forces. Whatever his true character, Confederates were determined to end his depredations. In October 1863 Captain C.H. Taylor, a Valley River Cherokee serving in the Thomas Legion, led an Indian detachment that pursued Bryson, killed him, and scattered the gang. A short time later some of the Indians paraded through the streets of Murphy wearing "portions of Bryson's bloody and bullet-pierced uniform." While this was hardly "civilized" behavior, the Cherokees could be forgiven their elation for evening an old score. Besides, bushwhackers had no compunction about murdering them as well as whites—and did so from time to time. This kind of violence was a distressing yet natural phenomenon in a ravaged land where loyalties were so sharply divided.[34]

There is reason to believe that in many respects the Cherokees were much like their white enlisted counterparts. No doubt they found the army tedious and monotonous and yearned for the warmth of their own hearths. In those simpler days of warfare when white troops amused themselves with games or tunes played on a mouth organ, the Cherokees had their own diversion—the traditional ballplay. Whether performing for appreciative audiences or merely contenting themselves, the Cherokees could quickly lose themselves in the ebb and flow of this ancient competition. In fact, one Indian detachment assigned to guard a bridge became so engrossed in a contest that it barely escaped capture by a Union force that suddenly appeared.[35]

As the federal threat to western North Carolina became more pronounced after 1863, General Robert B. Vance, Confederate commander of the region, clearly saw the wisdom of Thomas's long-standing obsession with defending the mountain passes. The idea was to block all the passes from Ducktown, Tennessee, northward to Hot Springs, North Carolina; the Confederates could then stage raids through the passes to hit federal forces in Tennessee or to capture badly needed supplies. Shortly after New Year's Day 1864, Vance ordered Thomas and his Indians to accompany him on a raid to obtain provisions. Vance's force totaled about 500 men, including 150 Cherokees. Thomas advised against the move, but the general was adamant. Crossing into Tennessee by way of Oconaluftee Gap, Vance left most of his men with Thomas at Gatlinburg and proceeded toward Sevierville with nearly 200 cavalry. On January 13 he captured a Union wagon train of provisions and then headed toward Newport. Stopping for a rest at Shultz's Mill on Cosby Creek, Vance's force was surprised by Union cavalry under the redoubtable Colonel William Palmer, who had fought the Cherokees just a month before. Palmer completely routed the Confederates, taking Vance and a number of his men prisoner.[36]

Soon the Yankees became increasingly bold in their own raids, crossing into western North Carolina from Tennessee and challenging Confederate defenses. Less than a month after Vance's capture, General Samuel D. Sturgis of the U.S. Army learned that the Legion was operating along the Little Tennessee River and ordered Major Francis M. Davidson of the Fourteenth Illinois Cavalry to attack. Davidson, with about 400 men and two howitzers, left his encampment on the morning of January 31 and headed into North Carolina via Cade's Cove and the valley of the Little Tennessee. On the morning of February 2 the federals heard that perhaps as many as 300 Indians were camped at the mouth of Deep Creek. About two in the afternoon they overran the Cherokee pickets and immediately rode on to attack the main body of Indians. Quickly recovering from their surprise, the Cherokees grabbed their weapons, scrambled to the top of a nearby bluff, and fiercely defended themselves. In "close and desperate" fighting, they were finally driven from this position. After taking some prisoners, Davidson returned to Tennessee.[37]

The various accounts of Davidson's attack differ in many respects and reflect the vagaries of warfare as perceived by opposing soldiers. The substance of federal reports was that the Fourteenth Illinois had won a great victory over Thomas. "This nest of Indians," General Sturgis said, "may be considered as entirely destroyed, nearly 200 of them having been killed." Union casualties were announced as two dead and six wounded.[38] Thomas, in contrast, insisted that they had "arrested the progress" of the Yankees, killing eight while suffering only two deaths themselves. He admitted the enemy had captured between twenty and thirty Indians and whites. Regardless of which side won, the Union raid was impressive enough to worry Thomas and his superiors about the vulnerability of western North Carolina.[39]

Some of the captured Indians were taken to Knoxville, where federal officers tried to cajole them into renouncing the Confederacy. Southern newspapers reported with glee that the Indians tricked their captors. While in that city "they were flattered and feasted, big talks held, and magnificent promises made, if they would abandon the Confederacy and join the Lincoln government. They were promised their liberty and *five thousand dollars in gold*, if they would bring in *the scalp! of their Chief, Col. Wm. H. Thomas!* The Indians seemed to pause—consult—and finally agreed to the proposition. They were released, returned to their native mountains, sought the camp of their Chief, told him all, and have ever since been on the warpath—*after Yankee scalps*!"[40]

While some Indians no doubt did renege on their pledge of loyalty to the Union, the fact remains that others willingly served the United States. According to the *Knoxville Whig and Rebel Ventilator*, the captured Cherokees claimed they had been deceived into fighting against the United States. Two were allowed to return to the band and relate "the real facts," and a few days later their chief came in with others to take a loyalty oath. Since their pledge, the newspaper said, they had been abused and threatened by rebels. James Mooney, who worked among the Cherokees about twenty years after the war, related a similar story—that some Indians had "become dissatisfied" with the Confederacy and "were easily persuaded to the Union side." Their headman was able to convince a few other Cherokees to do likewise.[41]

In any case, there were anywhere from a dozen to thirty Indians who accompanied Colonel George W. Kirk on a spectacular Union raid from Tennessee deep into North Carolina in June 1864. For the rest of the war these men continued to serve in Kirk's outfit, the Third North Carolina Mounted Infantry Volunteers. Most of them probably came from Cherokee County, which was a hotbed of toryism and readily accessible to federal forces. The Indians of this region, moreover, did not have the same personal loyalty to Thomas that those of Quallatown did. Like many poor whites, they probably saw no reason why they should defend the interests of slaveholders, and at least one Cherokee deserter was married to a slave.[42] Though the Unionist Indians were clearly a minority of their tribe, their disaffection was an ominous portent. They sometimes referred to their pro-southern tribesmen as Anighisgi, the name of a people that, according to Eastern Cherokee lore, were mortal enemies.[43] The bitterness and threatened violence that attended the Unionists' return home after the war was symptomatic of the factionalism that ravaged the Band.

The final year of the war was a time of turmoil and controversy for the Legion. Despite Thomas's continued pleas for the return of his troops in Tennessee, they were instead dispatched to the bloody battlefields of Virginia, where their ranks were quickly decimated. Most of the survivors finally rejoined the Legion in North Carolina during the fall of 1864, but a few Indians were supposedly assigned to other regiments in Virginia "and were present at the final siege and surrender of Richmond."[44]

In the spring of 1865 there were rumors the Legion planned an offensive against the federally controlled railroad in East Tennessee, but Union counterthreats required Thomas to remain east of the Smoky Mountains. In February, Colonel George Kirk returned with about 600 men and burned Waynesville before portions of the Legion repulsed him at Soco Creek, on almost the same spot where Tecumseh had exhorted the Cherokees to join him against the Americans during the War of 1812. Detachments of the Legion helped ward off one Union advance on Asheville, but on April 25 another federal force occupied the city.[45] Coupled with Lee's capitulation at Appomattox two weeks before, this setback made it clear there was no point in prolonging hostilities in western North Carolina. Sometime early in May, in a skirmish on the outskirts of Waynesville, units of the Legion and some Union soldiers exchanged what were apparently the last shots of the war on North Carolina soil. Thomas put a final scare into the Yankees by threatening them with destruction at the hands of his gaudily painted warriors and then, almost meekly, he and other officers surrendered to Lieutenant Colonel William C. Bartlett. Present were Thomas, Lieutenant Colonel James R. Love, and Brigadier General James G. Martin, Confederate commander of the region. Martin's depleted forces consisted solely of the Thomas Legion, which included a regiment and two battalions; the Cherokee troops made up one of the latter. Complying with the magnanimous terms of surrender already offered at Appomattox, Bartlett paroled all Confederate officers and men after they surrendered their weapons.[46]

Accompanying Thomas to the surrender council was a bodyguard of about twenty Cherokees, his constant companions in that bushwhacker-infested country. He told Bartlett that these men and a number of other armed Indians had never been mustered into Confederate service and therefore should be allowed to retain their own weapons to defend themselves. Bartlett had his word that the Indians would never fire on a Union man.[47] The officer agreed, and Thomas wearily turned for home. The war was over, the Confederacy vanquished.

Now sixty years of age, Thomas had been reduced by the rigors of command to a shell of his former self; he had suffered physical, emotional, and financial loss. Friends soon noticed occasional erratic behavior and whispered that there had been telltale signs of mental instability even before the war ended. At first these were momentary lapses, and he could still focus on certain problems with vigor and lucidity. But some of his difficulties appeared beyond remedy. He owed large sums of money and lacked any means of paying them beyond selling the lands he had acquired in the Indians' behalf. And it must have pained him to realize that he had involved the Cherokees in a war that was contrary to their interests—and worse, a war they had lost. He had been partially discredited and would never again exercise the kind of leadership that he had before secession.

Thomas later maintained that he had never intended to involve the Indians in the Civil War, that in fact he wanted them to remain neutral. Only after outside pressures on them to enlist had become unbearable, he said, did he organize them under his command in order to keep them in their homeland and prevent their being abused by officers unfamiliar with their ways.[48] These arguments are not convincing. The fact is that Thomas campaigned for creation of a Cherokee battalion very early in the war, long before passage of the conscription law. For a while he was even willing to countenance the possibility of Cherokee soldiers being sent to the swamps and lowlands of coastal North Carolina. Then, after losing his race for the Confederate Congress, he saw himself as the logical leader of a large military force which included Indian units. It was through his initiative that the Cherokees became participants.

The war had been a disaster for the Indians. Immediately upon its

Cherokee Veterans of the Thomas Legion, photographed at the 1903 Reunion of Confederate veterans in New Orleans. William W. Stringfield, one of their white officers, is third from the left in the back row.
(Courtesy of the Museum of the Cherokee Indian.)

conclusion a devastating epidemic raged among them, bringing to a superstitious people what appeared to be retribution for joining a war that did not concern them. Those who survived were hungry, dispirited, and bedeviled by a host of problems and uncertainties. Most ominous of all was the bitter division among themselves, a factionalism resulting in part from the war and in part from the vacuum of leadership left by Thomas. The old days of harmony and consensus—the virtues so esteemed by traditionalists like Enola and Swimmer—were gone forever.

6

TROUBLED TIMES

Simple survival was the foremost concern of North Carolina Cherokees following the war. Their afflictions were many, but most frightening was the smallpox epidemic that raged among them like an out-of-control fire. Apparently brought home by a warrior who had served with Union forces, the disease seemed a final and horrible retribution for Cherokee participation in the war. Superstitious Indians attributed it to Yankee witchcraft, inspiring an oral tradition that persisted into the twentieth century. Immediately after the war, the story goes, two recently released Cherokee prisoners in Knoxville were ushered into a room where they were shown a red fish swimming in a bowl of water. After watching the fish for a while, they were allowed to return home, where they quickly became ill and infected others. To the Cherokees the connection between these events was obvious. Like many other Indians, they believed disease is the natural consequence of the machinations of spirits, ghosts, or human enemies.[1]

William Thomas helped as much as he could by hiring a doctor from Tennessee, but the physician was unable to halt the smallpox. Desperate, the Indians resorted to traditional remedies like the cold water douche and sweatbaths followed by plunges into icy streams. Modern physicians would be horrified by such practices for smallpox victims, and apparently most who resorted to them died. Other responses included medicine dances and hanging the carcasses of skunks over doorways to keep the pox at bay. Eventually, in 1866, the disease ran its natural course after killing about 125 Cherokees; many of the most prominent perished, contributing to the lack of postwar leadership.[2]

Certainly Thomas no longer qualified as undisputed leader, though he showed impressive initiative in procuring medical attention and food for the Cherokees during this period. Distracted by financial losses and recurring mental instability, stigmatized by having led the Cherokees into a disastrous war, he was as much an object of scorn as respect. Most of the Quallatown Indians still esteemed him, but even they were reluctant to follow him unquestioningly. Unfortunately, they had so long been mesmerized by the man that they were incapable of competing for the mantle of leadership with more acculturated Indians from Macon and Cherokee counties—men like George W. Bushyhead and James Taylor.[3]

Other afflictions besetting the Cherokees were almost biblical in nature and scope. Their fields were in ruin, their lands in jeopardy. Factionalism, virtually nonexistent before the war, proved even more virulent than smallpox. The old sense of propriety, the striving for consensus based upon an ethic of harmony, was fast disappearing at a time when they were most threatened as a people. Those who had served the Union were ostracized or vilified or, in at least one instance, even murdered. Demoralization was pervasive. Their children were undernourished, clothed in rags, and growing up in ignorance. And it appears that the temperance pledges inspired by Yonaguska back in the 1830s were too often forgotten; alcoholism now threatened them as it did many other tribes. It seemed the only thing not afflicting the Cherokees was a plague of locusts.[4]

As if it really mattered in the midst of such chaos, the state of North Carolina finally took steps to recognize the Indians as permanent residents. For years authorities had equivocated when asked for an explicit affirmation of the right of Cherokee residency. Now, at last, under the prodding of Governor Jonathan Worth, the General Assembly granted such permission on February 19, 1866. Worth had pointed out that it was the only way the Indians could obtain the money promised them in 1848 and again in 1855. But it was also probably a recognition of their loyalty to the state during the war. The act declared "That the Cherokee Indians who are now residents of the State of North Carolina, shall have the authority and permission to remain in the several counties of the State where they now reside; and shall be permitted to remain permanently therein so long as they may see proper to do so, any thing in the treaty of eighteen hundred and thirty-five to the contrary notwithstanding."[5] Nowhere did the act mention, or even imply, citizenship for the Cherokees. The legislature also passed a resolution asking the secretary of the interior to hold the funds owed the Cherokees and pay only their accrued annual interest; or, if the government preferred, the state treasurer would take charge of the money and pay the interest.[6]

Without amelioration of their condition, the belated recognition of the Cherokees' right of residency was a meaningless concession. They needed assistance, and the man who did the most to educate the public about their plight was George Bushyhead, headman of Sand Town in Macon County. He had periodically visited Washington before the war in behalf of family claims, and early in 1866 many Indians from Cherokee and Macon counties granted him power of attorney to represent their interests. His first step was to apply to North Carolina for a large reservation where his people would be able to raise their children in peace, protected from avaricious whites. In the meantime, he requested clothing and other necessities. The state provided no such assistance, but the legislature did appropriate $100 to enable "Chief" Bushyhead to travel to Washington and plead his case.[7]

Where before William Thomas had represented the North Carolina Indians in the corridors of Capitol Hill, now Bushyhead was their spokesman. On his visit there in March 1866 he claimed that a tribal council had appointed him official delegate for his people, though many Cherokees were unaware of such action. After describing the misery of his tribesmen, he requested payment of the interest on the transportation and subsistence fund of 1848 in order to alleviate their suffering. He also wanted federal assistance in obtaining a North Carolina reservation. But Commissioner of Indian Affairs Dennis N. Cooley said the government lacked authority to provide relief to the Cherokees since they were presumably citizens of their state.[8]

John B. Jones, the U.S. agent to the Cherokee Nation and a member of its Washington delegation, believed the logical solution was for the North Carolina Indians to move west. It is ironic that after thirty years of successful resistance to removal, thirty years of seeking acknowledgment of Cherokee rights by state and federal governments, the Indians would again hear and consider this suggestion. Commissioner Cooley, however, correctly noted that all previous attempts at removal had been "wholly unavailing." Besides, the only money available for such a purpose was the 1848 fund, and the Cherokees may have forfeited their rights to it by their recent disloyalty. But Cooley then softened his tone somewhat by saying that if the Indians *really* desired to move west, the government would do what it could to help.[9]

One way the Cherokee Nation and the United States could both encourage the North Carolina Indians to move was to include an appropriate clause in the new treaty that was being negotiated. Commissioner Cooley favored a provision whereby the Nation would welcome as citizens any North Carolina Cherokees who emigrated there. But the final treaty of July 1866 contained no such measure, probably because there were too many unanswered questions regarding the full range of rights any newcomers would enjoy. Despite this lack of formal incentive, sentiment clearly existed in Washington for removal.[10]

The Indians were divided on the issue of moving west, as they increasingly divided on most issues affecting them. A number desired to go, but, as in the early 1840s, they demanded their transportation money in advance. They insisted that the 1848 fund remain intact, available for any tribal member who wished to emigrate. Some were ready to leave as soon as the summer heat and malarial fevers in Indian Territory abated. Others, especially the fullbloods of Quallatown, were determined to remain in their homeland and asked the government for money to return those kinsmen who had fled to Georgia and South Carolina during the war.[11]

As the government became more interested in the possibility of removal, it asked the new Principal Chief of the Cherokee Nation, W.P. Ross, what his people could do to help. Of particular concern was whether the newcomers would be able to obtain free land and share in national funds. Lewis V. Bogy, the current Indian commissioner, also asked for certain information from Gilbert Falls, a Cherokee mixed-blood living in Georgia. Bogy wanted a report on the Indians living in that state, one assessing their attitudes toward removal and providing any other relevant data concerning them.[12]

Ross and his associates said they would welcome their North Carolina brethren "as citizens of the Nation upon the most liberal terms," but they lacked any funds with which to help them move. This posed a major obstacle, for the federal government discovered that during the Civil War it had diverted the funds under the 1848 act to other uses. Congress would have to mandate any financial outlay, and if Bushyhead were correct in his assertion that 800 Indians wanted to move, it would obviously entail considerable expense. Falls meanwhile reported that almost all of the Georgia Cherokees—whose number he admitted he did not know—would also emigrate if assisted. Sensing a potential federal windfall, he offered himself as their enrolling agent. Rumors of a possible emigration quickly attracted others who hoped to make money as agents or contractors. In the meantime, poor Bushyhead literally had to beg officials for money to get back home. Even in those days, $100 did not go far in Washington.[13]

In the midst of all this, the Indians' legal standing remained murky. The federal government seemed to view them as citizens of the state, but this status had never been confirmed. The new state constitution, drafted early in 1868 as part of Reconstruction, nowhere defined citizenship. It did specify that all males born in the United States who were twenty-one or older, and who had resided in the state for at least one year, were entitled to vote. This obviously included Indians as well as recently liberated blacks. But were voters necessarily citizens? The newly ratified Fourteenth Amendment to the U.S. Constitution granted citizenship and equal protection under the law to individuals born within the United States and subject to its jurisdiction. It was intended to apply to blacks, but it was unclear whether it extended to such anomalous Indian groups as the North Carolina Cherokees.[14]

Unfortunately, Cherokee needs could not await resolution of legal complexities. Immediate assistance was required from Congress if the Indians' distress was to be alleviated. Payment of their interest on the 1848 fund, undisbursed since 1859, was essential for the purchase of food, clothing, and other necessities. Dr. R.J. Powell, a mixed-blood from Cherokee County, had already prepared a revised roll of those entitled to interest, but there was still no money to make any payments. Many Indians also looked to the federal government for assistance in saving their homeland. A number of Valley River Cherokees, for example, advocated federal guardianship and a reservation within the state. Bushyhead's delegation echoed these sentiments by telling the Indian commissioner the Eastern Cherokees wanted "to be taken, like other Indians, under the jurisdiction of your office, and to have extended to them the same fostering care."[15]

Congress finally responded on July 27, 1868, by formally recognizing the North Carolina Cherokees as a distinct tribe, similar to other tribes having relations with the government; most important, it gave the Department of Interior supervision over their affairs. Before this, the only formal responsibility for their welfare accepted by the government was the periodic payment of interest by the Treasury Department. The act also specified preparation of yet

105

another payment roll, a clause that, according to one critic, had been inserted by outsiders seeking to enrich themselves. In view of what soon happened, the charges were well founded. Yet this complaint could not obscure the significance of the government's accepting responsibility for the Indians, offering them at last a semblance of protection—or so they thought.[16]

The new development was a tonic for Cherokee morale. Much of the earlier sentiment for emigration quickly faded as the Indians apparently believed that, like western tribes, they would soon have their own reservation. Almost overnight they brought to Washington a veritable shopping list of requests. Now that they were wards of the government, they wanted federal assistance in establishing schools and churches; they wanted their own agent; they needed food and clothing; and, of course, they wanted federal protection of their lands. Their long and frustrating experience with officials over the previous thirty years should have prepared them for the fact the government usually works slowly and sometimes not at all. And, as events were to demonstrate, many officials in the Indian Office continued to operate on the assumption that the newly recognized tribe would be better off assimilated into the body politic of the Cherokee Nation.[17]

Prominent on the Eastern Cherokees' list of demands was one that dated back well before the war—their insistence that the government protect their rights to tribal lands in the West, especially the Neutral Lands in Kansas and the region beyond the Ninety-Sixth Meridian. The Cherokee Nation did not need these lands, and the federal government, as trustee, proposed to sell them. Having completed arrangements to dispose of the Neutral Lands, in July 1868 it negotiated a treaty with the Nation providing for sale of the rest. But the North Carolina Indians argued that they, too, had been forced to make sacrifices under the Treaty of New Echota and were therefore entitled to a proportionate share of the proceeds from any sale of the tribal lands. Cherokees from Georgia and as far away as California claimed the same for themselves. Senator John Pool of North Carolina asked the Indian commissioner if the pending treaty took into consideration the interests of his constituents, and the official admitted it did not. He said it was still established policy to persuade all Cherokees to move to the Nation and, once that was accomplished, there would no longer be this sort of problem. For its part, the Nation denied that kinsmen outside its territory were entitled to a share of the land sales and complained that such claimants were only disrupting negotiations. They were so disruptive, in fact, that they helped prevent ratification of the treaty even though, as a "carrot," it offered automatic citizenship in the Nation to any Eastern Cherokee emigrating within three years.[18]

Another feature of the new relationship with federal officials was the struggle to determine who would represent the Indians in Washington. Squabbling factions sent rival delegations and petitions, leading the Indian commissioner to suggest that the Eastern Cherokees select just one man to represent their interests. Agreeing on a suitable individual, however, was impossible amid such acrimony. In particular, fullbloods like Flying Squirrel and Enola at Quallatown were suspicious of the motives of any acculturated mixed-blood who presumed to speak in their behalf. Always there was the dread their opponents might bargain away the North Carolina homeland. A group of Qualla residents, probably at Thomas's behest, sent a petition to President Andrew Johnson describing Bushyhead and his cohorts as "vagabond Cherokees who subsist by begging and misrepresentation" and who were intent on removing the Cherokees from the state.[19]

Supporters of Bushyhead and James Taylor, Thomas's Civil War subordinate, organized a tribal council at Cheoah in December 1868, the first of what was to be an annual meeting. While there had been occasional meetings of North Carolina Cherokees, this was the first postwar gathering that could truly be called a general council. But it was clear from the outset that Bushyhead's group was dominant. The council appointed "wardens" for the poor, selected a delegation to go to Washington, decreed that claimants to tribal funds must prove their Cherokee blood, asked for clarification of their status within the state, and even drew up a rudimentary constitution. As a final gesture—on Christmas Day, no less—the Cheoah council revoked all previous powers of attorney that had been given Thomas, whose mental aberrations had resulted in his temporary confinement in an asylum.[20]

The new constitution, drawn up without approval from the Indian Office, specified that each Cherokee community elect one delegate for every 150 people to represent the town in a general council which would convene the first Monday of each October. The council would then elect a chairman, who would also serve as "President or chief" of the Eastern Cherokees for a term of not more than four years. Other council responsibilities included defining the duties of each officer, preparing laws to govern the tribe, establishing school systems in each community, and fixing the time and place for a national fair. Until the first election the following year, an appointed executive committee would handle tribal affairs. But not all Indians recognized the legitimacy of the constitution, and anytime enough of them could agree to meet they would hold their own councils and send their own delegations to Washington.[21]

The first responsibility of the Indian Office under the 1868 act was to prepare another roll of the Eastern Cherokees. In doing this, the government unwittingly became party to an intrigue of crassness and effrontery worthy of the fictional Senator Abner Dilworthy in *The Gilded Age*. Originally there were several candidates to take the census, but John T. DeWeese, a Raleigh attorney and congressman, was instrumental in convincing North Carolina's Senator Joseph Abbott to support Silas H. Swetland, a Washington lawyer. One of those shady minor characters who seemed so plentiful in a notably opportunistic age, Swetland had already done some claims work for the Cherokees and thus received the endorsement of Bushyhead's faction. There was a pause while questions were raised about his alleged criminal past, but the secretary of interior soon approved his nomination as special agent. He was to prepare two rolls, one a revised list of those entitled to payments of interest under the 1848 act, and the second a census of all the Cherokees East, including information on their status.[22]

As he prepared to visit North Carolina, Swetland and his associates were concocting a scheme that would be more lucrative than the government's employ. Not coincidentally, he appeared at Cheoah when the council met in December. It was he who encouraged the Indians to draw up a constitution. He was then able to convince many of them that he should be their Washington attorney for a commission of from one-quarter to one-third the value of all claims successfully prosecuted. The Indians agreed on condition that he would not claim a percentage of the money already promised them under the 1848 act, the payroll for which Swetland was preparing. Swetland hoped the government would also appoint him disbursing agent to pay the claimants on his new roll, and in such an event he promised to avoid a conflict of interest by finding another attorney to represent the Indians. By mid-January 1869, after an arduous trek through North and South Carolina, Georgia, Tennessee, and Alabama, he was back in Washington with his preliminary rolls and the coveted Cherokee power of attorney. He had a second, identical contract which the Cherokees had obligingly signed and left blank for an attorney's name to be added later.[23]

Swetland's payment list was basically a revision of the Mullay Roll. Predictably, there were anguished wails of protest from some Indians—and their lawyers—who objected either to being left off the new list or to its inclusion of claimants who were thought undeserving. During the next few months Swetland regularly added names to those he had already enrolled. His other roll, the census, listed 2,335 Cherokees in the Southeast.[24]

There remained the task of paying $48,540 in interest which had recently been appropriated for those Indians on the new roll. And despite renewed questions regarding his honesty, Swetland himself was appointed to perform this task. It was at this point that James G. Blunt strode onto the stage and made the melodrama his. A Civil War general from Kansas turned Indian lawyer, he was a habitué of Washington and familiar with its ways. He and DeWeese had been partners in some earlier claims work for the Eastern Cherokees, and it was he who posted the $12,135 required for Swetland's performance bond; the following day, having received the Indians' $48,540, Swetland dipped into it to repay Blunt. It was quite illegal. In addition, he entered Blunt's name on the blank power of attorney, which was then backdated. The Eastern Cherokees had no idea that Blunt now "represented" them and would claim 25 percent of the interest money that Swetland was about to disburse. Blunt would then share the money with DeWeese, Swetland, and possibly a few others.[25]

Unknown to the Indian commissioner, Swetland went to North Carolina with only about $32,000, which was still enough that he refused to travel through the robber-infested mountains without a military escort. Also accompanying him were G. F. Jocknick, a clerk in the Indian Office, and John Askew, Blunt's personal agent. Then, at the various communities, Swetland amazed the Cherokees by demanding they pay 25 percent of their interest to Askew for Blunt's alleged services in getting Congress to appropriate the money. When some Cherokees had the temerity to protest, Askew made thinly veiled threats and even intimated that the military escort was there to enforce compliance. Both Askew and Swetland said that if the Indians did not pay Blunt's commission he would use his influence in Washington to drop them from the rolls and deny them their money. Several mixed-bloods, apparently in league with the conspirators, urged payment by emphasizing Blunt's supposed power. Not surprisingly, almost all of the Cherokees grudgingly handed over $8 out of the $32 each had received.[26]

As they progressed from Quallatown to Sand Town, Cheoah, and Murphy, Swetland and Askew made some of the payments out of the funds they had already collected, nursing their $32,000 into about $41,000 in disbursements. But simple mathematics dictated a limited future for this sort of chicanery, and at Murphy, Swetland announced to a startled audience that he had run out of money and would send the rest from Washington. With more than $6,000 in unpaid claims, he left behind a number of bewildered and enraged Indians who waited in vain for him to make good on his promise. It is amazing that throughout the entire episode the only threat of violence emanated not from the Indians but from a white liquor dealer and his friends in Quallatown who took a personal dislike to Jocknick, threatening to lift his scalp before he left the mountains.[27]

The Indians and their sympathizers lost no time in protesting about Swetland's actions to Secretary of Interior Jacob D. Cox, who was shocked by what had happened. The conspirators maintained that Swetland had carefully followed instructions, paying the Indians individually all that each was entitled to receive; then, because the Cherokees had a "contract" with Blunt, they had paid his agent. Swetland said he did not pay everyone because some could not be found and in other cases the claims of a multitude of heirs were too difficult to unravel. He did not mention that he had actively abetted Askew, nor did he submit his records until the Indian Office threatened legal action. As for the Cherokees, Secretary Cox could do no better than advise them not to hire agents or attorneys in the future but to indicate their desires through their council or elected officers. The Indians, needless to say, were convinced that once again they had been victimized. And they were correct. Not until a few years later were they able to take action against their defrauders.[28]

A more pressing concern for the Indians than this swindle was protecting their lands so they would not have to move west. A few had fee simple title, but most occupied property that was still in Thomas's name. It had been clearly understood, however, that he was holding it in trust for them. Some of the Indians had already made payments to him, and others held his bond for title when he was paid off. But Thomas owed nearly $34,000 to William Johnston of Asheville, who held a lien on all his property; Johnston thus had first claim on almost all the lands the Indians had been living on and cultivating for years. He was not unsympathetic to their situation, but he was a businessman. He wanted his money. And during the summer of 1869, when Thomas was unable to pay after numerous extensions of time, the sheriffs of several counties sold most of his lands at auction. Because of their clouded titles, Johnston himself was able to purchase them at a fraction of their value. Being a reasonable and compassionate man, he agreed in September to sign the land over to the Cherokees if they paid him $30,000; if they could not do this within eighteen months, he would give them an undivided tract that was proportionate to what they had paid. Or, if the Indians chose, they could cancel the contract and reclaim any money they had already paid minus the accumulated interest. Until the sale was consummated, the Cherokees were to pay all taxes on the land. As earnest money they managed to pay Johnston $6,500 out of Swetland's recent payments, a remarkable sum considering how little they had actually received and their natural fear of being swindled again. Raising the remaining $23,500, however, appeared a hopeless task.[29]

The uncertain status of their lands understandably led many Cherokees to believe they had again been defrauded by *someone*— Thomas, Thomas's friends, other agents, Johnston perhaps, or maybe all of them together. Subtleties of the white man's law were not readily grasped, but the Indians well realized they were in danger of losing lands that, morally at least, were *theirs*. In fairness to Thomas, it is clear that he never intended to cheat them, that he retained title in order to guarantee they would pay him and, ironically, to protect them from being dispossessed. Nonetheless, in order for the Indians to secure their lands it was necessary to bring suit against him on grounds that he had been a careless or criminal administrator of the land he held in trust. James Terrell, as a former agent who had handled their money, was to be a codefendant, as well as Johnston, who now owned the lands in question.

There was only one obstacle. Because of their uncertain status, the Indians could not file suit in any court. Previous Supreme Court decisions made it clear that Indian tribes could not institute suit in federal courts, but on the other hand the North Carolina Cherokees could not undertake tribal action in state courts, either. Despite Governor W. W. Holden's belief that they were citizens of the state, the judiciary committee of the state senate firmly disagreed. While notably sympathetic to the Indians' dilemma, the committee could merely recommend that the Cherokees be empowered to sue their alleged defrauders. If and when they secured their lands, the committee said, they should sell them on the best possible terms and join the Cherokee Nation in the West.[30]

As the months passed, many Indians despaired of ever preserving their homeland. The ominous prospect of losing their birthright prompted many to look more favorably on removal to the West. By early 1869 the Cherokee Nation had formally invited them and their other scattered kinsmen to reunite in Indian Territory and enjoy the benefits of tribal citizenship. Already, since 1848, some two hundred or more Eastern Cherokees, "heartsick from poverty and disappointment," had somehow emigrated on their own. The majority were mixed-bloods who settled in the Flint District in the Nation's eastern section. Only a minority were on the Mullay Roll, and even these had no assurance the government would ever pay their long-delayed transportation and subsistence money. Despite the hardships of a move, the Nation's Principal Chief, Lewis Downing, insisted it was only logical for the North Carolina Indians to join their brothers. For years, he said, men like Thomas had systematically cheated them until they were "mere peons" who were even now "driven about from farm to farm like so many cattle." This sort of hyperbole from Downing is understandable, considering that his contacts in North Carolina were with the Bushyhead-Taylor party.[31]

Thomas, in turn, was capable of formidable invective, histrionics, and even biblical metaphor when denouncing his detractors. In March 1870 he directed a tirade against his favorite targets, Bushyhead and Taylor. Turning then to the gullible nature of the Cherokees, he lamented that since his health had failed "The Indians have been like bees without a king [sic], in the hands of bankrupts swindlers and vagabond Indians. And they have been very much like the Israelites in the days of Moses when they worshipped the calf. They have become deaf to the advice of their old friends and blind to their best interest. Hence they believe in false prophets and all kinds of slanders against me. . . ."[32]

Downing's invitation to join the Nation simply heightened the disagreement among the North Carolina Cherokees over the efficacy of moving west. While more were in favor than in the previous few years, others, notably fullbloods, remained "irreconcilably opposed." The energetic James Taylor became removal agent for a number of Georgia Cherokees who wished to leave and announced himself in favor of a general exodus. But the council that met at Cheoah in October 1869 said that while the Georgia Indians might wish to emigrate, few in North Carolina were similarly inclined. This was shortly after Johnston had signed the contract to return their land upon payment of $30,000. By February 1870, after the difficulty of recovering their property had become apparent, many Cherokees were not sanguine. Their delegation, headed by Bushyhead, reported that there was considerable sentiment at home favoring emigration. As if on cue, Lewis Downing reiterated again that his people would welcome their eastern brothers.[33]

While visiting Washington in 1866, Bushyhead had normally used the modest appellation of "chief," which was justified by his status as headman of Sand Town. In 1867, however, Swetland referred to him as "Chief of the Cherokee Indians of North Carolina," while Bushyhead styled himself "Chief of the Hill Cherokees of North Carolina." Then in 1869 the Cheoah council reaffirmed his status as foremost delegate and also elected him council chairman. Under the 1868 constitution, the elected council chairman became chief of the Eastern Cherokees; this was the obvious authority for his assuming the title of Principal Chief when he visited Washington in 1870, the first postwar instance of a North Carolina Cherokee's doing so. Though Quallatown fullbloods like Flying Squirrel and Enola denied the council's legitimacy and its choice of leader, most Indians living in Macon and Cherokee counties apparently recognized Bushyhead's authority.[34]

It was a joyous occasion indeed when, through the efforts of Bushyhead, Taylor, and various white supporters, Congress included in the Indian appropriations act of July 15, 1870, a provision authorizing the attorney general to institute suits in federal courts in behalf of the tribe against their present and former agents. (This, incidentally, was the first time the government officially designated the Indians as the Eastern Band of Cherokee Indians.) Unfortunately, the elation was short-lived. Despite Taylor's relentless attempts to begin proceedings, bureaucratic confusion and foot-dragging delayed action for several years.[35]

Tribal factionalism meanwhile became white-hot. Bushyhead, at least, was no longer a factor, having become ill and retired to South Carolina. His nominal successor was John Ross, who was selected as chairman of the council which met at Cheoah early in November 1870. The council also passed a series of resolutions relating to the Cherokees' legal status and the many swindles that had victimized them through the years. Most ominous were denunciations of certain fellow Cherokees for their alleged role in the schemes of Swetland and Blunt; these included Lloyd R. Welch of Cheoah, John and David Owl, Hugh Lambert, and Henry Smith and his relatives (one of whom was Nimrod J. Smith, later to become chief of the Band). In a petition to President Ulysses Grant, the council linked the swindles with the machinations of the William Thomas "*ring*."[36]

Later that same month Henry Smith, Welch, and others who were attacked at the Cheoah meeting helped organize a rival "Grand Council" of Cherokees at Quallatown. Though most Cherokees were represented, members of the Ross-Taylor camp were conspicuously absent. The Grand Council elected Flying Squirrel Principal Chief of the Cherokees and John Jackson, of Sand Town, as Second Chief. A new constitution was drafted which provided that all males sixteen and older could vote annually for their representatives to the council; that body was to govern the entire Eastern Band, and no other so-called council had any authority. There were a number of other actions by the council, the most revealing of which was the appointment of a six-man delegation to represent the Indians in Washington. Four of the appointees had been denounced by the Cheoah council: Welch, the two Owls, and Hugh Lambert; a fifth, Henry Smith, was to accompany the delegation as its interpreter. Flying Squirrel, it was later decided, would also go to Washington. The council continued its business in January and February 1871, elaborating on the start that had been made.[37]

There was a fairly sharp division in policy between the two factions. Lloyd Welch and Flying Squirrel headed one, with Welch the de facto leader while the old fullblood chief hovered suspiciously in the background. Welch well realized that his major support was in Quallatown, where the fullbloods still composed the most numerous block among the Eastern Cherokees. He and his fellow delegates appreciated the devoted attachment of this group to its homeland and consequently opposed removal. In fact, they favored payment of both the interest and principal mentioned in the 1848 act. Since they were not going to move west, there was no longer any point in merely collecting their annual interest on the transportation and subsistence fund. The Cherokees wanted all the money now. Quite logically, they attempted to enlist the support of William Johnston, who would be an immediate beneficiary by finally receiving the money for his lands. The Ross-Taylor faction, in contrast, represented many mixed-bloods as well as some fullbloods

114

and was more open-minded about the possibility of removal. Both Ross and Taylor on occasion supported emigration, and in fact both moved to Indian Territory during the 1880s. In general, they were more aggressive in their pursuit of real and alleged swindlers than their rivals.[38]

Meanwhile, as the threat of dispossession loomed ever larger, some Cherokees resigned themselves to what seemed the inevitable necessity of moving. In the spring of 1871 about ninety of them set out under James Obadiah on the long trek to Indian Territory. Just a year before, Obadiah, a headman of Cheoah, had denounced removal. He and his followers got only as far as the railroad at Loudon, Tennessee, before exhausting their means to continue. Plaintive messages went to Lewis Downing and the federal government, requesting assistance in continuing the trip by rail. Brigadier General Alfred Terry was finally instructed to furnish army rations to the stranded Indians, but the question of what to do with them remained unresolved. When the secretary of interior inquired if the War Department could provide rail transportation, the answer was negative. The Eastern Cherokee delegates in Washington then asked the secretary of interior to solicit assistance from the president.[39]

Obadiah's group camped in the sweltering Tennessee countryside throughout the spring and summer while perplexed officials reviewed the situation. Late in September John D. Lang and David C. Cox were appointed agents to visit Loudon, determine the number and condition of the Indians, provide them with necessary clothing, and make arrangements to send them west by rail if they were entitled to assistance under the 1848 act. The Swetland payment roll was to be used in determining this. Lang was a prominent Quaker who was serving on the Board of Indian Commissioners, a quasi-governmental agency made up of prominent citizens who were supposed to keep a keen eye on the Indian Office. Quakers also figured quite prominently in President Grant's so-called Indian Peace Policy, a program shaped in theory by honesty, efficiency, and humanitarianism. Cox was a functionary within the Indian Office assigned to assist his more dynamic associate.[40]

John Ross and about fifteen other Cherokees came over to Loudon from Cheoah to confer with Lang on what was to be done regarding removal of Obadiah's entourage, whose number had swelled to over one hundred. Lang, a no-nonsense personality, said he wanted to reach agreement with the Principal Chief—an embarrassing situation because since Bushyhead had retired no one in the Cheoah faction had assumed that lofty status (in Cherokee society it was easier to lose power than to gain it). Ross had an argument in his favor, if he dared use it. Under the 1868 constitution, he was entitled as council chairman to be chief of the Eastern Cherokees. But the 1870 Quallatown council, representing a majority of the Indians, had established a new constitution and elected Flying Squirrel Principal Chief. These matters of Cherokee legality and protocol made no impression at all on Lang. He insisted that the delegation from North Carolina confer among themselves, select their Principal Chief, and then Lang would deal through him. The group finally concluded that the most logical man was Ross. And so it was that Ross, through Lang's peremptory demand upon the Cherokees, became the Eastern Band's "Principal Chief," an event resembling Alexander Cuming's recognition of Moytoy as Cherokee "King" back in 1730. Flying Squirrel and 118 other Cherokees protested to the Indian commissioner that Ross was not and had never been chief, while Flying Squirrel was acknowledged as such by at least three-fourths of the tribe. Blithely ignoring this clamor, the Indian Office thereafter preferred to deal with "Principal Chief" Ross. This, of course, simply deepened intratribal animosities.[41]

The ongoing drama at Loudon had meanwhile led President Grant to assure the Eastern Cherokees that the government would assist any who wished to move west and that the move would not jeopardize their existing rights and claims. Ross, for one, believed the number emigrating would soon swell because of the impending loss of their lands; in fact, he was seriously considering going himself. In contrast, Flying Squirrel and other Quallatown fullbloods vociferously denied that many wished to leave. To accommodate those who did, the efficient Lang hired Q. A. Tipton to assist any who might arrive in Loudon seeking transportation to the West. Then, early in October 1871, Lang escorted 125 émigrés by rail to the Cherokee Nation, where they quickly discovered that their troubles were not over. Within a short time many were complaining of being treated like second-class citizens, having their crops devoured by grasshoppers, and being denied their share of federal relief funds.[42]

During the next year Tipton periodically dispatched small groups of Indians to the Nation, though none appeared for weeks at a time during the harsh winter of 1871–1872. He sent his last detachment in October 1872. Of those transported to the Nation, less than half were on the Swetland roll, meaning the federal government simply ignored for the moment its stated policy and transported the migrants at its own expense. This emigration of 1871–1872, then, was not the result of a program planned by the government; it was simply an ad hoc action brought on after months of indecision and prompted solely by the fact that a bedraggled group of Cherokee men, women, and children were camped in hungry isolation by a railroad track in Tennessee, waiting.[43]

By 1872 the most conspicuous figures among the Cheoah faction were Ross and Taylor. As a reflection of the vagaries of tribal politics, the former spokesman for that faction, George Bushyhead, now came under attack by his erstwhile associates. A council meeting in June accused him of betraying his people by submitting fraudulent claims to the government. Lacking funds to send a delegation to Washington, the council struck up a temporary alliance with the Cherokee Nation by authorizing its delegates to serve the North Carolina Indians as well. In his letter of appointment to the western delegates, Ross stressed the need for immediate payment of their interest—the first since the Swetland debacle—and then lamented the lack of harmony among his people. Too many individuals, whites and Indians alike, were misleading them for "ignoble purposes." In closing, he remarked that he had "no language to express our wants, only Suffering, Suffering, Suffering, and the echo is, Suffering." Not surprisingly, the delegates soon found it impossible to serve two groups that had diametrically opposed interests in regard to the sale of western lands.[44]

In November 1872 the attorney general's office at last secured indictments against James Blunt, John DeWeese, and other real or alleged defrauders. Swetland, however, was safely beyond reach, having long since died. Marcus Erwin, the assistant U.S. attorney for the Western District of North Carolina, had charge of the case, but the Eastern Cherokees were determined to be participants, too. An October council in Cheoah had appointed James Taylor to return as delegate to Washington, where his major responsibility would be to help with the pending suit. By February 1873 he and Erwin were assiduously "ferreting out" information vital to the case. At almost the same time, Ross used his authority as "Principal Chief" to hire Wallace W. Rollins as tribal counsel. Rollins was a Madison County attorney who had been involved in litigation concerning the Western North Carolina Railroad. His appointment was another blow to the beleagured Blunt, who still considered himself the legal representative of the Eastern Band.[45]

It required a long time to prepare the case against Blunt and his associates, primarily because some federal authorities were less than helpful. Most of the testimony and evidence focused on Blunt himself, the star defendant. He fought every step of the way during circuit court proceedings in North Carolina, but in October 1874 a jury found him guilty of fraud. According to one of the U.S. attorneys, the members had entertained no doubts as to Blunt's corruption. His conviction was disallowed, however, because the matter had dragged on longer than allowed by the statute of limitations. A federal grand jury then indicted him on perjury charges, which were later dropped. Blunt retaliated with savage attacks on his accusers, particularly Ross and Taylor. Those two men, he said, were the true defrauders. Ross, far from being a chief, was an "ignorant lying, perjured vagabond" to whom the Cherokees "would not confide a side a bacon, nor a sack of corn meal. He is simply the ignorant, and pliant tool of his more intelligent, and cunning confederate (Jas Taylor)." Taylor, he asserted, had betrayed his people by working for their enemies almost from the first day he had appeared in Washington. And Rollins's alleged contract with the tribe was fraudulent because Ross never had authority as chief to hire him; Rollins, moreover, was claiming a commission for services that Blunt had already performed for the Band.[46]

Blunt also intimated that federal officials were aiding and abetting Ross and Taylor in their defrauding of the Cherokees. The Indian Office responded in typical fashion, by appointing another investigative committee to review Blunt's various charges. But the three-man board had nothing new to add to the conclusions of the federal court. Taylor was willing to agree with Blunt at least to the extent of believing there was corruption in the government, but his main target was a cabal of officials—part of Blunt's "ring," he said—that had sabotaged legal proceedings by endless procrastination and theft of pertinent documents. During the next few years the specter of Blunt the bogeyman continued to haunt the Eastern Cherokees, evoking bitter recriminations and fault-finding. His maneuverings serve as a modestly proportioned paridigm of corruption in Indian affairs during the Gilded Age. He eventually slipped into insanity and died in Washington in 1881.[47]

At the same time the case against Blunt was in litigation, the

Eastern Band was involved in two other suits that were of much greater significance to its members. One was a suit in equity filed in May 1873 in the U.S. Circuit Court for the Western District of North Carolina. The Band brought this action against Thomas, Terrell, and Johnston in an effort to force an accounting of the money Thomas had received as the Cherokees' representative from 1836 to 1861—money he used to buy lands for the tribe. That land had remained in his name, of course, and was sold because of his indebtedness. Johnston was codefendant because he had taken sheriffs' titles to the land, well realizing the Indians' equitable interest. Terrell had served as Cherokee disbursing agent between 1853 and 1861 and allegedly had transferred money to Thomas. The second suit, an action at law, listed as defendant Terrell and several sureties on his performance bond as agent, including Thomas and Johnston.[48]

The primary suit was the one in equity against Thomas and Johnston, since it directly affected Cherokee lands. A particularly delicate problem was Thomas's mental state, which ranged from lunacy to lucidity. It was difficult to assess what credence should be attached to his comments and reminiscences. Another problem was the pitiful state of his personal records, which proved to be almost impossible to piece together. The lands in his name were in scores of tracts scattered over several counties. Some of the titles had been recorded but most had not, making the investigation even more complicated. Many Indians were willing to concede they still owed him for the lands he held as trustee, but they had only a vague idea of what the amount might be. Terrell, as a former business associate of Thomas, worked diligently to make sense out of the older man's affairs. William Johnston, aging and exasperated by the proceedings, left the legal battles to his son, Thomas D. Johnston, a prominent Asheville attorney and politician. The son quickly made it clear that he favored arbitration.[49]

Finally, in May 1874, all parties involved agreed to combine the two suits and submit the matters still in question to binding arbitration by three prominent Carolinians: Rufus Barringer, John H. Dillard, and Thomas Ruffin. The three began their deliberations in August and worked through most of October, conducting an exhaustive inquiry into all aspects of the cases. They examined nearly 150 witnesses, "most of them Indians, speaking only Cherokee" and took "many hundreds of pages" of depositions, findings, and testimony. As chairman Barringer noted, "All this had to be done in the midst of that confusion and chaos necessarily caused by the peculiar condition and doubtful legal status of these people through near a century of mixed tribal and civilized life."[50]

Thomas was among those testifying, leaving no doubt in the minds of anyone that the Indians were entitled to the lands. He was so pro-Indian, in fact, that Terrell despaired because he was not protecting himself adequately. Be fair but concede nothing was Terrell's philosophy. He told one friend how at a hearing one day Thomas stood outside the courtroom door, ranting and raving like the maniac he was, audible for half a mile. When he was finally admitted, however, he was so reasonable, articulate, and precise in his recollection of various land transactions that the court, despite voluminous medical evidence to the contrary, declared him sane at least for the purpose of testifying. As one acquaintance remarked, Thomas "may have been non compos mentis in general matters, but on anything connected with Indian affairs he seemed perfectly at ease." And everything he said supported the Indian claims while working against his own interests. It is little wonder the Indians later said that theirs was simply a "friendly" suit against him.[51]

On October 23, 1874, the arbitrators finally made their awards. They found that Thomas had indeed acquired thousands of acres over the years for the Indians, in part with their money and in part with his. A few Indians had already received deeds from him for individual units, while others held his bond for eventual title. But almost all of the Qualla Boundary, amounting to some 73,000 acres, had been purchased for them as a tribe or community. After calculating all the sums that Thomas had received as their agent, and his work and expenditures in their behalf, the arbitrators concluded that the Cherokees still owed him $18,250 for the Boundary. They noted that the Indians had paid Johnston $6,500 as a pledge of good faith when they agreed to buy the lands from him; with interest since September 1869, that now amounted to $8,486. Johnston was to credit this sum on his judgment against Thomas as money paid by the Indians toward what they still owed the latter, reducing the balance to $9,764.[52]

As for Terrell, the arbitrators decided that he was liable to the Cherokees for $2,697.89 that he had diverted (without criminal intent) to Thomas as attorney for the Indians. Thomas had claimed the Cherokees owed it to him. This sum was therefore deducted from the $9,764, leaving the Indians still owing Thomas $7,066.11. They were to pay this amount, with 6 percent interest from the date of the award, to Johnston as a credit on his judgments against Thomas. When this was done, Johnston was to convey to the Cherokees—or their trustees—legal title to the Qualla Boundary. Those Indians who still owed Thomas for their individual tracts would also receive title when they completed payment. In a separate decision the arbitrators held that Thomas still owed Johnston $18,335, so they appointed Terrell and Thomas Johnston commissioners to sell any of Thomas's property not encumbered by the Indians' equitable interest; proceeds from these sales would be used to pay off the elder Johnston.[53]

Of particular concern were some of the Indian-held lands in Graham County (recently carved out of Cherokee County). In 1850 Thomas had agreed to purchase for the Cherokees a large tract near the Cheoah River, comprising a "boundary" that would be similar to the common lands in the Qualla Boundary. True to his word, he had bought thousands of acres on which Indians had been living in peace for years. But the arbitrators concluded that the Cherokees had never taken the required steps to make the contract binding upon Thomas. They did not possess an equitable interest in the Cheoah Boundary, and commissioners Terrell and Johnston could sell those properties to help satisfy the judgment. They could legally evict the Indians, though Terrell doubted that anything short of military force could accomplish it. Fortunately, he and Johnston agreed to give the Eastern Band first chance to buy those properties. A few Indians living there already held perfect titles, making the surrounding land less attractive to prospective white purchasers. For that reason, the commissioners reasoned, it was in the best interests of all parties to sell to the Band. Another reason, less openly discussed, was startling in its import: if the Cheoah lands were sold to whites, the Indian residents would probably move to the already occupied common lands in the Qualla Boundary. The resulting pressures on the land would likely lead to intratribal arson and throat-cutting.[54]

The decisions of the administrators, and the subsequent arrangements between the land commissioners and Cherokees, seemed to please all parties to the litigation. Thomas's staunch defense of their rights and the realization they still owed him made the Cherokees effusive in their gratitude toward the man who so recently had been defendant to their suit. At the Cheoah council of November 1874 they expressed great satisfaction with the arbitrators' rulings and then offered a paean of praise for Thomas, whose financial misfortunes, they said, had necessitated their suits against him. Without him, they acknowledged, they would never have been allowed to remain in North Carolina. After describing how he had become a tribal member while a youth, they proceeded to a listing of all he had done for them in the intervening years. He had provided them with necessities; protected their rights to western lands; purchased lands in North Carolina for them; instructed them in Christianity and civilization; assisted their orphans, aged, and infirm; and throughout the years he had been their "steadfast friend and protector." In gratitude for his many services, they adopted his children and grandchildren as members of the Eastern Band and granted them all the "privileges, benefits and immunities" thereof.[55]

The Cherokee council also appointed James Taylor and Terrell to assist in procuring the money necessary for purchasing the Qualla and Cheoah boundaries. The only way to accomplish this was to have the government use both the principal and interest from the 1848 fund. The Cherokee arguments in favor of this were so persuasive that Indian Commissioner Edward P. Smith recommended diverting the fund from its original purpose, transporting and subsisting removal to the West, and using it as a common fund for tribal acquisitions. Money left over would finance the government's civilization programs for the Band.[56]

Before these complicated transactions could be completed, it was necessary to specify exactly which lands would be involved. Even before the arbitrators reached their decisions, Congress had appropriated $15,000 for a comprehensive survey of all Cherokee lands in North Carolina. Lacking enough information even to frame detailed instructions to a surveyor, the secretary of interior designated Francis A. Dony to ascertain the general nature of the land and the Indian titles to it, as well as any likely problems in surveying it. His report would be the basis for specific guidelines that the General Land Office would give the surveyor, M.S. Temple of Tennessee. While visiting North Carolina during the summer of 1874, Dony concluded with wry understatement that "A remarkable looseness seems to have prevailed here in connection with Indian lands for a long series of years." Nevertheless, he was able to make detailed recommendations for the preparation of Temple's survey.[57]

On March 3, 1875, Congress enacted legislation allowing the Indian commissioner to use the 1848 money as a common fund for acquiring lands and promoting agriculture and civilization

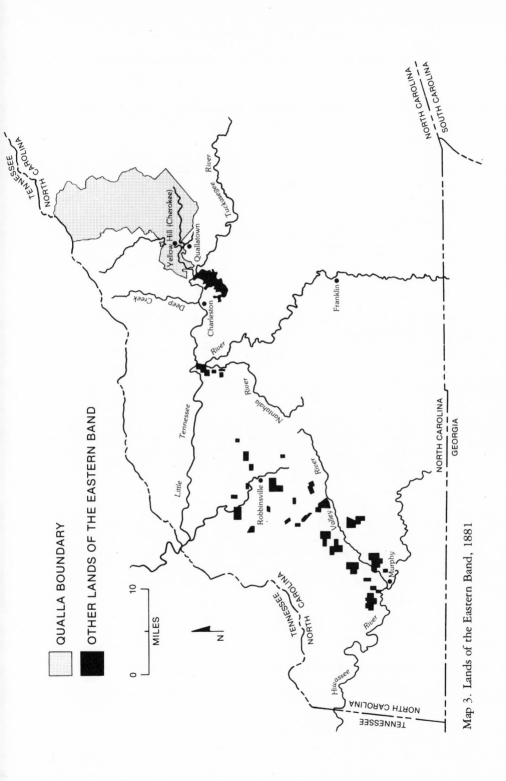

QUALLA BOUNDARY

OTHER LANDS OF THE EASTERN BAND

Map 3. Lands of the Eastern Band, 1881

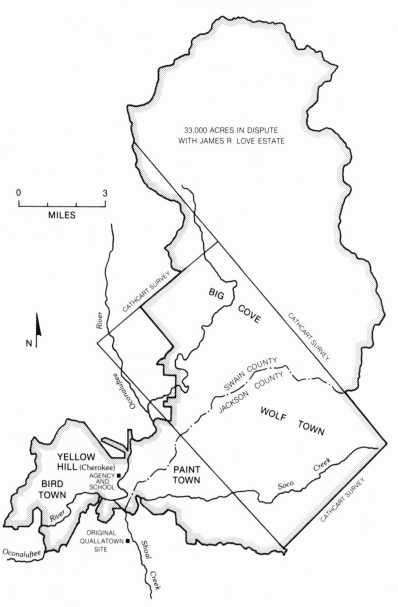

Map 4. Qualla Boundary, 1881

among the Eastern Band. The Indian Office then paid Johnston $7,242.75—the amount due him in one judgment plus interest—for the Qualla Boundary. Title was vested in the Eastern Band in common and was not alienable without the assent of the tribal council and the president. Later the government purchased the rest of Johnston's judgments, becoming, in effect, Thomas's creditor. This guaranteed that most of his outlying lands, after adjustments, would also become Cherokee property. And that same year Temple completed his survey of the Boundary, the first precise demarcation of Indian lands in North Carolina since the 1830s.[58]

Finally, in 1876, the government acquired preliminary title to thousands of acres outside Qualla, including part of the so-called Cheoah Boundary. But there were a number of conflicting white claims, so the Indians had to appoint a series of committees to select and appraise substitute lands and await completion of surveys. Enola and James Taylor were members of one such group. When all this had been completed in 1880, the total acquisition outside the Boundary was 15,211 acres. Title to these lands was held in trust for the Band by the Indian commissioner and his successors, a provision that quickly incurred the wrath of some of the more acculturated Cherokees.[59]

With the events of 1875, the Indian Office was at last convinced of the permanence of Cherokee residence in North Carolina. Now, seven years after federal recognition of the Eastern Cherokees as a tribe, the government was prepared to undertake a program to assist them. First on the agenda was selection of an agent who would be able to establish a systematic program of education. A group of Indiana Quakers, having already undertaken such work among Appalachian whites, expressed interest in serving the Cherokees, but the Indian Office first offered the position to a Baptist, the Reverend Horace James of Worcester, Massachusetts. When James became ill, the American Baptist Board of Home Missions recommended the Reverend William C. McCarthy, a New Yorker about forty years old, with experience in teaching and managing schools. In February 1875 McCarthy became special agent for the Eastern Cherokees, the first appointed official since the government assumed responsibility for the Band. He was to receive $1,500 a year. He arrived in North Carolina totally unprepared for the bitter factionalism that would soon engulf him, nor did he appreciate the difficulties of "civilizing" a people attached to traditional ways.[60]

7

A CHANGING SOCIETY

The Reverend William McCarthy had reason to feel abused. The American Baptist Board of Home Missions had nominated him to establish schools among the Eastern Cherokees and help liberate them from generations of ignorance. And yet, by governmental fiat, he had suddenly become a special agent and factotum for the Indian Office. Assuming his post in February 1875, he quickly discovered that his responsibilities were too demanding for someone of his background. He was expected to prepare reports, handle complaints, travel over many miles of mountainous terrain, sit on a board investigating James Blunt's activities, and fill out countless federal forms in accordance with instructions that were impossible to fulfill—all this on a shoestring budget.[1]

McCarthy lacked even an agency office. A possibility was the Echota Mission, about three miles from Yellow Hill (present-day Cherokee), but he believed Quallatown would be even better. Though it was just outside Qualla Boundary, it was the most convenient meeting place for Indians in Jackson and Swain counties, who continued to trade there. While he awaited instruction regarding an agency, he rented a private residence in Quallatown, moved his family down from New York state at a quarter of his annual salary, and began his work.[2] The problems he and the Cherokees confronted were many: poverty; lack of education; factionalism; and, despite the 1874 award by arbitrators, uncertain land titles. All were interrelated and would require the wisdom of Solomon and patience of Job to overcome. Reverend McCarthy at least had the perserverance of a good Baptist.

It did not require a teetotaler like McCarthy to recognize that sobriety was a prerequisite for Cherokee advancement. This had been no problem before the Civil War, when Yonaguska's temperance society enjoyed remarkable success, but afterward drunkenness became common. In January 1869 the Cheoah council asked the

Cherokees to take a temperance pledge, imposing a fine of five dollars for each violation. This was obviously ineffective, for a few months later an obstreperous liquor dealer was present at Quallatown when Silas Swetland made his disbursements. That same year George Bushyhead complained that a "great many of the Cherokees" were subject to alcohol "and wild natured when drunk."[3] McCarthy quickly became aware of the problem, noting that "Meetings for public worship on the Sabbath day are frequently disturbed by drunken persons, white and Indian. Assaults by and fights with and between drunken persons have been frequent." Once the agent went so far as to halt a whiskey-laden wagon that was approaching the Boundary, but despite such efforts alcohol remained a strong and insidious enemy.[4]

Even more important than temperance was the necessity of improving the Indians' economic base. Their arable land was limited in extent, and the typical farm, as in 1838, consisted of just a few cleared acres in a mountain cove or along a stream. Probably no more than 5 percent of the tribal domain was cultivated, the rest consisting of mountains, forests, and overgrown, abandoned fields. Here and there were neglected orchards that perversely continued to bear fruit, while tucked away in secluded spots were Indian cabins. A few Cherokees sharecropped for white landowners.[5]

Although outsiders usually portrayed the Cherokees as a contented people whose farms were no worse than those of poor non-Indians, knowledgeable visitors believed they were in desperate need of instruction in modern farming and animal husbandry. If anything, their agriculture had deteriorated since 1838 because of erosion, soil exhaustion, and periodic insect infestations. Their standard implements continued to be the hoe and bull-tongued plough, which merely scratched the surface and left shallow furrows exposed to the ravages of wind and water. William Stickney, a federal official who traveled through the area in 1875, found not one Cherokee farm that was outwardly prosperous, though he saw some along Valley River that were "tolerably well improved." Most of the latter were owned by mixed-bloods who were almost indistinguishable from whites.[6]

The Cherokees, like most whites, fenced in their small fields and allowed their livestock to roam through the forests and mountain meadows. Swetland's 1869 census shows 5,266 head of livestock distributed among the 489 Cherokee households in the Southeast. More than half were hogs worth a mere two dollars each, followed in order by cattle (including oxen), sheep, and horses. The mixed-bloods owned most of the animals, while many fullblood households had none. Among the fullbloods on Qualla Boundary, Flying Squirrel and Enola possessed the greatest wealth; the former owned thirty-three head of livestock and occupied thirty acres of improved land, and the latter had twenty-three animals and forty acres of improved land. Their wealth was inconsequential, however, compared with that of certain mixed-bloods and Cherokees by marriage living along Valley River—people like Jesse Raper, Elizabeth Welch, and Henry Smith.[7]

The North Carolina Cherokees had proportionately fewer draft animals than the more acculturated Indians in Georgia and Tennessee, and hardly any owned wagons. A few possessed crude carts, but these were unsuited to heavy hauling over the frequently impassable roads. Even if there had been adequate roads, wagons, and markets, Cherokee argiculture was too inefficient to produce much of a surplus. When the Indians were lucky enough to have some extra corn, they bartered it for such necessities as bacon, salt, or clothing. Or, if hard-pressed, they hired themselves out to local whites and worked for next to nothing. By mid-decade, a white man complained, the Indians had raised their rates to twenty-five cents a day in salt, corn, or pork.[8]

McCarthy's favorite cure for the Cherokees' economic malaise was to establish model farms among them, a proposal others had already made. The government should buy suitable land, provide the requisite implements and livestock, and educate the Cherokees in techniques of modern agriculture. Both he and William Stickney advocated two such farms, one at Cheoah and the other on Qualla Boundary. As a first step McCarthy recommended the purchase of 247 acres of farmland from Calvin A. Colvard in Graham County. This tract was within a mile of the county seat of Robbinsville and was strategically situated for the Cheoah Indians, who predictably supported the scheme.[9]

Money was an obvious requirement for any serious program of improving Cherokee status. One tempting source was the 1848 transportation and subsistence fund, and even before McCarthy became agent a bill was pending in Congress to divert this into a common tribal fund for securing land titles, making agricultural improvements, and promoting civilization. After it passed in March 1875, the Indian Office used this fund to purchase the lands discussed in the previous chapter, as well as to buy several thousand dollars of farm implements and livestock for the Eastern Band. But the Office considered a model farm an extravagance and rejected McCarthy's plan.[10]

Another possible use for the common fund was to pay delinquent Cherokee land taxes. Before the war William Thomas had attended to this, and local assessors were rather lax in carrying out their responsibilities. But things were different under the new state government that arose out of Reconstruction. When a number of Indians could not or would not pay, sheriffs from several counties threatened to sell their lands. To prevent this, Indian Commissioner Edward P. Smith instructed McCarthy to pay $923 for four years of back taxes, insisting this was to be a loan from the common fund and not a gift. The great object, he said, was to prepare the North Carolina Indians "at an early day to receive each his own land and other property and to become citizens of the State of North Carolina." This policy—severalty or allotment—would be a means of assimilating Indians into American society; afterward they would manage their own lands and pay their own taxes.[11]

For the present, however, this long-range goal was obscured by Cherokee exigencies. By late 1875 there was a new crop of tax delinquents, and McCarthy asked what was to be done. Both he and the competing factions believed the government should use the common fund to pay these obligations, but the Indian commissioner argued that it would destroy the Indians' self-sufficiency and lead to an unequal distribution of money from the fund; the slackers would profit at the expense of those who had paid their taxes. Somehow, the Cherokees managed to pay almost all their taxes during the next few years, but the specter of losing their lands because of tax delinquency would return to haunt them in the 1880s.[12]

Indians also paid other taxes—including, from time to time, a state poll tax. This levy was totally incomprehensible to them, and they cited it as a reason for moving to Indian Territory, where they would not be subject to the whims of a white-dominated government. When asked upon what grounds the tax was imposed, North Carolina's attorney general replied that in the absence of any law specifically exempting the Indians they should "be considered as other citizens in respect to the benefits and burdens of government." By the 1880s the Cherokees had worked out an arrangement that usually allowed them to escape the poll tax in return for disavowing certain forms of assistance from the counties.[13]

This dispute over taxation brought into sharp relief, once again, the question of whether the Cherokees were state citizens. They paid taxes, were allowed to vote, and were subject to North Carolina law, but on the other hand they had a special relationship with the federal government. The United States recognized them as wards under the 1868 act, but wards of a peculiar sort. It never protested the state's taxation of them and in effect acquiesced in North Carolina's assertion of at least a limited authority. At times, however, it could assert its prerogatives with dogged persistence. In short, it was a "mixed system" of government, with neither the state nor federal government defining its respective authority. The Eastern Band's anomalous status continued.[14]

Despite their squabbles among themselves, the Eastern Cherokees were in accord on one matter: their children needed education. Since even before the 1838 removal the Indians had been without formal instruction, except for an occasional teacher hired by Thomas for a few months at a time. In 1868 the United States spent $1,000 for books to distribute among them, but these were meaningless without teachers and schools. When the writer Rebecca Harding Davis visited Quallatown in 1875, she found the Indians totally lacking in education. They appeared capable and eager to learn, however, and she told a poignant story of her shy but intelligent interpreter who hoped he might someday attend school.[15]

According to Swetland's census, taken nearly fifty years after Sequoyah's invention of the syllabary, less than half of the North Carolina Cherokees could read or write in their own language. There were a number of households on Qualla Boundary and at Cheoah where not a single individual was literate in Cherokee. In contrast, the mixed-bloods had a high rate of literacy, either in Cherokee or English, or sometimes both. Recognizing the problems and ambiguities inherent in Swetland's data on literacy, one can still find enough evidence to support the conclusion that progress in education had been painfully slow.[16]

Agent McCarthy was determined to correct this by establishing Cherokee schools and had the strong support of Indian Commissioner Edward P. Smith, who believed there was no better purpose for which to use the Band's common fund. The Cheoah Indians were especially enthusiastic about the prospect of a school connected with a model farm, and without awaiting approval began constructing a large frame school house on the Colvard tract—apparently believing the government would buy the land as McCarthy had recommended. Both the Indians and Colvard expected to be paid by McCarthy, but the agent refused to do this without Indian Office approval, creating considerable dissatisfaction.[17]

In October 1875, McCarthy recommended the government hire Mary A. Manney, of Robbinsville, to take charge of the Cheoah school at a salary of thirty dollars a month for a five-month term. By early 1876 he had four other schools in operation, all on Qualla Boundary: at Yellow Hill, Bird Town, Big Cove, and the Echota Mission. The one at Cheoah was a boarding school, while the others were basically day institutions. Of the 111 pupils enrolled at Cheoah, most came from more than twenty miles away. Some boarded with whites or mixed-bloods at five dollars a month (paid from the common fund), while others huddled in tents or makeshift cabins built near the school. A number of fullbloods camped with their families in the woods, shivering in the rain and snow, anxious to avail themselves of education yet suspicious of whites and mixed-bloods. But the parents were not timid about demanding five dollars a month to support their children, too.[18]

A basic problem at all the schools was the students' extreme poverty. McCarthy noted that "Scarcely any have shoes, and many of both sexes are nearly naked." He urged the government to use the promise of clothes as an inducement to get them to attend, recommending distribution of three hundred pairs of brogan shoes, calico for new dresses, and jeans for the male students. Unfortunately, he was not appealing to a very sympathetic government. Only a few months before, the Indian Office had warned McCarthy against giving handouts to destitute Cherokees. The Indians had managed to keep from starving and freezing to death without assistance so far, the commissioner said.[19]

While McCarthy struggled with the Band's economic and educational problems, he became progressively mired in the tar baby of tribal factionalism; the more he struggled against it, the more he became a part of it. At the fall 1875 council meeting in Quallatown, he tried to remain aloof as the tribe elected officers and amended its constitution. Flying Squirrel and John Ross had been the rival claimants to chieftainship for the previous few years. At this meeting Lloyd R. Welch assumed the mantle of Flying Squirrel's leadership by winning election as Principal Chief for a four-year term. Experiencing his first taste of politics, McCarthy was appalled by what he viewed as the victor's electioneering excesses. Most Indians, he believed, had been unaware of the pending elections, enabling the Welch faction to rig the proceedings. Delegates from Tennessee and Georgia had been allowed to vote and gave their support to Welch. They and the new chief, McCarthy said, conspired to overturn the recent legislation creating the common fund and instead have the money distributed per capita. In addition, the agent accused Welch of being in league with James Blunt, still the bête noire of Cherokee affairs. The proper course was for the Indian Office to order a new election. Instead, the Office sent Inspector E.C. Watkins to investigate. Inspectors outranked agents in the hierarchy of the Indian Office and were often called upon to assess their competence. In this case Watkins concluded that Welch had been honestly elected and that McCarthy should stick to educational matters.[20]

Despite Watkins's barbed suggestion, McCarthy could hardly ignore the contagion of factionalism. Gradually, however, he reconciled himself to Lloyd Welch while increasingly taking note, as only an indignant Baptist minister could, of Ross's frailties. In April 1876 he reported that Ross was implicated in the murder of a fellow Indian during a drunken fracas at a grocery in Charleston, the Swain County seat. McCarthy did not believe Ross could be convicted for murder, but the "quasi" chief was hiding in the mountains. Though Ross was a kindhearted man of sound judgment when sober, when drunk he was "a very dangerous man. He has twice attempted the life of Captain Terrell." Ross soon resolved his difficulties with the law, whatever they were, but he, James Taylor, and Enola became vocal critics of McCarthy. Enola, now in his late fifties, served as Ross's assistant chief, occasional delegate to Washington, and Cherokee land commissioner. He was the most prominent Quallatown member of the Ross-Taylor faction.[21]

Meanwhile the Indian Office seriously considered closing the agency. Inspector Watkins had concluded in December 1875 that the Indians were far enough advanced to take care of themselves and that state jurisdiction might soon be appropriate. The Indian commissioner's report of that year suggested the same thing. In January 1876, Representative Robert B. Vance of North Carolina introduced a bill for that purpose, and this apparently prompted Secretary of Interior Zachariah Chandler to order the closing of McCarthy's agency effective February 1, less than a month after he had approved plans for construction of an agency office.[22]

Reverend McCarthy was outraged. In a lengthy letter to the Indian Office he detailed his personal sacrifices and travail during the past year. After overcoming many obstacles, he had supervised the opening of five schools among the Cherokees and had carefully selected their teachers. The students, despite their poverty, were making real progress. And now it would end. As agent, he had been expected to do "many difficult things . . . but Mr. Commissioner, you have set me the hardest task yet—to tell my Indians the schools must stop." He then listed several reasons why the agency should remain open: its fostering of morality; its value in protecting the Cherokees from lawless whites; its necessity for controlling the liquor traffic; and its promotion of Indian education and civilization. McCarthy acknowledged that he had made some powerful enemies as agent, and he believed this had been a factor in the agency's shutdown. The implied criticism of him by this action was a personal affront. He closed with a stinging rebuke, saying he had expected support and *this* was his reward.[23]

His impassioned appeal had a temporary effect. Vance's bill had not been enacted, and Indian Commissioner John Q. Smith recommended to Chandler that, in view of the recent progress among the Cherokees, the agency continue operation—with the stipulation that McCarthy limit himself to the educational interests of the Cherokees and to "a general oversight of their condition and affairs." There were changes pending for the agency, and Smith obviously did not want to hear of any more political disputes involving McCarthy.[24]

Despite a promising start, the Cherokee schools were McCarthy's undoing. After closing them on June 1 for summer vacation, the agent admitted his growing disillusionment. A variety of developments had caused attendance to drop off rapidly in the last few months: Cherokee poverty; the need for students to return to the fields during the growing season; the uncertainty of boarding arrangements at Cheoah; the shortage of blackboards, books, and other necessities; and the "mischievous" actions of a few whites in undermining the Big Cove school. Nonetheless, McCarthy retained confidence in his teachers and believed the Cherokees were eminently educable, if treated with firmness and patience.[25]

While the educational program began to crumble, Ross and Taylor increased their attacks on McCarthy; even Principal Chief Welch stated that the Indians did not require an agent to manage their affairs. It is hardly surprising, therefore, that in its appropriations act of August 1876 Congress directed that McCarthy's agency close on September 1. The secretary of interior would continue to spend $6,000 a year from the Band's common fund for farm implements and education, but the fund could no longer be used for land acquisitions or paying back taxes. Part of the money would go to the superintendent of common schools in North Carolina, who would supervise Cherokee education under the direction of the Indian commissioner. This provision reflects a mutual recognition of joint state and federal responsibility for the Indians, an acceptance of the "mixed system." for the next few years there would be no federal agent living among the Eastern Cherokees, though special agents and inspectors would periodically descend upon them, like locusts, to conduct investigations.[26]

To his mortification, McCarthy could not make a graceful exit from his Indian responsibilities. Taylor and others accused him of fraud, profiteering, and, cruelest of all, being a "Bluntite." For a time he was even defendant to charges of financial mismanagement brought by the Indian Office. His defenders insisted he had been victimized by poor health, excessive demands on his time, and an unfamiliarity with federal bookkeeping procedures. And they were probably correct.[27]

The transfer of Cherokee education to the state superintendent of schools soon proved unwise, for that official found it impossible to oversee Indian matters when he was more than two hundred miles away in Raleigh. In 1877 the government terminated its arrangement with the state, and the Indian Office appointed Dr. J.D. Garner, a Quaker from Maryville, Tennessee, to oversee educational affairs among the Cherokees of North Carolina, Tennessee, and Georgia. He was to harmonize his work as much as possible with North Carolina's school law and to operate about the same as a county school superintendent. Local Cherokee school boards were to assist him.[28]

As it turned out, Cherokee education was just another prism refracting tribal factionalism. Garner quickly chose sides, supporting Lloyd Welch as chief and characterizing Ross and Taylor as, respectively, a dupe and a scoundrel. Even more bitter was the feud he and Welch carried on with John and Kate DeVaughan, who were associated with the Cheoah school. Mrs. DeVaughan was an experienced teacher from Washington who had moved to North Carolina hoping to help the Indians, but she tended to ignore diplomatic niceties and bureaucratic red tape. In so doing she was accused of, among other things, misappropriating tribal funds. Her husband blamed Garner for the difficulties, accusing him of incompetence, criminality, and intimidation of the local Cherokee school board. Amid such a politicized and vindictive atmosphere, it is little wonder Cherokee schools suffered.[29]

Finally, in July 1879, Secretary of Interior Carl Schurz terminated Garner's appointment and let the schools die. A local Methodist proposed using the tribal common fund to establish a school at Echota Mission, but the government embarked upon a different plan.[30] Federal agents would select the most promising students and send them to nearby academies and "colleges." This would cut overall costs and keep the Indians away from the tribal milieu, enabling them to adjust more rapidly to "civilized" life.

Placing Indians in boarding schools was a concept dating back to the colonial period, and by the late nineteenth century many officials and humanitarians came to view it, along with allotment, as a primary means of assimilation. The most famous Indian boarding school was Carlisle Institute in Pennsylvania, founded by Captain Richard Henry Pratt in 1879. Even before Pratt began instructing his young charges in the ways of civilization, Garner placed three Eastern Cherokees in the Friends Normal School in Maryville, hoping they would be successful scholars and return to their people as teachers.[31]

By 1880 Cherokee pupils were also enrolled at Weaverville College, Asheville Female College, and Trinity College, all in North Carolina. In truth, these so-called colleges were little more than glorified grammar schools and were so hard-pressed financially that they competed in seeking federally sponsored students. As an example, the principal of Weaverville College proposed in 1879 to treat the Indians the same as other students and to board, educate, and clothe a dozen or so for ten months at $150 each. He hastened to add, however, that this did not include the costs of medical attention or burial. The directors of Asheville Female College offered a full calendar year of instruction for $150 each.[32] Indian Commissioner Ezra A. Hayt preferred this sort of arrangement, for otherwise "the home influence brought to bear upon the Indian Children will neutralize in (2) two months, the good work of the other ten (10) months."[33]

The special agents who selected the students had to take care that the various factions and districts of the tribe were represented. Occasionally a would-be student was lucky enough to be acceptable to all factions, bringing a sigh of relief from the agent. In March 1880 Special Agent John A. Sibbald selected twelve males and eleven females, ranging in age from eight to sixteen and representing all groups within the Band. After a physical examination in Asheville, all of the males but one went to Weaverville College and all but one female to Asheville Female College.[34]

Trinity College, in Randolph County, was different from the other institutions. This impoverished Methodist predecessor of Duke University was more than one hundred miles from the mountains and might as well have been on the far side of the moon as far as most Cherokees were concerned. Nonetheless, the Indian Office planned to send twelve Indian boys there in the fall of 1880. Agent Sibbald doubted that Cherokee parents would want their children to go so far away, and he was right. His successor, A.F. Fardon, encountered strong opposition when he tried to select the prospective students. At a special council the Indians complained that the school was too far away; the low country was unhealthy; they needed their children to help at home; and they objected to the use of common funds for the education of only a few.[35] After considerable difficulty Fardon was finally able to select twelve boys for Trinity and one for Weaverville. It took three days by wagon for them to reach Asheville, and from there Fardon escorted the students by train to Trinity. Nearly all were fullbloods, and the two who could read and write English were to serve as interpreters for their classmates. The Reverend Braxton Craven, president of Trinity, had leased and furnished a separate building where the Indians were to board with his son.[36]

Considering how little educational background Cherokee children had, the curricula at these schools appear demanding enough. At Weaverville Indian males studied English, reading, spelling, arithmetic, and geography as their academic curriculum, in addition to gardening and general farmwork. The girls at Asheville also studied English, and at least one worked in arithmetic; mostly, however, they concentrated on sewing and housework.[37]

If one believes the principals' monthly reports, Cherokee pupils made about as much progress as other students; most were middling, a few quite bright, and even fewer disruptive and pugnacious. At Weaverville two Cherokee boys with a solid background in English entered the contest for a declamatory medal and one of them, according to the principal, had a good chance for success. All of the other Indian students, he said, were rapidly learning English. At the other end of the spectrum was the Weaverville mixed-blood who bullied and terrorized his classmates with drunken tirades and profanity. The principal quickly expelled the miscreant and asked for a better replacement. [38]

There remains the tantalizing question of whether the designated pupils really wished to attend school. Some, like Rebecca Davis's eager interpreter, probably needed no encouragement. Others were so unenthusiastic they appear to have been shanghaied, and teachers had to watch them closely to prevent their running away. Then, when vigilance was relaxed, they would escape and head for their mountain homes while white officials literally tried to "head them off at the pass." Eventually, as agent Sibbald expressed it, most were "captured." Despite such efforts to retain pupils, some who returned home for sanctioned vacations refused to go back to school. [39] Sometimes it was the parents who prevented their children from continuing their education. On one occasion, a drunken father appeared at the college and, over the protests of teachers and principal, took his child home. [40] Quite possibly he had to resort to alcohol to overcome the normal Cherokee aversion to unpleasantness, particularly when dealing with whites. It must have required considerable effort for him to travel to a strange town and confront an educator in his own school.

Acculturated Cherokee parents were likely to be more forceful and self-confident, especially when they believed their children were being abused. David Taylor angrily declared that he would not allow his two daughters to return to Asheville because they were allegedly treated like servants; they were required to wash clothing, wait on the wife of a college official, clean up rooms, and "pack out pots full of excrement" for the whites. Reflecting the legalistic bent that was peculiar to Cherokees, he wanted to charge the college sixty dollars for the services of his daughters over a three-month period. Nor was Weaverville any better, he said, for his sons came home with lice and tales of treatment "beyond humanity." He was outraged that their common fund was being "squandered" in this way. [41] But a tribal official visited Weaverville about the same time and, according to the principal, was pleased with the situation. [42]

Some Cherokees were jealous of those families whose children were going away to school. It was not that they necessarily wanted their own offspring to leave, but like all Cherokees, they resented unfair distinctions among themselves, especially when the common fund was being used. This is why Agent Sibbald recommended reestablishing a day school on Qualla Boundary. It would not only help those children still at home but also assuage some of the jealousy. Acting upon his suggestion, the Indian Office appointed the Reverend J.W. Bird as teacher at the Echota Mission. He was not especially well educated, but he knew the Indians and was the most qualified person living around Quallatown. Within a few months, however, he came under systematic attack by discontented tribal officials who wanted to replace him with more experienced Quaker teachers.[43]

The arrival of the Quakers—or Friends—marks the real beginning of educational progress for the Band. Since the late 1860s they had become a powerful force in American Indian policy, conducting a wide-ranging crusade for pacifying and uplifting the red man and reforming the Indian Office. As early as 1875 they had expressed interest in working among the North Carolina Indians, and, of course, J.D. Garner and the Quaker School at Maryville had figured prominently in Cherokee education. In May 1881, with the government's approval, the Quakers contracted with the Eastern Band to provide a ten-year educational program featuring Christian morality, a strong work ethic, and an emphasis on the practical. Each year during that period they would renegotiate a separate contract with the Indian Office. The system of contracting with Christian denominations for Indian education was necessary because of the lack of any comprehensive federal educational program.[44]

Most active in the Quakers' Cherokee work was Barnabas C. Hobbs, who represented the Western Yearly Meeting of Indiana, which included a number of Friends from North Carolina. With the aid of this group and the North Carolina Yearly Meeting, Hobbs agreed to reopen the day schools that had been abandoned, using the interest from the tribal fund as well as money from his organization and the government. He appointed Thomas C. Brown as the first superintendent of these schools and hired experienced teachers who, despite some local animosity toward outsiders, quickly proved their worth. In 1884 Henry W. Spray, former superintendent of the Maryville school, succeeded Brown.[45]

By the time Spray arrived, the Quakers were constructing large boarding schools for boys and girls at Yellow Hill and had established a small model farm that was like what the much-maligned William McCarthy had advocated a decade before. By favoring mechanical and agricultural instruction, the Friends provided on-reservation education that most Indians could appreciate. The girls concentrated on domestic skills, while the males worked at gardening, farming, carpentry, and smithing. Students of both sexes also studied English, arithmetic, and a few other academic subjects, besides submitting to Quaker pronouncements on religion and temperance. In addition, a few Cherokees continued to attend college at Maryville, Trinity, and elsewhere.[46]

In the meantime, tribal politics had undergone significant changes. Lloyd Welch had steadily consolidated his power at Quallatown, and in 1877 he was also able to dominate a tribal council convened at his old home of Cheoah. This was a stunning setback for the Ross-Taylor faction, which had been firmly entrenched there. As additional humiliation, Nimrod Jarrett Smith, a Welch lieutenant, introduced a successful motion to create a tribal council ground at Yellow Hill and to lay out a number of town lots there, a clear sign the Welch group intended to establish the Cherokee capital on Qualla Boundary. During the next few years, moreover, Welch and his coterie increasingly won the support of the Indian Office.[47]

But the not-so-loyal opposition was far from dead and continued what one Cherokee called "the shallow mockery" of electing rival officials and drawing up conflicting petitions and resolutions. Taylor and Ross used the supposed authority of their own councils to send delegates to Washington, issue proclamations, and even hire a Washington attorney, Mrs. Belva A. Lockwood, to prosecute tribal claims. Perhaps unaware of the vagaries of Cherokee politics, she worked in their behalf well into the 1880s before the Quallatown faction disavowed any connection with her.[48]

The year 1880 marks a clear transition in tribal politics. Lloyd Welch had recently been reelected to another four-year term, and Special Agent John Sibbald confirmed that he enjoyed the support of a majority, while the Ross-Taylor faction merely reflected the opportunism of Taylor. Then, acting upon Sibbald's suggestion, the Welch faction decreed that henceforth the seat of government would be at Yellow Hill. From that time on, the Quallatown Indians had the tribal political apparatus in their own backyard. Of more immediate concern was the growing awareness early in 1880 that Chief Welch was dying, stirring speculation as to his successor. He resigned shortly before his death in June, delivering a touching farewell to his people, and the next month, to no one's surprise, the general council elected Nimrod Smith as Principal Chief. For the next eleven years he would be the most powerful political figure within the Band, though not without opposition.[49]

Smith (Tsaladihi) was one-quarter Cherokee and the son of Henry Smith, long a leading resident of Cherokee County. The younger

Smith acquired "a fair education," became fluent in Cherokee and English, served as a sergeant in the Thomas Legion, and acted as secretary of the 1868 Cheoah council that had drawn up the first tribal constitution. Following the denunciation of his father and Lloyd Welch by Ross and Taylor, he had slowly built a political career among the Quallatown faction. Six feet, four inches in height and well proportioned, he enhanced his dramatic appearance by affecting a drooping mustache and long, black hair that curled over his shoulders; this, coupled with his air of self-assurance, made him resemble George Armstrong Custer, a comparison Smith would have found amusing. The Indian Office soon discovered that he was about as dynamic and headstrong as the general.[50]

As Smith's election signified the political preeminence of the Qualla Indians, so the 1880 census confirmed their numerical superiority. Since Swetland's 1869 census, their population had risen from 730 to 825, while the number of Cherokees living in Graham, Macon, and Cherokee counties had plummeted from 912 to 398.[51] During that period, especially 1871–1872, many had moved from those counties to the Cherokee Nation, and others had shifted to Qualla Boundary. Perhaps the latter felt more secure living on common lands among their own kind, or, in the case of individuals like Nimrod Smith, it may have been a wish to find political preferment. Certain enclaves in Graham County, like the Snowbird Community, retained their lands and Cherokee identity—and continue to do so—but it was clear long ago that Qualla Boundary was the center of Cherokee life in North Carolina.[52]

The ascendancy of Smith was a signal to Dennis Bushyhead, chief of the Cherokee Nation, who renewed the invitation to unhappy Cherokees to move west. Despite the experiences of those who had emigrated in 1871–1872, he promised that any newcomers would receive citizenship and the full range of rights within the Nation. Late in 1880 the dispirited John Ross led a contingent of Eastern Cherokees to Loudon, Tennessee, where, like their predecessors a decade before, they awaited federal assistance. Once again a reluctant government intervened and during the next year used the Indian Civilization Fund to transport 161 to Indian Territory. A bit later James Taylor also moved and, together with Ross and other émigrés, continued his attacks on Nimrod Smith. Taylor called him "the pliable tool of the Indian ring" and claimed that under the 1868 constitution Enola was actually chief.[53] Not content with this

Chief Nimrod J. Smith, ca. 1890
(Source: *Eleventh Census of the United States: Extra Census Bulletin* [Washington, D.C., 1892].)

long-distance vituperation, he eventually returned to North Carolina, engaging in his old tricks and fomenting discord.

Some Eastern Cherokees moved on their own to Indian Territory and then requested repayment, only to find that the removal money had been designated for other purposes by the act of March 1875. Furthermore, Chief Smith and his faction bitterly opposed any diversion of this fund for the transportation of malcontents. There was no way to reimburse those who had moved on their own unless Congress made a special appropriation. Arguments over this matter injected another dose of vitriol into Cherokee factionalism.[54]

In the meantime, the Eastern Cherokees' uncertain status came one step closer to being defined. Their former attorneys, Wallace W. Rollins and Otis F. Presbrey, attempted to collect more than $42,000 for services in helping them acquire the lands awarded by arbitrators in 1874. When the federal government allowed only $5,200, the lawyers sued the Eastern Band in a state court. After a ruling that the state lacked jurisdiction, Rollins and Presbrey appealed to the North Carolina Supreme Court. The Indian Office was secretly delighted, viewing the appeal as a heaven-sent opportunity for a top-level judicial decision on the Cherokees' status. In its October 1882 term the supreme court upheld the lower tribunal by affirming that the Eastern Band was a tribe like any other, under the jurisdiction of the United States and therefore immune to suit in state courts. The United States had exclusive authority over the Band's contractual affairs.[55]

Perhaps in anticipation of this decision, the Indian Office had shortly before taken action to quell Nimrod Smith's unexpected manifestation of independence. Without consulting federal officials, the Principal Chief had attempted to raise tribal revenue by signing contracts with outsiders for cutting timber on Qualla Boundary. And it was he who had been most active in wooing the Quakers. This assertiveness, along with the Band's growing difficulties and the likelihood of a favorable decision in the Rollins suit, probably explains the government's appointment in September 1882 of Samuel G. Gibson of Swain County as special Indian agent for the Band. For the first time since William McCarthy's dismissal, the Eastern Cherokees had a resident agent. Clearly, the federal government intended to exercise its authority.[56]

At the same time Gibson became agent, the government appointed Joseph G. Hester to take yet another census of all Cherokees living east of the Mississippi River.[57] At stake for the North

Carolina enrollees was a share in any future distribution of the Band's assets and, perhaps, those of the Cherokee Nation. (The Band was at that moment attempting to bring suit against the Nation for a proportionate share of past land sales and annuities.) Of particular concern to Hester was the enrollment of children who had been born to unions of blacks and Indians. This had been a problem for David Siler when he prepared his 1851 roll, and by the early 1880s there had been even more Cherokee intermingling with both blacks and whites. The solution, Indian Commissioner Hiram Price said, was for Hester to list all children of mixed unions who were recognized by the Indians as tribal members. The Cherokees, true to their matrilineal traditions, generally refused to acknowledge those whose mother was not of Cherokee blood, though they allowed Hester to decide on a few cases.[58]

Apparently the Cherokees felt the same ambivalence toward blacks that many whites experienced. Despite occasional miscegenation, the Indians still looked with disfavor on Negroes, perhaps fearful of themselves being mistaken for mulattoes. Cherokees who lived with blacks risked social ostracism, as did their children. When the daughter of such a union was selected to attend college, a tribal official took the white agent aside; putting his fingers in his hair, he gave them a twist and pointed to the girl, indicating that her hair was kinky and that she had Negro blood. The agent selected someone else.[59]

Hester's final roll of January 1884 included 2,956 Cherokees, 1,881 of them living in North Carolina. Georgia had 738, Tennessee 213, Alabama 71, and eight other states shared the rest.[60] The North Carolina figure was more than 50 percent above what federal census-takers had reported in 1880. Hester invited Chief Bushyhead from the Cherokee Nation to attend the official reading of the census at Yellow Hill, but the chief was unable to attend and had to content himself with a copy of the roll to inspect. After the Yellow Hill council accepted Hester's census, some Cherokees complained that a host of non-Indians had gained inclusion. Whatever its accuracy, the Hester roll signified the breakdown of a relatively homogeneous, though factionalized, Eastern Band. As outsiders increasingly settled around and even among the Indians, it was inevitable there would be intermingling. The Cherokees were a society in transition.[61]

A major headache for Agent Gibson and his successors was protection of Indian land; always it was the land that preoccupied the

Cherokees and always the land that seemed to be just beyond their secure grasp. The 1874 decision by the board of arbitration was simply a way station on the long road toward undisputed possession of their patrimony. The greatest threats were the trespassers who had settled on the Qualla Boundary and some of the outlying tracts. Trespassing resulted in part from an absurd law allowing the state to issue grants to anyone who cared to file on a piece of property, regardless of prior ownership or possession. The state then let rival claimants resolve their disputes in court at their own expense. As one horrified federal agent expressed it, North Carolina, "like some great big fish on her spawning grounds, went right on breeding and hatching out more titles to the same land." In other cases, according to William McCarthy, whites had simply driven Indians off their own property or "rented" land from them and then refused to pay. The Cherokees were in a quandary. They owned the Qualla Boundary in common but lacked standing as a group in state and federal courts; as for privately owned tracts outside the Boundary, few individuals could afford to bring suits of ejectment. This legal lacuna left them facing possible dispossession by unscrupulous whites.[62]

When the Indians appealed to federal authorities, the government found it had few options. Amazingly enough, most of the titles conveyed in 1874 had disappeared. Wallace Rollins, who was supposed to have recorded them in the appropriate courthouses, said he had received less than a dozen from the board of arbitration. The others had been misplaced, secreted, or destroyed, partly through carelessness and partly through malice on the part of some whites who hoped to obtain Cherokee lands. Without such documentation, it was difficult for the government to take action against supposed trespassers. In 1884 the Indian Office finally asked the attorney general to look into the matter, but nothing could be done until agents tracked down the surviving records.[63] For the next ten years the Band attempted to hold off trespassers while a sometimes bewildered government muddled its way toward a solution.

Although many Cherokees looked to the government to protect their lands, others insisted that federal authorities had already done too much, to the Indians' detriment. Some objected to the government's control of the common fund, claiming it had been nearly depleted without any compensating benefits. Some grumbled because they believed they could not buy and sell improvements within the Boundary without the president's approval. And a few mixed-bloods like James Taylor opposed federal trusteeship over the lands outside Qualla Boundary, claiming—correctly—that it violated the terms of the 1874 award, which stipulated fee simple titles for certain individuals. After finally obtaining his title and moving west, Taylor asked the government to sell the Band's remaining lands and distribute the proceeds on a per capita basis. After all, those who had recently moved to Indian Territory were still entitled to a portion of the tribal domain. Nimrod Smith favored selling some of the more remote outlying lands but not the Qualla Boundary. To sell it would mean the end of the Band as a tribal entity.[64]

One crucial matter remaining unresolved since the 1850s was the claim of the Eastern Band to a share of the land sales in the Cherokee Nation. Shortly after the Civil War, Congress sold the Neutral Lands and then prepared to sell other tribal lands west of the Ninety-Sixth Meridian. The Eastern Band continued to insist that it was entitled to a proportionate share of the proceeds, an argument that strained relations with the Nation. An exhaustive inquiry by Inspector C.C. Clements supported the Band's position and was strongly endorsed by the Indian Office.[65] But because they lacked any standing in court, the Eastern Cherokees could only appeal to Congress for assistance. In 1883, after years of debate, Congress authorized the Band to bring suit in federal court against both the Cherokee Nation and the United States for recovery of a proportionate share of land sales and annuities. Chief Smith hired Samuel J. Crawford, a former governor of Kansas, as their Washington attorney and initiated the suit.[66]

Eventually the case worked its way to the U.S. Supreme Court, which in March 1886 decided against the plaintiffs. The Eastern Cherokees, it said, had separated from the Cherokee Nation and had refused to emigrate west; they could therefore have no claims to any of the tribal lands.[67] Going beyond the immediate point, the Court contended that the Eastern Cherokees had never been recognized as a tribe and were in fact citizens of North Carolina. Their supposed constitution had merely been a social and business arrangement among themselves.[68] This *obiter dictum*—a nonbinding point not germane to the case at issue—was mistaken on several points and completely ignored the complexity and ambiguity of the Eastern Band's historical and legal context. It also contradicted the position taken in the Rollins case of 1882. It is the only instance in the nineteenth century of federal courts contending that the Eastern Cherokees were citizens.

A few of the more acculturated Cherokees were delighted at least with the *obiter dictum*, believing their supposed citizenship would free them and their property from the heavy hand of federal control. James Taylor, now in his late sixties and back in North Carolina, said it meant the Indians could do as they pleased, without regard to the wishes of their agents and the government. They could sell their own land, cut their own timber, even buy whiskey.[69] In contrast, most Cherokees found nothing worthy of joy in the Court's decision. Not only had they failed to win their share of the land sales and annuities, but their tribal organization had been declared invalid as a means of regulating and structuring their lives. The possibility of losing the federal government's sometimes bumbling guardianship, of being on their own, was also frightening. In response to this anxiety, Indian Commissioner John D.C. Atkins suggested a familiar "solution": they should rejoin their noncitizen brothers in the West. Even though Chief Smith and other Indians considered this alternative, it was only a momentary aberration; they would struggle to remain where they were. Besides, it was not at all certain that the Cherokee Nation would welcome their recent legal adversaries.[70]

It was probably just as well that Enola had died the year before the Supreme Court's decision; he would have been distressed by the fear and uncertainty that pervaded his people. Throughout his long years of creative cultural adaptation, he had never renounced the old ways, "at last dying, as he was born, in the ancient faith of his forefathers."[71] It must have been harder for Swimmer, carefully trained by his elders to learn and preserve the ancient lore that had sustained the Cherokees since antiquity. He was only about fifty, but already his was a voice from the past. Now the whites had settled among his people; there were new towns like Charleston and Robbinsville where Indians got into trouble; there were Quakers and teachers and government agents and trespassers and laws that seemed designed to deceive and dispossess them. It was an era of change.

8

Always a Cherokee

For the Eastern Cherokees the years from the late 1880s to 1900 were a turbulent period, rife with uncertainty. Previously isolated from the major currents of American development, they now confronted an expanding white population and myriad changes. Their legal status, anomalous since the 1830s, became even more confused. Factionalism again confounded them. They lacked a viable economic base, were unable to pay all their taxes, and faced a swarm of trespassers. Educators encouraged them to shed their Indian ways and become homogenized "Americans," while ethnologists, paradoxically, sought to preserve their traditional culture. Through all these difficulties, the Indians struggled both to adapt and to retain their identity.

The Cherokees' legal standing was especially confusing. The United States claimed to be their guardian but had allowed an undefined, mixed system of state and federal authority to evolve. The Cherokees voted, paid taxes, and otherwise acted as citizens of North Carolina, but this status had never been openly asserted until the Supreme Court's *obiter dictum* of 1886. Thus, as one lawyer noted, a strange dichotomy existed: the Indians were "quasi citizens" and "quasi wards."[1] As such, they had no idea what their rights and responsibilities were.

Of more immediate import than this legal conundrum was the threat to Cherokee lands. With their titles misplaced or stolen, there was no way they could protect themselves against trespassers. Whites already claimed most of the best property in Bird Town on the basis of state grants and were cutting timber on much of the unoccupied outlying lands. Late in 1885 Special Agent Eugene W. White described the various frauds committed by trespassers and concluded that "The manner in which the affairs of the Band have been attended to since the war of the rebellion is positively shocking." Like many special agents before him, he made a number of recommendations for improving the situation and then left.[2]

The Eastern Band could not initiate suit against the trespassers because it lacked standing in either state or federal courts. Individual Indians could bring suit on the state level, but few possessed the means to do so. It was obvious the federal government would have to do something to protect Cherokee lands. In 1888, after collecting what title documentation it could, the Justice Department brought two suits in behalf of the Band against William Thomas, his guardian, and other parties to the 1874 arbitration. The object was to force them to abide by the terms of that settlement and present valid titles to the Indians. To the dismay of the Cherokees, these suits dragged on until 1894, allowing the trespassers to become even more firmly entrenched.[3]

Linked with the title disputes was the exasperating matter of land taxation. Most Indians managed to pay the taxes on their own farms, but it was another matter to pay for the unoccupied common lands—thousands of acres in remote sections of several counties that were largely worthless for agriculture. Many Cherokees advocated their sale in order to buy better land closer to Qualla Boundary, where their children could also obtain an education. In the meantime they had to pay the taxes, sometimes on property occupied by trespassers or which had been logged over by whites. After the early 1880s the Indians were consistently remiss in meeting their obligations, and almost every year the sheriffs advertised the sale of lands for nonpayment.[4]

There were few means of paying these back taxes and redeeming the lands that had been sold. The Cherokees' primitive agriculture yielded no sufficient marketable surplus, they lacked any alternative employment, and their tribal fund was designated exclusively for agricultural and educational advancement. Nor was the Band able to exploit its supposed mineral resources, despite its allowing Theodore H. N. McPherson, a Washington attorney and entrepreneur, to mine the stream beds of the Oconaluftee River and Soco Creek. He was required, if and when he found valuable minerals, to pay the tribal land taxes as well as a percentage of his mining income. But a Cherokee bonanza was illusory. Though McPherson's company briefly stationed a dredge on the Oconaluftee, it never actually began operations. By 1887 the mining project had collapsed.[5]

As tribal leaders well understood, Cherokee forests represented their only sure source of income. Along Soco Creek alone, according to government experts, there were readily available about 5.2 million board feet of "the finest hard wood timber that we have ever seen." There were another 10 to 20 million feet in the same area (much of it almost inaccessible) and 15 to 25 million board feet in the Oconaluftee watershed. The foresters did not even survey the considerable timber still available on outlying lands.[6]

Control of Cherokee forests quickly became a major point of contention between tribal officials and the Indian Office. As early as 1881 Chief Smith, with the backing of his council, contracted to sell some valuable walnut trees in Big Cove on Qualla Boundary. Indian Commissioner Hiram Price was offended by this display of initiative and haughtily asked the chief by what authority he had made such a transaction. A number of trees had already been cut, and the logs simply lay on the ground while federal officials tried to decide what to do. The resident agent, Samuel Gibson, recommended their sale before they rotted and periodically sought permission to cut additional timber. He and later agents noted that construction of the Quaker schools and the Western North Carolina Railroad offered promising markets for Cherokee timber, shingles, and crossties, but the Office was suspicious of such opportunities. At best, it would allow cutting of only enough timber to pay the back taxes, usually with enough restrictions to dissuade lumbermen from bidding. About the only way the Cherokees themselves could legally cut trees was in clearing land for farming. A few attempted to use this as a means of getting around government restrictions, but with little success.[7]

Throughout the 1880s the reports of resident agents became almost a litany of familiar complaints: white trespassing, back taxes, impending sale of Indian lands for nonpayment of taxes, and requests for the cutting of timber to raise revenue. Julius L. Holmes succeeded Gibson as agent in January 1885, quickly became dissatisfied, and tendered his resignation later that year. Robert L. Leatherwood of nearby Charleston (soon renamed Bryson City) was an interim replacement and then officially succeeded Holmes in March 1886.[8] He encountered the usual problems but was especially troubled by James Taylor, who scurried between North Carolina, Indian Territory, and Washington. Taylor and some of his Indian supporters openly defied federal restrictions on timber cutting, arguing they were citizens and could do as they pleased with "their" property.[9]

The one bright spot in Cherokee affairs—for a while—was education. Barnabas Hobbs remained in overall control of the Quaker educational program and paid frequent visits from his home in Indiana. The resident superintendent, Henry Spray, was a dynamic individual who was assisted by an energetic wife and a corps of dedicated teachers. Together they nourished a program of practical education that included day schools at Big Cove, Macedonia (site of the old Echota Mission), Bird Town, and Snowbird Gap in Graham County. But the pride of the Band was the training school at Cherokee, where males and females attended as day students or boarders. The Quakers had purchased the site from the Indians and then conveyed the title to the United States; in addition, the Friends spent much of their own money in constructing buildings, acquiring livestock and tools, and paying teachers. Other money came from the government and interest on the Band's common fund. The Indians did not ordinarily receive state or county funds, in return for which local officials agreed not to collect the state poll tax.[10]

During the first few years the Quakers enjoyed near universal acclaim for their work. Everyone admitted that Cherokee children were making significant progress in education and "civilization," some having learned to read and write in English. But white attitudes toward the Quakers soon hardened because of Spray's personality, his policies, and especially his alleged influence with Indian voters. Since adoption of the 1868 state constitution, Cherokees had voted and local politicians had solicited their support. They represented a significant block of potential voters, leading one to suspect that this had been a factor in 1871 when Swain County was carved out of Jackson and Macon counties. The boundary line was drawn in such a way as to divide the Indians of Qualla Boundary between Jackson and Swain counties, lessening their political influence in either. It was a neat bit of gerrymandering that is still in effect. Even with such a division, the Cherokees represented a swing vote in those sparsely populated counties. As one election approached, an observer noted that in Swain County "the balance of power will probably lay in the hands of the Indian vote."[11]

Most seemed satisfied with the situation as long as the Cherokees followed the lead of their old mentor, William Thomas, and voted Democratic. But in the bitter national election of 1884, the Indians defected en masse to the Republican candidate, James G. Blaine. (The outcome reflected their bad luck when attempting to play white games. Grover Cleveland was elected president, the first

Democrat to hold that office since the Civil War.) The most common explanation for this shift is that Chief Smith was impressed when he heard that Blaine's running mate, John A. Logan, had Indian blood. The prospect of having an Indian vice president was sufficient to convince Smith to support the Republicans and, the story goes, he persuaded almost all the Cherokees to do likewise. [12]

Local Democrats, however, charged that Henry Spray had persuaded the Indians to switch to Blaine and had even rewarded them with free tobacco. Spray vehemently denied he had done anything to influence them, though he admitted he had always supported the Republican national and state tickets. His disclaimer notwithstanding, the political charges against him mingled with other complaints: the teachers at the Quaker school were outsiders, they did not understand the local population, and they were attempting to turn the Indians against their white "friends." Spray was even charged with assaulting an elderly Cherokee, an accusation that must have shocked the pacifistic Quakers. [13]

There was also the fact that Quakerism was an exotic transplant in a garden of religious fundamentalism. Stories circulated that the Friends were trying to indoctrinate the Indians and that Spray would not allow representatives of other denominations to use the Cherokees' own buildings for services. Yet the Indians, who were now mostly Baptists with a sizable Methodist minority, never seemed to feel pressured by Quaker influence. Only a relatively few sided with local whites against Spray. [14]

In Washington the Democratic administration paid careful attention to these developments. The defection of the Indians to the Republicans may have been one reason Commissioner John Atkins encouraged them to join their noncitizen—and nonvoting—brothers in the West. And when the yearly Quaker contract came up for renewal in 1886, the Indian Office dispatched Special Agent H.G. Osborne to North Carolina to investigate. After noting the strong white opposition to Spray and the whole Quaker educational system, Osborne expressed grudging admiration for the training school at Cherokee. The day schools, in contrast, were "very inferior" because they were open only seven months a year. When he called a meeting to hear the Indians' views, he was startled by the turnout—so many that some had to stand outside and listen through the windows. They voiced overwhelming support for Spray and Quaker education. Osborne then asked if they would object to another group's taking over the schools if it could run them as efficiently as the Quakers but at reduced expense to the Band's fund. With this kind of cue, the Cherokees agreed that such an arrangement, if possible, would be desirable. Osborne then recommended to the Indian commissioner that the day schools be terminated and the training school continue on a quarterly basis, presumably until a better contractor was found. None ever was.[15]

Still the storm clouds gathered around Henry Spray's head. As the 1888 national elections approached, a former Indian pupil of his offered a deal from the Democrats of Swain County. If Spray would use his influence to restore the Cherokees to their Democratic allegiance, the opposition to Spray and Quaker education would cease. According to Spray, he told the emissary that he lacked the power to deliver the Indian vote even if he had been so inclined, which he was not. By then a number of influential people had rallied to his defense. Chief Smith and practically all of the Cherokee council were vehement defenders, as was Charles C. Painter, the powerful Washington agent for the Indian Rights Association. He exonerated Spray by blaming the brouhaha on politics and the supposed desire of Methodists to take over Cherokee education. His published report may have given pause to some of Spray's enemies in the Indian Office. In any case, Benjamin Harrison's election seemed to guarantee Spray's position, at least for the present.[16]

Amid all this controversy, Nimrod Smith was the articulate, dynamic representative of his people, making frequent trips to Washington and conferring with officials on a variety of issues. He spoke in behalf of Spray and the Quakers, responded to the accusations of James Taylor, complained about trespassers, begged for federal confirmation of Cherokee titles, sought clarification of their legal status, and argued for proper use of tribal resources. He became widely respected for his imposing appearance, poise, and force of personality.[17]

Among those impressed by Smith was James Mooney, a young ethnologist at the Smithsonian Institution who first met him in 1885. Mooney was a former newspaperman who had developed a singular obsession for the systematic study of Indians. He so impressed John Wesley Powell, founder of the Smithsonian's Bureau of American Ethnology, that he obtained employment and began a distinguished career in his chosen field. During the summers of 1885 and 1886, he interviewed Smith while the chief was in Washington. Together they prepared a Cherokee grammar, and Smith offered enough tantalizing insights into Cherokee culture to whet the ethnologist's interest. In 1887, at the age of twenty-six and with the blessing of Powell, Mooney went to North Carolina to conduct more than three seasons of fieldwork among the Eastern Band. Plunging into his research, he learned the Cherokee language and quickly became a fixture in tribal life, conversing with young and old and melting away initial suspicions. He was immeasurably assisted by the good offices of Smith, Spray, and several educated mixed-bloods, the most important of whom was James Blythe, the tribal interpreter.[18]

With the luck of a novice, Mooney had arrived during a critical period for Eastern Cherokees, a transitional phase when they were shedding some of their ways and, outwardly at least, becoming increasingly acculturated. During the next few years he observed this process of change and attempted to preserve the legends and lore that were already fading from tribal consciousness. Quite possibly his inquiries and interest reawakened in some Indians an appreciation of their heritage. Others, like Swimmer, had always gloried in their Cherokee identity. It was Swimmer, in fact, who became Mooney's foremost informant, revealing much about his people and their traditions. He was even maneuvered by the wily ethnologist into a professional rivalry with other tribal shamans. It was a matter of pride that he knew more than they did, and to Mooney's joyous amazement he produced a carefully kept notebook of sacred rites. For months the two men were almost inseparable, attending tribal ceremonies, invoking ancient rites, identifying and picking medicinal plants, discussing Cherokee cosmology, and exchanging stories and legends. Swimmer was a magnificent teller of stories and loved to act them out, even to the point of imitating appropriate animal sounds. Mooney rewarded his friend with money and by relating Irish folk myths.[19]

Other important informants for Mooney were James Terrell and William Thomas, the latter now in his eighties and still lucid when discussing Indians. Confined to a mental institution and largely ignored by whites and Cherokees alike, the old gentleman must have been delighted by the attention Mooney paid him. The ethnologist, in turn, was gratified to have access to a man who, along with Swimmer, probably represented the greatest living storehouse of Cherokee information. Thomas's recollection of events was sometimes faulty, as archival records have shown, but he was able to provide valuable background information. Mooney's historical sketch of the Band owes a large debt to his memory.[20]

James Mooney
(Source: *Bulletin* 99, Bureau of American Ethnology.)

In his published work Mooney said little about contemporary Cherokee problems, especially the factionalism that was resurfacing in the late 1880s. Perhaps in helping to shape the new discipline of anthropology he instinctively avoided controversial topics that transcended the merely descriptive. Or, more likely, it was simply too painful to discuss the internecine warfare that involved good friends on both sides. Privately, he did express alarm over the high mortality rate among the Eastern Cherokees and noted that many enrolled by Joseph Hester a few years before had already died. He attributed this largely to their ignorance of proper health and sanitation measures and urged remedial action and greater concern on the part of the government. Tuberculosis was especially troublesome and, despite Mooney's efforts, continued to be a major cause of death among the Band well into the twentieth century.[21]

Mooney seemed less concerned about another Cherokee health problem, alcohol. Resident agents consistently viewed this as a threat and sometimes inquired whether the Band, with its muddled status, was protected by federal laws against peddling whiskey to Indians. But few of the Cherokees' neighbors considered such activity a sin. Moonshining was part of mountain culture, and local distillers resented any effort to limit their business. When Special Agent Eugene White visited the Indians late in 1885, he was briefly threatened by a group of roughnecks who suspected him of being a federal revenue agent. And in 1898 Joseph C. Hart reported, "There is a distillery just outside the Boundary where Indians of all ages can get liquor for money or corn. As a result, most of our young men are growing up worthless drunkards."[22] Unfortunately, the periodic attempts to prosecute liquor dealers met with little success.

During Mooney's last full season of fieldwork among the Band, the Cherokees took a significant step toward defining their status and defending their property. For years there had been talk of incorporating the Eastern Band under state law, a course that was clearly appropriate if the Cherokees were indeed citizens. It would also render moot the Supreme Court's contention that their existing tribal organization was invalid. Therefore, in March 1889, the North Carolina General Assembly recognized the Eastern Band as a corporate body that could sue and be sued in property matters, but the act would not prejudice any titles that others might claim adverse to those of the Indians. The Cherokees would have to challenge those in court. This incorporation, viewed with equanimity by the Indian Office, was a classic reflection of the mixed system of authority under which the Cherokees functioned. As later amended, the act also established a political and economic structure by which the Indians could function with or without federal assistance. To this day the Band operates under its provisions.[23]

Coincidental with the Band's incorporation, certain administrative and political changes occurred that were to have important consequences. When the Harrison administration took office early in 1889, Agent Robert Leatherwood was removed, though an official admitted that his only fault was being a bit dilatory and imprecise in submitting his accounts. But he had also antagonized a few prominent Indians by his impatience with their deliberations in council, once going so far as to suggest the Cherokees needed "more labor and less legislation." His replacement was James Blythe, the agency interpreter who had studied at the Quaker college in Maryville, Tennessee. It was the first time the federal government had selected a local Cherokee for such a lofty position.[24]

Nimrod Smith was at first delighted with Blythe's appointment, in part because the new agent had married one of the chief's daughters. But cordiality soon became strained as Blythe and Henry Spray came to head a faction that increasingly opposed Smith. The origins of this feud are obscure, but it did not help that after the 1888 election Smith returned to the Democratic fold and unsuccessfully attempted to convert the rest of the Band. (In the "offyear" elections of 1890, the Cherokees cast a total of 137 Republican votes in Swain and Jackson counties, and only 39 for Democrats.) Even more decisive in the growing estrangement between factions were the stories of the chief's moral lapses: drunkenness, assaults, corruption, and other sins. Spray and Blythe, Quakers by faith or education, were indignant over these alleged indiscretions. For his part, Smith came to view Spray, Blythe, and their cohorts as dangerous rivals for tribal influence.[25]

By 1890 the schism had reached such a point that Smith was willing to defy his council and veto a decision to renew indefinitely the Quaker contract for education, accusing Spray of misusing the Band's common fund and of exercising near-dictatorial control over Cherokee buildings. Some of the local whites and a minority of the tribe joined the attack on Spray. Because of his strong support for Quaker education, Blythe found himself aligned against his father-in-law. Despite Smith's objections, the Quakers continued in charge of tribal schools and the factions became irreconcilably opposed to each other. Of particular concern to Smith was his growing estrangement from the tribal council, which remained firmly committed to Quaker education. The culmination of this growing fractiousness came in February 1891, when Smith sent a lengthy letter to Indian commissioner Thomas J. Morgan in which he leveled a number of charges against Spray and Blythe. The great "mistake of my life," he confessed, had been his earlier support for those two men.[26]

Morgan immediately dispatched the Reverend Daniel Dorchester, a Methodist clergyman and the government's superintendent of Indian schools, to conduct an investigation. Smith was apparently surprised by the prompt response to his accusations and refused to testify before Dorchester, claiming he needed time to locate more witnesses. By then, according to the council, Smith had "alienated himself" from his people and degraded the office of chief. His transgressions were such that the council had "no expectation of his being re-elected next September."[27] After conducting a lengthy investigation and interviewing scores of witnesses, Dorchester prepared a report of 172 pages which dealt with most aspects of Cherokee affairs and boldly attacked the chief's character in what can only be described as an exposé. According to the testimony, Smith was a drunk, a brawler, an adulterer, and worse. Two of Smith's daughters claimed that he had forced their older sister to live with a white trader out of wedlock in exchange for certain favors to the chief. In addition, his alleged adultery had broken up a Cherokee family and resulted in the woman and her cuckolded husband being excommunicated from their Baptist church, she for sleeping with Smith and he for refusing to forgive the sinners.[28]

These and other unfavorable reports touching on Smith's character destroyed his reputation within the Indian Office. He was no longer a man to be trusted, no longer fit to lead his people. Eleven years of leadership had seemingly corrupted him completely. Both the Indian Office and Agent Blythe were determined that he would not remain in power. Blythe informed the Office that Smith's defeat in the forthcoming election was certain unless the chief could convince people that he retained influence in Washington; the agent asked Morgan for a statement as to Smith's status within the Office. Morgan, a former Baptist minister and educator, attached a handwritten memorandum to Blythe's letter that was curt and emphatic: "Reply that this office does not regard Mr. Smith as a suitable person for chief and will not recognize him as such if he should be elected. He [Blythe] will notify the Indians of this action[.]" The federal government was clearly willing on this occasion to wield its full authority over the Eastern Band. Not surprisingly, Smith lost the September election to Stillwell Saunooka.[29]

The embittered Smith stepped up his attacks on Spray and Blythe and claimed that the newly elected chief and council were their tools. Oddly enough, while having little effect in Washington, these charges struck a responsive chord with Barnabas Hobbs and others in the Quaker hierarchy. Though they had supported Spray in his conflict with local whites, they were dismayed that the troubles persisted. Apparently the criticisms diminished Hobbs's confidence in Spray, and the notably businesslike Quakers also objected to his sloppiness in filing his financial accounts. In 1891, as they were concluding their tenth year among the Cherokees, they asked Spray and his wife for their resignations, selecting as replacements Mr. and Mrs. Simon Hadley. To the chagrin of Hobbs, the Sprays refused to leave or turn the facilities over to the Hadleys. Rather than face further unpleasantness in a situation that had already deteriorated, the Quakers decided not to continue their administration of Cherokee schools. The federal government would have that responsibility after the fiscal year ended on June 30, 1892.[30]

Commissioner Morgan viewed this new responsibility as an opportunity to embark upon a program that he and other reformers had long advocated—gradual abandonment of contract schools on reservations and their replacement with federally run institutions. Among other things, such a change would presumably bring unanimity of purpose to Indian instruction. In addition, Morgan believed that a federal superintendent of schools on Qualla Boundary could carry out the administrative tasks performed by Agent Blythe and his predecessors. In this way Morgan wished to modify the agency system, to "prepare the way for its complete abolition by placing the agency affairs, in certain cases, in the hands of school superintendents."[31] This would work best at an agency like that in North Carolina, where the Indians had already demonstrated some progress. If this streamlining of administration worked among the Eastern Band, it could be applied at certain other agencies as well. The Eastern Cherokees, then, were to be a modest vanguard of bureaucratic reform.[32]

George H. Smathers, a Waynesville attorney assisting the government in its ongoing litigation against Thomas, argued strongly against abolishing the agency. He noted that Blythe had performed many crucial functions for the Indians, and the confusion over land

James Blythe, 1888
(Negative 1014, National Anthropological Archives, Smithsonian Institution.)

Walini, a Cherokee Woman
(Source: *Nineteenth Annual Report,* Bureau of American Ethnology.)

Cherokee Councilmen, 1891. Rear group: Rev. John Jackson of Graham County and Morgan Calhoun of Big Cove; front group: William Ta-la-lah of Bird Town and Wesley Crow of Wolf Town.
(Source: *Eleventh Census of the United States: Extra Census Bulletin* [Washington, D.C., 1892].)

titles alone warranted his continuance. Nonetheless, the agency was closed at the end of the fiscal year. After that, federal responsibilities on Qualla Boundary devolved upon Andrew Spencer, the newly appointed school superintendent from New York City. He was to receive $1,500 a year for his educational work and an additional $200 for handling Blythe's former duties.[33] That fact alone demonstrates how little federal officials valued the efforts of their resident agents.

Spencer's immediate problem was obtaining the school buildings from Henry Spray, who remained stubbornly ensconced on the premises. Backed by former agent Blythe, he would neither vacate the buildings nor allow them to be used as schools. In December both men were arrested and fined, but Spencer claimed that a henchman of Spray remained in the latter's house armed with a gun. Finally, in January 1893, Assistant Indian Commissioner R.V. Belt arrived and arranged for Spray to surrender the buildings so that Spencer could restart the school under a government contract with the Band. It was assumed that Spray would return to his home in Tennessee. Instead, he acquired some land from the Indians near the school and continued as a daily influence among his devoted followers, much to the irritation of Spencer. (Later, during the McKinley administration, Spray himself would become school superintendent.)[34]

Spencer and his successors had basically a twofold objective: to maintain and improve the Indian schools, and to serve as symbols of federal authority over the Band. Education was their chief concern, and they busied themselves elaborating on the start made by the Quakers. Attendance at the training school remained high, but the day schools were open only sporadically. By the mid-1890s, 294 out of 440 school-age Indians were receiving at least part-time education. The training school's curriculum had changed little since Quaker days, with boys concentrating on farming and industrial arts and girls on housework. The school also offered a variety of extracurricular activities, including a brass band which gave concerts twice a week and drilled with the state militia. The boys were able to compete on organized baseball and football clubs, while girls played croquet and tennis. There was even a semi-monthly "sociable" which was supposed to promote "gentility" among pupils.[35]

Spencer's successors, Thomas W. Potter, Julian W. Haddon, and Joseph C. Hart, sent a number of the older or more promising students to Indian boarding schools like Carlisle, Hampton Insti-

Bird Town Day School, ca. 1890
(Source: *Eleventh Census of the United States: Extra Census Bulletin* [Washington, D.C., 1892].)

Eastern Cherokee Training School at Yellow Hill (Cherokee), looking westward across the Oconaluftee River, ca. 1890
(Source: *Eleventh Census of the United States: Extra Census Bulletin* [Washington, D.C., 1892].)

Eastern Cherokee Training School, ca. 1890
(Source: *Eleventh Census of the United States: Extra Census Bulletin* [Washington, D.C., 1892].)

Boys' Dormitory at Eastern Training School, ca. 1890
(Source: *Eleventh Census of the United States: Extra Census Bulletin* [Washington, D.C., 1892].)

Cherokee Training School, 1893
(Courtesy of the Museum of the Cherokee Indian.)

Teacher and Pupils at Training School, 1893
(Courtesy of the Museum of the Cherokee Indian.)

tute in Virginia, and Haskell Institute in Kansas. Continuing a custom dating back before the Quaker era, an occasional Cherokee also attended Trinity College. The superintendents placed much of their hope for Indian civilization on such individuals, but apparently none completed the full curriculum at the boarding schools before returning home. Those at Carlisle appeared to be somewhat less satisfied with their regimen under Captain Pratt than those attending Hampton. Even if the pupils learned something, Hart noted, the lack of opportunities upon their return to Qualla Boundary was likely to lead them into idleness and drunkenness.[36]

While federal officials attempted to foster Cherokee education, significant changes were occurring in tribal politics. Following the deposing of Nimrod Smith in September 1891, the new chief and council, backed by influential whites, challenged federal control of tribal resources. Without asking the Indian Office, they immediately voted to offer for sale all of the timber on the Cathcart Tract, a unit of 33,000 acres that was mostly on Qualla Boundary. Such a sale would raise more than enough money to pay present and future taxes and would bring about Cherokee employment in the logging and milling operations. But the most pressing need was to redeem a large portion of Qualla Boundary that had been "sold" for back taxes in 1890, at a sale which the Indians claimed had never been advertised. The property had then been resold to D. W. Kerr of Swain County. Redemption of this land became an obvious priority before enough time had elapsed to make Kerr's acquisition final.[37]

Not wishing to offend the Indian Office by what might seem a precipitous action, H.G. Ewart, the tribal attorney, patiently explained the Band's predicament. In February 1892, President Harrison agreed to the timber sale but in language that proved subject to differing interpretations. Following directions from the Indian Office, Ewart placed advertisements in local and national lumber journals describing terms of the sale and inviting bids. When there was not a single offer, he claimed the government had imposed too many conditions and expressed doubt that the Cherokees, as supposed citizens, even had to submit their contracts for approval.[38] Now, because of federal interference, they had no bidders and no means of reclaiming their property from Kerr. In August, Congress responded to this situation by authorizing the Band to draw from its common fund whatever was necessary to pay such back taxes. This was a right that had been denied the Cherokees since 1876. Once again they had adequate means for meeting their obligations, if they did not object to siphoning off the money available for education and agricultural improvement.[39]

Andrew Spencer quickly used $1,000 of the fund to redeem the lands held by Kerr, but he was reluctant to record the title because it conveyed the land to the Eastern Band as a corporation rather than to the Indian commissioner in trust. He said this would allow George Smathers and Henry Spray to control Cherokee property through a pliable tribal council. Smathers, who was daily gaining influence among the Band, thus joined Spray as Spencer's enemy. Spencer believed that most Indians opposed losing federal guardianship, and if the Indian commissioner knew their real conditions and sentiments he "would not feel like permitting what is now a minority of the band, by their foolishness, to destroy the only hope that these people have of ever attaining any considerable civilization." Acting Commissioner Belt replied with heavy-handed sarcasm that Spencer was making too much of his responsibilities and that his correspondence 'had become "too voluminous." The redeemed land therefore became property of the corporation but was still subject to the adverse claims of trespassers.[40]

Tribal leaders meanwhile continued their efforts to sell the Cathcart timber. Gifford Pinchot, a young forester later to become famous, provided some useful publicity by including sections of prime trees from Qualla Boundary as part of the state exhibit at the 1893 Columbian Exposition in Chicago.[41] More likely than not, however, it was the hard-working Ewart who was responsible for persuading W.C. Smith of New York City to buy all of the Cathcart timber for $15,000. The money was to be paid directly to the Band. The Indian Office responded that President Harrison had authorized cutting only enough timber to pay back taxes and that any money should be paid to it. The Office agreed to reconsider its stand if it could be shown there was a need to sell the entire tract and that the price was a fair one.[42]

After trying to meet federal objections, exasperated Cherokee councilmen were willing to accept Ewart's contention that as citizens they did not need to ask permission before selling their own property. By this time there was a suspicion that W.C. Smith was merely a speculator who hoped to profit from the legal confusion without making the first payment. And so, without consulting the Indian Office, the tribal council contracted to sell the same timber at the same price to David L. Boyd, of Newport, Tennessee. Ewart was to receive a commission of 20 percent of the purchase price.

This sale upset both the Indian Office and Smith, whose contract was still pending. There ensued a lengthy and complicated series of legal maneuverings that were to have profound consequences for the Band in terms of defining their status.[43]

Almost unnoticed amid these developments were the deaths in 1893 of two of the most prominent men associated with the Eastern Band, former chief Nimrod J. Smith and William Holland Thomas. The latter died at the age of eighty-eight on May 10 in the state insane asylum at Morganton.[44] For those Cherokees who could remember his varied services in their behalf, it must have been a sad occasion. Without his assistance they would never have remained in North Carolina. Without his constant support they would never have acquired the lands they were still fighting to retain. Without him there would have been no Eastern Band of Cherokees. Despite a normal measure of human shortcomings, he was the best friend the Indians ever had.

Nimrod Smith was in certain respects an even more pathetic figure than the enfeebled Thomas. He was a beaten man, rejected by many of his people, spurned by the Indian Office, his reputation in shambles. Yet posterity remembers him more kindly through the published work of his staunch friend, James Mooney. The ethnologist appreciated his many kindnesses, his powerful personality, and the good that he accomplished for his people. And he emphatically defended Smith's honesty and frugality in office. At the same time, however, Mooney was careful not to criticize Henry Spray and James Blythe, who had also befriended him.[45]

Not long after the deaths of Smith and Thomas, Captain W. W. Wotherspoon of the U.S. Army inspected Qualla Boundary as a possible site for relocation of several hundred Apaches, some of whom had fought at the side of Geronimo a few years before. (Fortunately, he decided that Qualla Boundary was unsuited to such guests.) Like other visitors, the officer found the Cherokees to be poor but industrious, generally satisfied with their way of life, and frequently victimized by whites. He noted that trespassers occupied much of the Cherokees' land and that negotiations were pending for its return.[46] In January 1894 these meetings resulted in a compromise whereby white claimants agreed to surrender their land for $24,552. The Indians also had the option of buying an adjoining tract of 33,000 acres from the heirs of James Love for $1.25 an acre. This land had been in dispute ever since the arbitrators had mistakenly ordered it surveyed as part of the Boundary. The following

August, acting on the recommendation of Attorney General Richard Olney, Congress appropriated the money necessary for both compromises. After years of litigation, the Cherokees held undisputed title to their lands.[47]

By this time the Indian Office and Eastern Cherokees were locked in a protracted struggle over the nature and extent of federal authority, occasioned by the long-simmering dispute over the management of Cherokee resources. The government was in the midst of a lawsuit against David Boyd, the lumberman who had offered to pay the Indians $15,000 for the Cathcart timber. Boyd had resold his contract to Harry M. Dickson and William T. Mason for $25,000. Those two men had begun logging operations on the tract, causing the government to enjoin them from further work on the grounds that Boyd's original contract was invalid without approval of the Indian Office. Attorneys for Boyd, including George Smathers, insisted the Cherokees were citizens and did not need federal permission to make contracts. Attorney General Olney was of the same opinion and advised dropping the suit, but the Department of Interior persisted, desiring a definitive judicial decision on the Cherokees' status.[48]

The attorneys for the tribal council and lumbermen cited certain specific grounds for the Band's self-determination: the Supreme Court's contention that the Eastern Cherokees were citizens; the Band's incorporation under state law in 1889; and the fact that titles resulting from the 1894 settlement had been vested directly in the Band. They also pointed out that in the midst of this litigation, in March 1895, the North Carolina General Assembly had amended the 1889 act by setting up a system of government similar to that which had earlier existed under the tribal constitutions. Most significant, the amended charter recognized the corporation's right to hold the fee simple title to tribal lands and invested the council with exclusive control of those properties. It also confirmed all previous tribal contracts and specifically those with Boyd and Ewart. Tribal leaders thus claimed to have both the legal right and means to control the Band's affairs.[49]

Thomas Potter, the resident school superintendent, blamed local whites for the desire of tribal leaders to separate from the government. He was particularly alarmed by the influence of Smathers, whom the council had recently hired as tribal attorney at $1,000 a year, and viewed him as part of a Waynesville "ring" of lawyers and speculators who intended to defraud the Cherokees. Potter also attacked Spray, Blythe, Ewart, and J.M. Moody, Boyd's partner; Moody and Ewart, he charged, had colluded with Smathers and used their collective political influence to obtain the legislature's approval of the 1895 charter amendments. He believed the Indians did not need Smathers's services and that the amended charter should be repealed. The superintendent sternly advised the Band not to oppose the government in the Boyd suit, warning that do do so would mean the loss of federal goodwill and financial assistance.[50]

According to Potter, his adversaries retaliated by harassing him and even challenging the legality of his marriage to a daughter of Nimrod Smith. Disgusted, he repeatedly requested transfer to a post in the West, preferably in Indian Territory, where his wife was applying for citizenship in the Cherokee Nation. In the summer of 1895 sympathetic officials finally arranged an exchange of posts between Potter and Julian Haddon, who had been in charge of an Indian school in Salem, Oregon.[51]

The 1895 decision of the U.S. District Court in the Boyd case satisfied neither side completely. On the one hand, it held that the Supreme Court decision was, in effect, *obiter dictum* and had not conferred citizenship on the Eastern Cherokees. Nor had any formal act by any legislative body done so. Regardless of the fact that North Carolina had usually treated the Indians as citizens, the Cherokees could not be considered such without federal action, nor could the state set aside federal guardianship established under the 1868 act. On the other hand, the court noted the Eastern Cherokees' peculiar history and said they were not identical in status to some of the western tribes. They were under the state's laws insofar as those did not interfere with federal guardianship. In line with this reasoning, the court held that the Indian Office's proper role in the Boyd case was merely to ensure that no fraud had occurred in making the contract. When an investigation later that same year concluded that none had been involved, the court lifted the injunction against Mason and Dickson.[52]

The United States appealed this decision on the grounds that its guardianship was complete, that it could invalidate any and all contracts negotiated by the Eastern Band. Eventually, in November 1897, the Fourth Circuit Court of Appeals in Richmond concurred with that reasoning and reversed the lower court ruling. The Indians were not citizens; they were in fact a tribe, and the federal government had a long-recognized right to supervise Indian affairs as it thought appropriate. The government could disallow the Boyd contract if it chose.[53] Its authority intact, the Department of Interior began a reassessment of the Boyd contract even as Mason and Dickson appealed to the Supreme Court. They promptly dropped their appeal when the department approved the contract, leaving the circuit court decision the definitive statement of federal authority over the Band, at least for the nineteenth century.[54]

Paradoxically, the Boyd decision muddied the Cherokees' status even more in certain respects than it had been before. Some North Carolinians pointed out the obvious differences between the 1886 and 1897 court decisions and continued to view the Cherokees as at least quasi-citizens. The Indians still functioned under their state corporate charter and amendments, with the obvious approval of the Indian Office. They continued to pay taxes and otherwise observe most state laws. But some local officials were reluctant to enforce these laws among the Cherokees, arguing in effect that as wards of the United States—"mere" Indians—they could not be expected to observe such legislation. A few Cherokees apparently reinforced this unflattering opinion by behaving irresponsibly and without fear of state authority. To the disgust of Henry Spray, who became superintendent in 1898, some even resumed their ballplay and other aboriginal customs, reasoning that if they weren't citizens they would at least be Indians. Recognizing the many uncertainties confronting them, the Cherokee council plaintively inquired, "What are we, where do we stand, and where are we at"?[55]

More immediate was another question raised by both Indians and whites: if the Cherokees were not citizens, did they have the right to vote? This matter had obvious political implications in Swain and Jackson counties, and Democrats, not surprisingly, were more likely than Republicans to favor disfranchising the Indians. Thus, at the same time that North Carolina and other southern states were limiting the franchise for blacks, the Cherokees were about to suffer the same fate for different reasons. It was a two-step process: first, the state required a separate voter registration list for Indians; and second, in 1900, Democratic registrars in Swain and Jackson counties refused to register them at all on the grounds they were noncitizen wards of the United States. Some Indians took legal action, but a decision in federal district court upheld the registrars. Not until 1930 did the North Carolina Cherokees gain an undisputed right to vote. Ironically, federal guardianship had entailed the loss of certain rights which the Cherokees had long enjoyed and which policymakers extolled as the ultimate objective for all Indians.[56]

The Boyd decision also meant the Indian Office could now consider implementing one of the key features of its civilization program—allotment. This had been an official policy since passage of the Dawes Severalty Act of 1887 and had already been applied to many other tribes. Before recognition of federal authority over the Band, Cherokee agents could merely express varying opinions as to the readiness of the Indians for taking their land in severalty. A recurring theme in the 1880s was that the Eastern Cherokees were not quite ready for allotment, a contention some acculturated mixed-bloods disputed.[57] In 1892 Andrew Spencer expressed the fear that the moment the Indians owned their land in fee simple unscrupulous whites would take advantage of them. The next year, however, he appeared more hopeful: "I trust that the time is brief which must elapse before they will be able, having received their land in severalty, to release the government from its charge over them, and to take their places as intelligent and energetic citizens."[58] And in 1895 Thomas Potter declared, "The Eastern Cherokees are ripe and ready for allotment." He acknowledged, however, that they would require a lengthy federal trusteeship before they could manage their property independently.[59]

Despite such qualified support for allotment, certain decision-makers must have wondered whether severalty was feasible for the Eastern Cherokees. First of all, their titles were still vested in the Band as a state corporation, complicating any unilateral federal decision to initiate the policy. More important, the Indians had already divided up most of the common lands among themselves and were farming almost every available acre. Though the property belonged to the tribal corporation, each head of household could occupy and improve land that for all practical purposes became his own.[60] What more could be gained by severalty? Besides, there was not enough arable land to provide each family with even close to 160 acres, the unit thought suitable for sustaining Jefferson's symbolic ideal of the self-reliant yeoman. That was another irony, of course—that industrial America, under the guise of modernity, was imposing on so many Indians the mythology of its own past. Logical or not, an attempt would be made in the twentieth century to extend that myth to the Band, and there are certain Cherokees still bitter that it never succeeded.[61]

175

Thus, as a bustling industrial nation embarked upon a new century and prepared confidently to assert itself on the world scene, nearly 1,400 Indians remained in the mountains and valleys of North Carolina, taking halting, tentative steps toward modernity.[62] The modest changes that had touched them were precursors of the coming age. They had become a more heterogeneous people as outsiders had crowded in and impinged upon them. The railroad now made western North Carolina accessible to the modern world, while small towns like Robbinsville, Murphy, Webster, and Bryson City offered convenient windows to that world. Many Indians had traveled beyond, over the Balsams to Waynesville or Asheville. And some of their children had studied at colleges so far away they could not see the mountains outlined against the sky. They had witnessed different vistas, different worlds.

The mountains and forests so central to Cherokee identity had recently attracted the interest of outsiders, who ranged from unscrupulous trespassers to honest lumbermen offering money and employment to a hard-pressed people. White reformers, harbingers of the twentieth-century conservation movement, were already envisioning other possibilities for that mountain fastness, including a national forest and an Appalachian park. The latter idea was the seed of inspiration that in another generation would blossom into the Great Smoky Mountains National Park. Like an enormous security blanket, the park would almost enfold Qualla Boundary, bringing federal largesse and a tribal livelihood—tourism—that few could have imagined in the nineteenth century.[63]

It was also in 1900 that James Mooney published his classic "Myths of the Cherokee," reflecting much of his research on the tribe. Sensitive to many of the outward changes affecting the Eastern Cherokees, he viewed them as a people in transition and saw the recent death of Swimmer as symbolic. With his demise, the chief conservator of tribal traditionalism had departed. Swimmer's had been a contracting world amid the ever-expanding possibilities of modern America. In his final years he could do little more than witness the many changes, practice the ancient rites, and through Mooney leave his heritage to a posterity that would find it curious and quaint. This is not to say we should pity him. A photograph shows him sitting ramrod straight, holding a gourd rattle that signified the authority given his kind by generations of tribal culture. But his eyes leave the most indelible impression—unblinking lasers emanating from the past that seem to dissect and probe the

Swimmer
(Negative 1008, National Anthropological Archives, Smithsonian Institution.)

present without acquiescence or deference. They are proud and knowing. When he died in 1899, not yet an ancient man, his friends took him high in the mountains and buried him according to the old ways. "Peace to his ashes and sorrow for his going," Mooney wrote, "for with him perished half the tradition of a people."[64]

To Mooney it appeared that the Eastern Cherokees were opting for the mysteries and opportunities of modern America rather than the past. But perhaps the cultural transition was less pronounced than he believed. Perhaps Swimmer's passing meant only the end of one individual or, at most, one phase of Cherokee identity. Despite the outward changes that were so apparent in 1900, one might question how fundamental they actually were. True, a higher percentage of Indians could speak and read and write in English. It was still a minority, however, and many children did not even attend school. Though a number of Eastern Cherokees had studied at places like Carlisle and Hampton institutes, their only effect as yet had been to make their people more aware of the outside world. Despite Swimmer's death, there were still a few conjurers around. The ballplay and other ancient games and ceremonies were even staging a minor revival, much to the dismay of Henry Spray. And Cherokee food, homes, agriculture, and land tenure were much like they had been twenty—or eighty—years before.

Even if we concede some truth to Mooney's claim that the Indians were becoming more like their white neighbors, certain reservations are in order. Though the line between Cherokees and whites had become less distinct during the previous few decades, a visitor seeking the stereotypical Indian could still find him easily enough. On Qualla Boundary most of the Cherokees still "looked" like Indians and were visible refutations of the assimilationist assumptions of modern America. Even many of those who could have "passed" for whites were as Indian in certain respects as their bronzed, raven-haired neighbors. A shared identity stretching back through the millennia separated them from Appalachian whites, regardless of outward appearances. That is the point. Like all humans, the Indians were changing, but within their own cultural context and at their own pace. They still perceived and defined themselves as Cherokees. In the new century, as the pressures of acculturation accelerated, they would quietly make whatever accommodations seemed necessary or desirable, yet somehow retain a core that was undeniably Cherokee.

NOTES

ABBREVIATIONS USED IN NOTES

CIA	Commissioner of Indian Affairs
FRCEP	Federal Records Center, East Point, Georgia (Cherokee Agency)
GLB	Governors Letter Book
GP	Governors Papers
LB	Letter Book
LR	Letters Received
LS (LD)	Letters Sent, Land Division
M-21	Microcopy 21. Letters Sent by the Office of Indian Affairs, 1824–1881, National Archives
M-234	Microcopy 234. Letters Received by the Office of Indian Affairs, 1824–1881, National Archives
M-348	Microcopy 348. Report Books of the Office of Indian Affairs, 1838–1885, National Archives
M-574	Microcopy 574. Special Files of the Office of Indian Affairs, 1807–1904, National Archives
M-653	Microcopy 653. Eighth Census of the United States, 1860, National Archives
M-950	Microcopy 950. Interior Department Appointment Papers: North Carolina, 1849–1892, National Archives
M-1059	Microcopy 1059. Selected Letters Received by the Office of Indian Affairs Relating to the Cherokees of North Carolina, 1851–1905, National Archives
NCDAH	North Carolina Division of Archives and History, Raleigh
OIA	Office of Indian Affairs
PC	Personal Collection
RFBCC	Records of the Fourth Board of Cherokee Commissioners, Record Group 75, National Archives
RG	Record Group
SHC	Southern Historical Collection, University of North Carolina, Chapel Hill

SI   Secretary of Interior
WCU   Western Carolina University, Cullowhee, North Carolina
WHTC   William Holland Thomas Collection, Western Carolina University
WHTP   William Holland Thomas Papers. 4 Microfilm Rolls. Newspapers and Microforms Department, Duke University Library

NOTES TO PREFACE

1. Walter L. Williams, "Patterns in the History of the Remaining Southeastern Indians, 1840–1975," in Walter L. Williams, ed., *Southeastern Indians Since the Removal Era* (Athens, Ga., 1979), 193.

2. *The Invasion of America: Indians, Colonialism, and the Cant of Conquest* (Chapel Hill, 1975), 14.

NOTES TO CHAPTER 1

1. James Mooney, "Myths of the Cherokee," *Nineteenth Annual Report*, Bureau of American Ethnology (Washington, D.C., 1900), Pt. 1, pp. 17–18; Duane H. King, "Introduction," in Duane H. King, ed., *The Cherokee Indian Nation: A Troubled History* (Knoxville, 1979), ix–x; Roy S. Dickens, Jr., "The Origins and Development of Cherokee Culture," in King, *ibid.*, 3–28; Grace Steele Woodward, *The Cherokees* (Norman, Okla., 1963), 17–22; John Phillip Reid, *A Law of Blood: The Primitive Law of the Cherokee Nation* (New York, 1970), 8.

2. Charles Hudson, *The Southeastern Indians* (Knoxville, 1976), 5.

3. Reid, *Law of Blood*, 11–14.

4. Mooney, "Myths of the Cherokee," 15, 297–300, 325–26, 336–37, 404; Reid, *Law of Blood*, 14; Charles Hudson, "Utkena: A Cherokee Anomalous Monster," *Journal of Cherokee Studies* 3 (Spring 1978): 62–75.

5. Mooney, "Myths of the Cherokee," 11; Woodward, *The Cherokees*, 22–31; Theda Perdue, *Slavery and the Evolution of Cherokee Society, 1540–1866* (Knoxville, 1979), 19–35; John Phillip Reid, *A Better Kind of Hatchet: Law, Trade and Diplomacy in the Cherokee Nation During the Early Years of European Contact* (University Park, Pa., 1976).

6. Perdue, *Slavery*, 19–35; Reid, *Better Kind of Hatchet*, 189–96; Gary B. Nash, *Red, White and Black: The Peoples of Early America* (Englewood Cliffs, N.J., 1974), 239–40, 248–52.

7. Reid, *Law of Blood*, 29–33; Woodward, *The Cherokees*, 60–67; David H. Corkran, *The Cherokee Frontier: Conflict and Survival, 1740–1762* (Norman, Okla., 1962).

8. Reid, *Law of Blood*, 35–48; Hudson, *Southeastern Indians*, 184–202, 229–32.

9. James Adair, *Adair's History of the American Indian*, ed. Samuel Cole Williams (Johnson City, Tenn., 1930), 152–53.

10. Reid, *Law of Blood*, 73–112; Perdue, *Slavery*, 11–12; Rennard Strickland, *Fire and the Spirits: Cherokee Law from Clan to Courts* (Norman, Okla., 1975), 10–33. See also John Phillip Reid, "A Perilous Rule: The Law of International Homicide," in King, *Cherokee Nation*, 33–45.

11. Woodward, *The Cherokees*, 71–79; Corkran, *Cherokee Frontier*, 142–272.

12. Woodward, *The Cherokees*, 88–116; James H. O'Donnell III, *Southern Indians in the American Revolution* (Knoxville, 1973), *passim*; Henry Thompson Malone, *Cherokees of the Old South: A People in Transition* (Athens, Ga., 1956), 9–10, 32–45.

13. Reid, *Law of Blood*, 14–15; act of 1783 in *Sen. Doc.*, 25 Cong., 3 Sess., No. 120 (Serial 315, Washington, D.C., 1838), 618, hereafter cited as *Sen. Doc.* 120 (Serial 315).

14. Ronald N. Satz, *American Indian Policy in the Jacksonian Era* (Lincoln, Neb., 1975), 2.

15. Woodward, *The Cherokees*, 105–106. For detailed discussion of Cherokee treaties and land cessions, see Charles C. Royce, "The Cherokee Nation of Indians," *Fifth Annual Report*, Bureau of American Ethnology (Washington, D.C., 1887).

16. For extended analysis of white views on the Indians' nature and capacity to "improve," see Bernard Sheehan, *Seeds of Extinction: Jeffersonian Philanthropy and the American Indian* (Chapel Hill, 1973).

17. *Ibid.*, 42–44, 89–181, 243–75.

18. Mooney, "Myths of the Cherokee," 93–97; Malone, *Cherokees of Old South*, 71–72.

19. Satz, *American Indian Policy*, 11; Francis Paul Prucha, *American Indian Policy in the Formative Years: The Indian Trade and Intercourse Acts, 1790–1834* (Cambridge, Mass., 1962), 224–25; Andrew Jackson, First Annual Message, Dec. 8, 1829, in James D. Richardson, ed., *A Compilation of the Messages and Papers of the Presidents: 1789–1897*, 10 vols. (Washington, D.C., 1896–1899), II, 456–59.

20. Malone, *Cherokees of the Old South*, 46–170; Woodward, *The Cherokees*, 117–56. for an overview of Boudinot's life, see Theda Perdue, ed., *Cherokee Editor: The Writings of Elias Boudinot* (Knoxville, 1983), 3–33.

21. Woodward, *The Cherokees*, 138–91; Wilson Lumpkin speech, May 17, 1830, in Joseph Gales, *Register of Debates in Congress*, 14 vols. in 29 (Washington, D.C., 1825–1837) VI, Pt. 2, pp. 1022–25. The most recent biography of Ross is Gary M. Moulton's *John Ross: Cherokee Chief* (Athens, Ga., 1978).

22. For perceptive commentary on various aspects of Cherokee acculturation see Theda Perdue, "Rising from the Ashes: The *Cherokee Phoenix* as an Ethnohistorical Source," *Ethnohistory* 24 (Summer 1977): 207–17; William G. McLoughlin and Walter H. Conser, Jr., "The Cherokees in Transition: A

Statistical Analysis of the Federal Cherokee Census of 1835," *Journal of American History* 44 (Dec. 1977): 678–703; and Mary Young, "The Cherokee Nation: Mirror of the Republic," *American Quarterly* 33 (Winter 1981): 502–24.

23. McLoughlin and Conser, "Cherokees in Transition," 702; see also William G. McLoughlin, "Thomas Jefferson and the Beginning of Cherokee Nationalism, 1806 to 1809," *William and Mary Quarterly* 3d ser., 32 (Oct. 1975): 551.

24. Jennings, *Invasion of America*, 58–84; Gary B. Nash, "The Image of the Indians in the Southern Colonial Mind," *William and Mary Quarterly* 3d ser., 29 (Apr. 1972): 197–230.

25. The Cherokees were well aware of the government's contradictory arguments. See Malone, *Cherokees of the Old South*, 69.

26. Article 8 of 1817 treaty and Article 2 of 1819 treaty in Charles J. Kappler, ed., *Indian Affairs: Laws and Treaties*, 5 vols. (Washington, D.C., 1904–1941), II, 143, 178.

27. List of North Carolina reserves accompanying letter of Robert Houston to Secretary of War John C. Calhoun, Nov. 21, 1820, M-574, 25/1303–1305. For a list of all Cherokee reserves, without delineation of their home states, see *American State Papers*, 38 vols. (Washington, D.C., 1832–1861), *Public Lands*, V, Doc. 625, pp. 396–97.

28. *Ibid.*; Mooney, "Myths of the Cherokee," 160–62, 164.

29. *American State Papers, Public Lands*, V, Doc. 623, pp. 391–92; *Eu-che-lah v. Welsh*, 10 *North Carolina Reports* 155–74; "Cherokee Lands Entries and Surveys, 1820–1824," Secretary of State Papers, NCDAH; "Report of the Commissioners under the Act of 1823 on Indian Reservations," Oct. 24, 1824, *ibid.*; 4 U.S. *Statutes* 268, 353.

30. "Report of Commissioners," Secretary of State Papers, NCDAH; "Haywood County—1828 Contracts A & B & C," *ibid.*; Deposition of Euchella, Claim 251 ("Oochella"), RFBCC; Mooney, "Myths of the Cherokee," 162–63.

31. Petition of citizens of Haywood and Macon counties, Jan. 31, 1836, WHTP, Roll 2; Mattie Russell, "William Holland Thomas, White Chief of the North Carolina Cherokees" (Ph.D. diss., Duke Univ., 1956), 32–33.

32. Mooney, "Myths of the Cherokee," 160; Russell, "William Holland Thomas," 14; Thomas to James Graham, Oct. 18, 1838, WHTC; Duane H. King, "The Origins of the Eastern Cherokees as a Social and Political Entity," in King, *Cherokee Nation*, 166–67.

33. For Thomas's entire career see Russell, "William Holland Thomas." His work in behalf of the Cherokees is discussed in Mattie Russell, "Devil in the Smokies: The White Man's Nature and the Indian's Fate," *South Atlantic Quarterly* 73 (Winter 1974): 53–69; and Richard C. Iobst, "William Holland Thomas and the Cherokee Claims," in King, *Cherokee Nation*, 181–201.

34. Quoted in McLoughlin and Conser, "Cherokees in Transition," 687.

35. Robert Fleming, *Sketch of the Life of Elder Humphrey Posey . . .* (Philadelphia, 1852), 57–63; William Gammell, *A History of American Baptist Missions . . .* (Boston, 1849), 323–24; Malone, *Cherokees of the Old South*, 106–109.

36. Fleming, *Sketch of Life*, 64–65; Gammell, *History of American Baptist Missions*, 324–27; Malone, *Cherokees of the Old South*, 108–10; Wool to Maj. Gen. A. Macomb, Oct. 12, 1836, *Sen. Doc.* 120 (Serial 315), 48.

37. Mooney, "Myths of the Cherokee," 165; Charles Lanman, *Letters from the Alleghany Mountains* (New York, 1849), 96.

38. Thomas to James Graham, Oct. 18, 1838, WHTC; memorial of citizens of Haywood and Macon counties, Jan. 31, 1836, WHTP, Roll 2; Memorial of Haywood County Court, Dec. 28, 1836, Legislative Papers 545, NCDAH.

39. Woodward, *The Cherokees*, 157–81; Moulton, *John Ross*, 34–53; Walter H. Conser, Jr., "John Ross and the Cherokee Resistance Campaigns, 1833–1838," *Journal of Southern History* 44 (May 1978): 191–212.

40. Satz, *American Indian Policy*, 19–31; Woodward, *The Cherokees*, 157–81; First Annual Message of Jackson, in Richardson, *Messages and Papers of the Presidents*, II, 456–59. Francis Paul Prucha has argued that removal was the only logical alternative available to Jackson. "Andrew Jackson's Indian Policy: A Reassessment," *Journal of American History* 56 (Dec. 1969): 527–39.

41. *American State Papers, Public Lands*, V, 394.

42. Woodward, *The Cherokees*, 173–74; Mooney, "Myths of the Cherokees," 163.

43. Satz, *American Indian Policy*, 39–51, 97–100; Moulton, *John Ross*, 34–75; Kenneth Penn Davis, "Chaos in the Indian Country: The Cherokee Nation 1828–35," in King, *Cherokee Nation*, 129–30. For analysis of the Worcester decision see Joseph C. Burke, "The Cherokee Cases: A Study in Law, Politics, and Morality," *Stanford Law Review* 21 (Feb. 1969): 500–531.

44. The census, called the Henderson Roll, may most conveniently be consulted in James W. Tyner, ed., *Those Who Cried: The 16,000* (n.p., 1974). For analysis of the census see McLoughlin and Conser, "Cherokees in Transition."

45. Woodward, *The Cherokees*, 171–91. A sympathetic view of the "treaty party" of Cherokees is in Thurman Wilkins, *Cherokee Tragedy: The Story of the Ridge Family and of the Decimation of a People* (New York, 1970). The treaty is in Kappler, *Indian Affairs: Laws and Treaties*, II, 439–49.

46. Kappler, *Indian Affairs: Laws and Treaties*, II, 444. For Ross's "nonviolent resistance" see Conser, "John Ross and the Cherokee Resistance Campaigns."

47. Supplementary Article 1 in Kappler, *Indian Affairs: Laws and Treaties*, II, 448. See also Mary E. Young, *Redskins, Ruffleshirts and Rednecks: Indian Allotments in Alabama and Mississippi, 1830–1860* (Norman, Okla., 1961), 191–93.

48. Power of Attorney, Jan. 31, 1836; and CIA C.A. Harris to Thomas, July 19, 1836, both in WHTP, Roll 2; Russell, "William Holland Thomas," 61–64; see also *Sen. Doc.* 120 (Serial 315), 612–17.

49. Instructions of Currey, Aug. 15, 1836, Claim 251, RFBCC; act of Dec. 30, 1836, *Laws of the State of North Carolina 1836–37* (Raleigh, 1837); 333; Article 12 in Kappler, *Indians Affairs: Laws and Treaties*, II, 444–45.

50. Mooney, "Myths of the Cherokee," 163; Lanman, *Letters from Alleghany Mountains*, 109–110; Russell, "William Holland Thomas," 69.

51. Deposition of Joseph McMillen, July 27, 1843, Claim 251, RFBCC. "Cherokee Valuations N.C. 1836 Welch and Garrett [*sic*]," Cherokee Property Valuations, 1835–39, RG 75, does not signify which Cherokees chose to remain, except for a handful of prominent mixed-bloods.

52. Memorial of Haywood County Court, Dec. 28, 1836, Legislative Papers 545, NCDAH; act of Jan. 21, 1837, *Laws of North Carolina, 1836–37*, 30; memorial of Qualla Town Cherokees, April 6, 1837, *Sen. Doc.*, 29 Cong., 1 Sess., No. 408 (Serial 477, Washington, D.C., 1846), 17–18; hereafter cited as *Sen. Doc.* 408 (Serial 477).

NOTES TO CHAPTER 2

1. See for example M. Killian to Governor Edward B. Dudley, Jan. 5, 1838, GLB 32, p. 148; H.G. Woodfin to Dudley, Feb. 26, 1838, GP 83, pp. 1364–65; Joab L. Moore to Dudley, Mar. 10, 1838, GP 83, pp. 1418–19; preamble and resolutions of Macon County citizens, Mar. 10, 1838, GP 83, p. 1423; all in NCDAH.

2. Killian to Dudley, Mar. 25, 1838, GP 83, pp. 1454–56, NCDAH.

3. Thomas to Dudley, Apr. 25, 1838, GP 84, p. 1590; Reuben Deacon to Col. N.J. King, Mar. 29, 1838, GP 83, pp. 1472–73; statement of various whites of Haywood County, July 26, 1837, GP 79, p. 689; all in NCDAH; Thomas to James Graham, Oct. 18, 1838, WHTC (reprinted in *Niles' National Register*, Dec. 1, 1838, p. 216).

4. Land Grants, 1836, WHTC; George E. Frizzell, "The Legal Status of the Eastern Band of Cherokee Indians" (M.A. thesis, Western Carolina Univ., 1981), 15–17.

5. Standard accounts of Cherokee removal are in Grant Foreman, *Indian Removal: The Emigration of the Five Civilized Tribes of Indians* (Norman, Okla., 1953); Marion L. Starkey, *The Cherokee Nation* (New York, 1946); Woodward, *The Cherokees*.

6. Lanman, *Letters from Alleghany Mountains*, 79. Hog Bite was listed as 110 years of age in David W. Siler's 1851 census.

7. Mooney, "Myths of the Cherokee," 131, 157–58.

8. The following is a shortened, revised version of my article, "The Saga of Tsali: Legend Versus Reality," *North Carolina Historical Review* 56 (Winter 1979): 1–18 (Copyright, 1979, by the North Carolina Division of Archives and History).

9. The pageant is staged throughout each summer tourist season; its script was written by Kermit Hunter and published as *Unto These Hills: A Drama of the Cherokees* (Chapel Hill, 1950). See also Paul Kutsche, "The Tsali Legend: Culture Heroes and Historiography," *Ethnohistory* 10 (Fall 1963): 329–57; and Duane H. King and E. Raymond Evans, "Tsali: The Man Behind the Legend," *Journal of Cherokee Studies* 4 (Fall 1979): 194–201.

10. Tyner, *Those Who Cried*, 140; King, "Origin of the Eastern Cherokees," 170–71; Frizzell, "Legal Status of the Eastern Band of Cherokee Indians," 17–18.

11. Lt. Smith to Lt. C.H. Larned, Nov. 5, 1838; Lt. Larned to Maj. Gen. Scott, Nov. 5, 1838, Records of the Bureau of Indian Affairs, Letters Received, 1824–1881 (Cherokee Emigration), RG 75, National Archives; hereafter cited as RG 75 (Cherokee Emigration). See also deposition of Joseph Welch, Aug. 16, 1843, RFBCC, Claim 251, RG 75. There are some discrepancies in these accounts, and it is unclear whether Tsali's band was under guard one or two nights.

12. Lt. Smith to Lt. Larned, Nov. 5, 1838, RG 75 (Cherokee Emigration). See also Lt. Larned to Maj. Gen. Scott, Nov. 5, 1838, *ibid.*; William Thomas to Gen. Scott, Mar. 7, 1846, William Holland Thomas Papers, Duke Univ. (hereafter cited as Thomas Papers, Duke); Finger, "Saga of Tsali," 7 (n. 13).

13. Ross to Scott, Nov. 4, 1838; Foster to Scott, Nov. 4, 1838, both on roll 1 of microfilm copies of Cherokee-related materials in National Archives (Newspapers and Microforms Department, Duke Univ. Library). Scott to War Department, Nov. 6, 1838, RG 75 (Cherokee Emigration).

14. Scott to Foster, Nov. 7, 1838, RG 75 (Cherokee Emigration).

15. Scott to War Department, Nov. 6, 1838, *ibid.*

16. In his 1839 account of this incident, Thomas indicated that the Oconaluftee Indians made the only contact with Euchella. Thomas, *Argument in Support of the Claims of the Cherokee Indians . . .* (Washington, D.C., 1839), 19, WHTP, Roll 2. In 1846, however, he said he had gone with a single guide to Euchella's lair and personally persuaded him to help. Thomas to Gen. Scott, Mar. 7, 1846, Thomas Papers, Duke. A similar version is in Lanman, *Letters from Alleghany Mountains*, 112–13. Thomas was seeking a favor from Scott in 1846, so it is possible he exaggerated his personal role in the events. See also the accounts of Euchella and others in RFBCC, Claim 251, RG 75.

17. Foster to Scott, Nov. 11, 1838, on roll 1 of microfilm copies of Cherokee-related materials in National Archives (Newspapers and Microforms Department, Duke Univ. Library). All of Foster's letters and enclosures to Scott after Nov. 11 were included with a letter Scott sent to the Adj. Gen. of Dec. 28, 1838, Records of the Adjutant General's Office, 1780s–1917, Letters Received, Main Series, 1822–1860, File Designation S-568-1838, RG 94, National Archives; hereafter cited as RG 94. See specifically Foster to Scott, Nov. 15, 1838 (enclosure "A" of S-568-1838), RG 94. See also George Archibald McCall, *Letters from the Frontier; Written during a Period of Thirty Years' Service in the Army of the United States* (Philadelphia, 1868), 346–62. McCall so completely altered his correspondence and memoirs in preparing them for publication that they can not be relied upon, especially for dates. For the wary reader, however, the anecdotes and details provide a vivid and fascinating backdrop for Foster's campaign.

18. Foster to Scott, Nov. 15, 1838 (enclosure "A" of S-568-1838), RG 94.

19. Foster to Scott, Nov. 19, 1838 (enclosure "B" of S-568-1838), RG 94.

20. Foster to Scott, Nov. 24, 1838 (enclosure "C" of S-568-1838), RG 94; Thomas, *Argument in Support of the Claims of the Cherokee Indians*, 19; Board of Inquiry, Nov. 21, 1838, in *Journal of Cherokee Studies* 4 (Fall 1979): 223.

21. Undated extract from Hamilton (Tenn.) *Gazette* published in *Niles' National Register*, Jan. 5, 1839, and *Daily National Intelligencer*, Jan. 7, 1839. Other details are found in McCall, *Letters from the Frontier*, 361; Captain John Page to CIA T. Hartley Crawford, Dec. 4, 1838, RG 75 (Cherokee Emigration).

22. Foster's letter of Nov. 24, 1838, mentions neither Tsali nor Washington by name, but the information it provides and later events justify inclusion of their names by this writer. Washington was about sixteen years old in 1838. Duane King and E. Raymond Evans have raised the question of whether he was actually Tsali's son, noting that the 1840 census shows another man as his father ("Tsali: The Man Behind the Legend," 194). But subsequent censuses list him as Tsali's son, and, more important, the Cherokees apparently did not deny his parentage when James Mooney conducted his investigation in the late nineteenth century. It is unlikely that as the legend of a heroic Tsali emerged, the Cherokees, jealous of unfair distinctions among themselves, would allow Washington's claim if undeserved. So why is he listed as another's son in the 1840 census? A plausible explanation is that as late as 1843 some people believed the surviving members of Tsali's band were under a sentence of banishment to the Cherokee Nation in the West. Deposition of Joseph Welch, Aug. 16, 1843, RFBCC, Claim 251, RG 75.

23. Contending that the Cherokees volunteered to execute their brethren are Thomas, *Argument in Support of the Claims of the Cherokee Indians*, 19; and John Preston Arthur, *Western North Carolina: A History (From 1730 to 1913)* (Raleigh, 1914), 578. In contrast, McCall, *Letters from the Frontier*, 359, says Foster requested them to perform the executions. For the Indians to do so of their own volition, according to John Phillip Reid, would be contrary to traditional tribal law rather than in accordance with it (*Law of Blood*). Yet such action was not unprecedented. See Wilcomb E. Washburn, *The Indian in America* (New York, 1975), 17–18; and comments of Bloody Fellow in *Knoxville Gazette*, June 2, 1792.

24. Foster to Scott, Nov. 24, 1838 (enclosure "C" of S-568-1838), RG 94; petition dated Nov. 18, 1838 (enclosure "D," *ibid.*); proclamation of Foster, Nov. 24, 1838 (enclosure "E," *ibid.*).

25. Depositions of Joseph Welch, Euchella, Edward Delozier, Jonas Jenkins, Joel Sawyer, and John Chambers, RFBCC, Claim 251, RG 75. Foster believed that, except for Euchella's band, there were not more than sixty Cherokee fugitives left in the mountains. Foster to Scott, Nov. 24, 1838 (enclosure "C" of S-568-1838), RG 94.

26. Foster to Scott Nov. 24, Dec. 3, 1838 (enclosure "C" and unlettered enclosure of S-568-1838), RG 94; deposition of Jonas Jenkins, Aug. 16, 1843, RFBCC, Claim 251, RG 75; William Thomas to Matthew Russel, Nov. 25, 1838, WHTC; Thomas, *Argument in Support of the Claims of the Cherokee Indians*, 19 (quote).

27. Foster to Scott, Dec. 3, 1838 (unlettered enclosure of S-568-1838), RG 94; Scott to Adjutant General, Dec. 28, 1838, S-568-1838, RG 94; *Sen. Doc.* 408 (Serial 477), 16. This writer believes that a possible "deal" with Euchella had been discussed during Scott's meeting with Foster and Thomas, and that Scott had approved it without committing himself in his written orders.

28. Deposition of Jonas Jenkins, Aug. 16, 1843, RFBCC, Claim 251, RG 75; Lanman, *Letters from Alleghany Mountains*, 113–14; Mooney, "Myths of the Cherokee," 131, 157–58; Finger, "Saga of Tsali," 17; for discussion of the literary "savage," see Robert F. Berkhofer, Jr., *The White Man's Indian* (New York, 1978), 86–96.

29. Mooney, "Myths of the Cherokee," 158. Paul Kutsche underestimates Thomas's role but is quite correct in saying that it had become exaggerated by Mooney's time. Kutsche "The Tsali Legend," 346–48.

30. Perhaps a qualification is in order. Though the Qualla Band had tacit permission to remain, the Cherokee commissioners did not officially approve their remaining until Dec. 5, 1838, immediately following the Tsali incident. It is possible the band's assistance in the episode contributed to that recognition. *Sen. Doc.* 408 (Serial 477), 19.

31. Moulton, *John Ross*; Morris L. Wardell, *A Political History of the Cherokee Nation, 1838–1907* (Norman, Okla., 1938); Gerard Reed, "Postremoval Factionalism in the Cherokee Nation," in King, *Cherokee Nation*, 148–61.

32. The following is a shortened version of my article "The Abortive Second Cherokee Removal, 1841–1844," *Journal of Southern History* 47 (May 1981): 207–26 (Copyright, 1981, by the Southern Historical Association).

33. The figures of William Thomas indicate there were at least 1,087 North Carolina Cherokees in 1840. "Census of the North Carolina Cherokees, 1840," Thomas Papers, Duke; compare with "Supplementary Report of Cherokee Indians Remaining in N.C., 1835–1840," compiled by William Thomas (microfilm at Museum of the Cherokee Indian, Cherokee, N.C.). For the 1840 Quallatown figures, see "Present state of civilization among the Cherokee Indians of Qualla Town," accompanying the letter of Thomas to William Wilkins, Mar. 3, 1845, M-234, 89/542-43. See also *Sen. Doc.*, 28 Cong., 2 Sess., No. 90 (Serial 451, Washington, D.C., 1845), 1–3.

34. Kenneth B. Pomeroy and James G. Yoho, *North Carolina Lands: Ownership, Use, and Management of Forest and Related Lands* (Washington, D.C., 1964), 94; Nathaniel C. Browder, *The Cherokee Indians and Those Who Came After: Notes for a History of Cherokee County, North Carolina, 1835–1860* (Hayesville, N.C., 1973), 73–87; George H. Smathers, *The History of Land Titles in Western North Carolina* (Asheville, N.C., 1938), 85; William Eaton, Jr., to Gov. David S. Reid, Aug. 28, 1851, GP 127, NCDAH.

35. Estimates of the total number of Cherokees remaining east range from an obviously low figure of 1,000 to 1,500 or more; 1,400 seems closest to the mark. Many letters in M-234 for the years after 1838 attest to the presence of relatively acculturated Cherokees in Georgia, Tennessee, and Alabama. Before the 1838 removal "Cherokees East" denoted the main body of Cherokees under John

Ross, distinguishing them from the tribal minority who had already moved west. In this book the term always refers to those remaining east after 1838.

36. Dudley to Joel R. Poinsett, Nov. 16, 1839, GLB 32, pp. 329–20, NCDAH. In Jan. 1839 Congressman Graham introduced a resolution asking how many Cherokees remained and why they had not been removed. *Cong. Globe*, 25 Cong., 3 Sess., 129 (Jan. 21, 1839). See also Graham to President Martin Van Buren, Apr. 29, 1840, M-234, 84/365–68; Graham to Secretary of War John Bell, July 6, 1841, M-234, 85/165–67; Crawford to John Kennedy et al., Feb. 11, 1839, GP 88, p. 2179, NCDAH; *House Doc.*, 25 Cong., 3 Sess., No. 224 (Serial 348, Washington, D.C., 1839), 1–2; "Report of the Commissioner of Indian Affairs," Nov. 25, 1839, *House Ex. Doc.*, 26 Cong., 1 Sess., No. 2 (Serial 363, Washington, D.C., 1839), 333; Crawford to Poinsett, Feb. 7, 1840, M-348, 1/411–12 (record book page numbers will be cited for M-348 rather than frame numbers); and Crawford to Poinsett, May 28, 1840, M-348, 2/106–107.

37. For different versions of Yonaguska's farewell see Mooney, "Myths of the Cherokee," 163; Lanman, *Letters from Alleghany Mountains*, 110.

38. Thomas to Edward Dudley, Sept. 22, 1839, GP 89, NCDAH; Wilson Lumpkin to Thomas, Sept. 25, 1839, Thomas Papers, Duke; Thomas to CIA Crawford, June 30, 1841, 1841, M-234, 85/474–75; Russell, "William Holland Thomas," 103–104; Iobst, "William Holland Thomas and the Cherokee Claims," 188–90; CIA to Thomas, July 8, 1840, M-21, 29/13–14; Flying Squirrel to CIA, Oct. 12, 1874, M-234, 107/856.

39. Moulton, *John Ross*, 127–30; Iobst, "William Holland Thomas and the Cherokee Claims" 192; Reed, "Postremoval Factionalism," 156–57.

40. Hindman to Lea, Sept. 21, 1841, M-234, 85/178–80; Hindman to Lea, [n.d.], M-234, 85/184–85; Moulton, *John Ross*, 37, 105.

41. Hindman to Lea, Sept. 21, 1841, M-234, 85/178–80; Hindman to Lea, [n.d.], M-234, 85/184–85. In a letter to Crawford of July 30, 1842, Thomas claimed he had already purchased 55,000 acres for the Indians. M-234, 86/713–14.

42. Crawford to Thomas, May 27, Aug. 21, 1841, M-21, 30/311; 31/42; OIA to Hindman, Sept. 29, 1841 (3 letters), M-21, 31/148–51; Acting CIA Daniel Kurtz to Lea, Sept. 22, 1841, M-234, 85/536–37. Gideon F. Morris was appointed Hindman's assistant but was too preoccupied with personal matters in Washington to return to North Carolina. In December his appointment was revoked, and Hindman continued with the assistance of a single interpreter.

43. Acting Secretary of War Lea [in behalf of President Tyler], "To the Cherokee People East of the Mississippi," Oct. 1, 1841, M-21, 31/160–61.

44. OIA to Thomas, Sept. 29, 1841, M-21, 31/148; Thomas to CIA Crawford, Oct. 17, 1841, M-234, 85/499–501; Thomas to Acting CIA Kurtz, Nov. 13, 1841, M-234, 85/509–10.

45. Hindman to Lea, Dec. 6, 1841, M-234, 85/226–28; Council of North Carolina Cherokees to Tyler, Oct. 22, 1841, M-234, 85/95–100.

46. Hindman to Acting CIA Kurtz, Dec. 13, 1841, M-234, 85/219–22; Hindman to Crawford, Dec. 20, 1841, M-234, 86/582–84.

47. Hindman to Crawford, Dec. 20, 1841, M-234, 86/584–87; William Holland Thomas Diary, 1840–41 [*sic*: actually Dec. 1841–Jan. 1842], 63–65, WHTC; Hindman to Crawford, Feb. 3, 1842, M-234, 116/115–17; Thomas to Hindman, Jan. 19, 1842, M-234, 116/118–19.

48. Thomas Diary, 1840–41 [*sic*], 63–65, WHTC.

49. Hindman to Crawford, Dec. 20, 1841, M-234, 86/586–87; Hindman to Crawford, Feb. 3, 1842, M-234, 116/114–17.

50. OIA to Hindman, Jan. 12, Feb. 1, 1842, M-21, 31/364–65, 418–19; Lea to Secretary of War John C. Spencer, Mar. 14, 1842, M-234, 87/711–13.

51. Timson to Graham, May 18, 1842, M-234, 86/569–70.

52. Graham to President Tyler, Dec. 16, 1841, M-234, 85/271–74; Graham to Secretary of War Spencer, May 13, 1842, M-234, 87/621; Spencer to John Ross et al., May 26, June 3, 1842, M-21, 32/206, 222; Crawford to Secretary of War James M. Porter, Jan. 13, 1844, M-348, 4/90; Ross et al. to Spencer, June 6, 14, 1842, M-574, File 75 (Cherokee Delegations, 1842–1844), 8/275–76, 278–80; Moulton, *John Ross*, 133–34.

53. *Cong. Globe*, 27 Cong., 2 Sess., 536, 737, 888–89 (May 25, July 9, Aug. 13, 1842), and *passim*; *House Rep.*, 27 Cong., 3 Sess., No. 288 (Serial 429, Washington, D.C., 1843); Satz, *American Indian Policy*, 192–95.

54. Spencer to Ross et al., July 9, 1842, M-21, 32/314; Ross et al. to Spencer, July 11, 1842, M-574, 8/286; *Cong. Globe*, 27 Cong., 2 Sess., 737 (July 9, 1842).

55. James Graham to President Tyler, Aug. 24, 1842, in J.G. de Roulhac Hamilton and Max R. Williams, eds., *The Papers of William Alexander Graham*, 6 vols. (Raleigh, N.C., 1957–1976), II, 372–73; Graham to Tyler, Sept. 1, 1842, M-234, 86/567–68; Crawford to Robinson, Sept. 2, 1842, M-21, 32/425–28; Senate resolution approving appointment of James Iredell and John H. Eaton as commissioners, Aug. 31, 1842, M-234, 86/673. Iredell declined his nomination and was eventually replaced with Edward B. Hubley.

56. Rogers's suspicion of Ross's connection with the removal program is apparent in his letters to William Thomas of Sept. 23, Dec. 28, 1841, and Apr. 7, 1842, Thomas Papers, Duke. For his change in attitude see his letter to John Timson, Dec. 7, 1842, M-234, 116/269–71.

57. For examples see Alfred H. Hudson to John Timson, Oct. 1, 1842, M-234, 116/263–65; Margaret Morgan to Timson, Nov. 18, 1842, M-234, 116/267; Timson to Crawford, Jan. 9, Feb. 15, 1843, M-234, 116/260–61, 276; Johnson K. Rogers to Crawford, June 14, 1843, M-234, 116/247; "Memorial of Wm. Henson and Other Cherokees" to J.W. Deadrick [*sic*], Aug. 1843, M-234, 116/152; Preston Starrett to Crawford, Nov. 8, 1843, M-234, 116/256–57.

58. *Journal of House of Commons*, 696, and *Journal of Senate*, 211, in *Journals of the General Assembly of the State of North Carolina at its Session in 1842–'43*

(Raleigh, 1843); memorial from citizens of Haywood County, Legislative Papers 583, "Cherokee Indians and Cherokee Lands" folder, NCDAH. See also petition of citizens of Macon and Haywood County, Aug. 17, 1842, *Sen. Doc.* 408 (Serial 477), 21–22.

59. J. Kerner to William A. Graham, May 31, 1842, in Hamilton and Williams, eds., *Papers of William A. Graham*, II, 319.

60. Legislative Papers 583, "Cherokee Indians and Cherokee Lands" folder, NCDAH.

61. "To the Chiefs of the State of North Carolina," in Senate, Jan. 13, 1843, *ibid.*

62. *Journal of Senate*, 312–13, 373, 377; *Journal of House of Commons*, 918; "Report of Joint Select Committee upon Indian Removals"; "Resolution in Relation to the Removal of the Cherokee Indians," Jan. 25, 1843, Legislative Papers 583, "Cherokee Indians and Cherokee Lands" folder, NCDAH.

63. Timson to Crawford, Jan. 9, 1843, M-234, 116/260–61; Robinson to Crawford, Jan. 10, Feb. 11, Mar. 18, Apr. 11, 1843, M-234, 116/236, 238, 241, 245; J.R. Siler to Secretary of War, June 16, 1843, M-234, 116/253–54; Timson to Crawford, June 17, 1843, M-234, 116/278–79; Johnson K. Rogers to Crawford, June 29, 1843, M-234, 116/250; Deaderick to Crawford, Aug. 10, 17, 22, Sept. 7, 18, Oct. 23, Dec. 4, 1843, M-234, 116/147, 149–50, 158–59, 166–68, 170–71, 173–74, 178–79; OIA to Deaderick, July 6, 1843, M-21, 34/94–95.

64. Axley (often spelled "Axly") to Crawford, Nov. 30, 1843, M-234, 87/108–10; Proceedings of a Council of Valley River Cherokees, Jan. 4, 1844, M-234, 88/273–78; J.W. King to Thomas, Feb. 6, 1844, WHTC.

65. Crawford to Deaderick, Dec. 5, 1843, M-21, 34/361–62; see also Crawford to Deaderick, Sept. 16, 1843, M-21, 34/244; Deaderick to Crawford, Dec. 18, 1843, M-234, 116/324–30; Crawford to Secretary of War J.M. Porter, Jan. 30, 1844, M-234, 116/388–89.

66. Deaderick to Crawford, Jan. 1, 23, 1844, M-234, 116/334, 338–39; Crawford to Porter, Jan. 30, 1844, M-234, 116/388–92; Crawford to Deaderick, Feb. 2, 1844, M-21, 34/460–61; Crawford to Timson, Feb. 2, 1844, M-21, 34/461.

67. For examples of emigrants during the 1840s and early 1850s see M-234, 116/305, 498, 541, 638–40, 681–82, 784, 796, 815, 881.

68. Francis Paul Prucha has shown that humanitarianism was a persistent theme in Indian policy during the 1840s. Prucha, "American Indian Policy in the 1840s: Visions of Reform," in John G. Clark, ed., *The Frontier Challenge: Responses to the Trans-Mississippi West* (Lawrence, Kan., 1971), 81–110.

69. Crawford to Secretary of War William Wilkins, Feb. 22, 1844, M-348, 4/132–36. Crawford's incomplete figures actually totaled only $1,487; Timson's later account added $367, and Deaderick's pay (which had not been calculated by Crawford) was estimated by this writer to have been from $500 to $600. For more on retrenchment in Indian affairs, see Satz, *American Indian Policy, passim*.

NOTES TO CHAPTER 3

1. For discussion of the Eastern Cherokees' legal status, see John R. Finger, "The North Carolina Cherokees, 1838–1866: Traditionalism, Progressivism, and the Affirmation of State Citizenship," *Journal of Cherokee Studies* 5 (Spring 1980): 17–29; Frizzell, "Legal Status of the Eastern Band of Cherokee Indians"; Ben Oshel Bridgers, "An Historical Analysis of the Legal Status of the North Carolina Cherokees," *North Carolina Law Review* 58 (Aug. 1980): 1075–1131.

2. Mooney, "Myths of the Cherokee," 12, 157; Russell, "William Holland Thomas," 32–33, 67; McLoughlin and Conser, "Cherokees in Transition," 686–87, 689; Thomas to James Graham, Oct. 18, 1838, WHTC; petition in *Sen. Doc.* 408 (Serial 477), 21–22; memorial "To the Chiefs of the State of North Carolina," Jan. 13, 1843, Legislative Papers 583, "Cherokee Indians and Cherokee Lands" folder, NCDAH.

3. Chapman J. Milling, *Red Carolinians* (Chapel Hill, 1940), 254–56; Iobst, "William Holland Thomas and the Cherokee Claims," 193; Mooney, "Myths of the Cherokee," 163–64.

4. Milling, *Red Carolinians*, 256–57; Douglas S. Brown, *The Catawba Indians: The People of the River* (Columbia, S.C., 1966), 298–302; Mooney, "Myths of the Cherokee," 165; Charles M. Hudson, *The Catawba Nation* (Athens, Ga., 1970), 65; Thomas to David Hutchison, June 26, 1841, Hutchison Papers, York County Library, Rock Hill, S.C.

5. Morehead to Joseph F. White, Sept. 8, 1841, GLB 34, pp. 165–66; see also White to Morehead, Aug. 10, 1841, GP 98; David Hutchison to Morehead, Apr. 26, 1842, GP 100; all in NCDAH.

6. Joseph F. White to William Thomas, Feb. 4, 1843, Thomas Papers, Duke.

7. Lanman, *Letters from Alleghany Mountains*, 93; Milling, *Red Carolinians*, 257, 259; Brown, *Catawba Indians*, 299–300; Hudson, *Catawba Nation*, 65–66. Some of the Catawbas sharecropped on the lands of whites who lived near the Cherokees.

8. William H. Thomas, *Explanation of the Fund Held in Trust by the United States for the North Carolina Cherokees* (Washington, D.C., 1858), 4–8. Examples of official comments are William Medill to James Graham, July 13, 1846, M-21, 38/239; and Luke Lea to Thomas, Apr. 11, 1851, M-21, 44/300.

9. CIA T. Hartley Crawford to Thomas, July 8, 1840, M-21, 29/13–14; Thomas to Crawford, July 30, 1842, M-234, 86/713–14.

10. *Laws of the State of North Carolina, 1844–45* (Raleigh, 1845), 71–72; indenture for Cherokee corporation, Dec. 4, 1846, Thomas Papers, Duke; Thomas to Graham, Mar. 8, 1847, GP 117, NCDAH.

11. Graham to Thomas, Mar. 24, 1847, Thomas Papers, Duke; Thomas Diary, May 19, 1847, WHTC; indenture of May 19, 1847, GP 118; Thomas to Graham, June 2, 1847, GP 118; Proclamation of June 22, 1847, GLB 37, pp. 358–60, all in NCDAH; Lanman, *Letters from Alleghany Mountains*, 94; Thomas,

Explanations of the Rights and Claims of the Cherokee Indians (Washington, D.C., 1851; facsimile reprint, Asheville, N.C., 1947), 7; Francis A. Dony, "Report . . ." to the Commissioner of General Land Office, Oct. 29, 1874, M-234, 107/571–75; Silas H. Swetland to CIA Ely S. Parker, Nov. 20, 1869, in *House Ex. Doc.*, 41 Cong. 2 Sess., No. 1 (Serial 1414, Washington, D.C., 1869), 897–98.

12. Thomas to Duff Green, June 20, Sept. 13, 1844, Duff Green Papers, SHC; Duff Green to Thomas, Dec. 13, 1844, WHTC; Duff and Benjamin Green to William Meredith, May 16, 1849, WHTP, Roll 2; Duff Green to CIA, Apr. 4, 1851, M-234, 95/836–38; Thomas to John H. Eaton and Edward B. Hubley, Cherokee commissioners, June 15, 1843, roll 4 of microfilm copies of Cherokee-related materials in National Archives (Newspapers and Microforms Department, Duke Univ. Library).

13. Finger, "The Abortive Second Cherokee Removal," *passim*. There are numerous communications from Axley, Starrett, Rogers, and other Cherokee agents in Letters Received by the Office of Indian Affairs.

14. Thomas to Polk, Aug. 6, 1846, M-234, 90/657; Sen. Willie P. Mangrum to Polk, Aug. 7, 1846, M-234, 90/661; H.L. Turney et al. to Polk, Aug. 6, 1846, M-234, 90/669; James Graham to Polk, July 10, 1846, M-234, 90/650; Polk to [OIA], Aug. 6, 1846, M-234, 90/656; Thomas, *Explanations of the Rights and Claims*, 10.

15. Kappler, *Indian Affairs: Laws and Treaties*, II, 561–65. Articles 9 and 10 on p. 564.

16. 9 *U.S. Statutes* 264–65. Duff Green described in detail the political maneuvering involved in passage of this act. Green to Thomas, Aug. 17, 1848, Thomas Papers, Duke.

17. Duff Green to William Marcy, Sept. 25, 1848, M-234, 92/190–91; and Greens to William Meredith, May 16, 1849, WHTP, Roll 2; *House Misc. Doc.*, 32 Cong., 1 Sess., No. 64 (Serial 652, Washington, D.C., 1852), 19–28.

18. 9 *U.S. Statutes* 264; Thomas to Gov. Charles Manly, Sept. 1, 1849 (quote), GP 123, NCDAH; Thomas Diary, July 11, 1848; Nov. 26, Dec. 7–8, 10–19, 1849, WHTC; OIA to John Ross, Aug. 23, 1848, M–21, 41/194; James C. Mullay to Thomas, Dec. 4, 1848, Thomas Papers, Duke; James W. Covington, "Proposed Catawba Indian Removal, 1848," *South Carolina Historical and Genealogical Magazine* 55 (Jan. 1954): 42–43. A first-hand account of the Catawbas is David Hutchison's lengthy article in the *Palmetto-State Banner* (Columbia, S.C.), Aug. 30, 1849; see also *Keowee Courier*, Dec. 8, 1849; *Sen. Doc.*, 54 Cong., 2 Sess., No. 144 (Serial 3471, Washington, D.C., 1897), 8–10; Hudson, *Catawba Nation*, 65–66.

19. Mullay to Medill, July 27, Aug. 21, 1848, M-234, 92/273–74, 271–72; Medill to Mullay, Aug. 26, 1848, M-234, 98/170–72.

20. Mullay to Medill, Sept. 11, Dec. 14, 1848, M-234, 92/276, 279–82; Mullay to CIA Luke Lea, Jan. 23, 1851, M-234, 95/624–27; John Owl to Secretary of War, Nov. 20, 1848, M-234, 92/137–42; Thomas Diary, Sept. 22–Oct. 3, 1848, WHTC.

21. Mullay to Thomas, Nov. 14, 1848; see also his letter to Thomas of Dec. 4, 1848, both in Thomas Papers, Duke.

22. A certified copy of the original Mullay Roll is in the James W. Terrell Collection, MS 1926, National Anthropological Archives, Smithsonian Institution, Washington, D.C.

23. B.M. Edney to Orlando Brown, n.d., received Jan. 2, 1850, M-234, 94/288; Felix Axley to CIA, Feb. 25, 1850, M-234, 94/8; T. Ewing to Luke Lea, July 18, 1850, M-234, 94/361; John B. Woodfin to Luke Lea, Aug. 1, 7, 1850, M-234, 94/554, 369–70; Mullay to Lea, Aug. 10, 1850, M-234, 94/429–31; Mullay to Lea, Jan. 23, 1851, M-234, 95/624–27; Mullay Roll, National Anthropological Archives.

24. Mullay to CIA Luke Lea, Jan. 23, 1851, M-234, 95/624–25; act of Jan. 2, 1847, *Laws of North Carolina, 1846–47* (Raleigh, 1847), 128.

25. Thomas to William Wilkins, Jan. 3, 1845, M-234, 89/535; Lanman, *Letters from Alleghany Mountains*, 95; Frizzell, "Legal Status of the Eastern Band of Cherokee Indians," 27–30.

26. Adolph L. Dial and David K. Eliades, *The Only Land I Know: A History of the Lumbee Indians* (San Francisco, 1975), 1–24, 39–41, 43–44.

27. *Eu-che-lah v. Welsh,* 10 *North Carolina Reports* 155–74; Dial and Eliades, *Only Land I Know*, 40–41, 43–45; Frizzell, "Legal Status of the Eastern Band of Cherokee Indians," 32–34; Bragg to SI R. McClelland, Sept. 26, 1855, GLB 43, pp. 276–78, NCDAH.

28. Indian taxes for 1853, WHTP, Roll 2.

29. Contract of Oct. 25, 1850, M-234, 107/951–52; also in WHTC, Addition 1.

30. David W. Siler to Gov. David S. Reid, May 19, 1851; Reid to Eaton, Aug. 8, 1851, GLB 40, p. 117; "Explanation of the condition of the Cherokee Indians of Buffalo Town, residing on unsurveyed lands in the county of Cherokee, owned by the State," GLB 40, pp. 117–20; Thomas to Reid, Aug. 8, 1851, GP 127; Eaton to Reid, Aug. 28, 1851, GP 127, all in NCDAH. Reid to Jacob Siler, Sept. 24, 1851, WHTC.

31. CIA Luke Lea to Felix Axley, Jan. 18, 1851, M-21, 44/144; Lea to Preston Starrett, Apr. 28, 1851, M-21, 44/352; Lea to Siler, May 24, 1851, M-21, 44/400–401; Sen. George Badger to SI A.H.H. Stuart, Feb. 25, 1851, M-234, 95/550.

32. Rogers to SI Stuart, July 24, 1851, M-234, 95/667; Rogers to CIA Lea, Sept. 1, 1851, M-234, 95/664–66; David Siler to Lea, May 26, June 20, July 6, Oct. 17, 1851, M-234, 95/729–30, 734–36, 738–40, 747–49; Siler to Charles E. Mix, Aug. 19, Sept. 17, 1851, M-234, 95/742–43, 745; Thomas to Mix, Aug. 7, 1851, M-234, 95/801; R.M. Edwards to Lea, Mar. 31, 1852, M-234, 95/1149–51; Mix to Siler, Aug. 20, 1851, M-21, 45/81. The roll is most conveniently consulted in David W. Siler, comp. *The Eastern Cherokees: A Census of the Cherokee Nation in North Carolina, Tennessee, Alabama and Georgia in 1851* (Cottonport, La., 1972).

33. Lea to Chapman, Nov. 20, 1851, M-21, 45/233–35.

34. Rogers to CIA Lea, Nov. 11, 1851, M-234, 95/690–96; Rogers to SI Stuart, Nov. 12, 1851, M-234, 95/1229–31; William K. Sebastian to Rogers, Sept. 12, 1851, M-234, 95/697–98; Clingman to Thomas, May 23, 1852, WHTP, Roll 2.

35. At issue were fees for the per capita payments. Thomas and the Greens had already collected $6,910 in fees for interest payments on the removal and subsistence fund. Thomas, *A Letter to the Commissioner of Indian Affairs upon Claims of the Indians Remaining in the States East* (Washington, D.C., 1853), 45 (quote). The strongest argument for payment of the fees was made by Benjamin Green in his letter to SI Stuart of Nov. 3, 1851, M-234, 95/490–95; see also Lea to Alfred Chapman, Dec. 5, 1851, M-21, 45/252.

36. Petition of North Carolina Cherokees to President, Dec. 23, 1851, M-234, 95/927; Chapman to CIA Lea, Feb. 7, 1852, M-234, 95/923–25; A. Austin Smith to Lea, Feb. 9, 1852, M-234, 95/919–21.

37. Petition to President, Dec. 23, 1851, M-234, 95/927; Chapman to Lea, Feb. 7, 1852, M-234, 95/923–25; A. Austin Smith to Lea, Feb. 9, 1852, M-234, 95/919–21.

38. Rogers to Lea, Feb. 12, 1852, M-234, 95/914–17.

39. Lea to A.H.H. Stuart, Feb. 18, 1852, M-234, 95/909–10.

40. Luke Lea to E.W. Chastain, Jan. 13, July 21, 1852, M-21, 45/356–57, 46/218; Lea to T.L. Clingman, Jan. 29, 1852, M-21, 45/404; Chastain to Lea, July 19, 1852, M-234, 95/988; act of July 31, 1854, in 10 *U.S. Statutes* 333; Charles E. Mix to Chapman, Sept. 7, 1855, M-21, 52/353–54; Chapman to Mix, Sept. 21, 1855, M-234, 97/135.

41. Secretary of Treasury to Terrell, Oct. 22, 1851, WHTC; Report of Arbitrators, Oct. 23, 1874, *House Ex. Doc.*, 43 Cong., 2 Sess., No. 51 (Serial 1645, Washington, D.C., 1875), 9. See also Terrell to Comptroller Elisha Whittlesy, Jan. 7, 1856, WHTP, Roll 2.

42. Terrell to Secretary of Treasury, Aug. 22, 1854; Terrell to First Auditor of Treasury, Nov. 28, 1854, both in WHTP, Roll 2.

43. Act of Mar. 3, 1855, in 10 *U.S. Statutes* 700; Thomas, *Explanation of the Fund Held in Trust*, 11–12.

44. SI R. McClelland to Bragg, Sept. 22, 1855, GP 139; Bragg to McClelland, Sept. 26, 1855, GLB 43, pp. 276–78, both in NCDAH; Thomas, *Explanation of the Fund Held in Trust*, 11–12.

45. James Taylor to SI McClelland, June 25, 1856, M-234, 98/302–303. An excellent account of the history of the payments under the 1848 act, as well as reasons why the federal government would not accept North Carolina's tacit permission is in a memorandum of Mar. [n.d.] 1855, M-234, 97/346–50. See also the detailed arguments for paying the Cherokees—despite their anomalous status and lack of sufficient funds to pay all claimants—in Joseph L. Williams to McClelland, Mar. 31, 1855, M-234, 97/325–31.

46. Thomas Diary, Mar. 9, 23, 1853, WHTC; T.L. Clingman to President Pierce, Mar. 6, 1853, M-234, 96/81–82; Cherokee petition to President, Mar. 22, 1853, M-234, 96/108–109.

47. Cherokee petition to President, Mar. 22, 1853, M-234, 96/108–109; petition of Qualla Town Indians to [President], n.d., referred to CIA, Apr. 27, 1853, M-234, 96/111. See also Cherokee petition, Sept. 17, 1853, M-234, 96/259–61; petitions under covering letter of Edmund Fallin, Dec. 23, 1853, M-234, 96/505–20. The Cherokee Nation's response to these and similar petitions is in "Conference with Cherokee delegation January 15th, 1855," M-234, 97/276–83. The Band's post–Civil War claims to lands in the Cherokee Nation are discussed in chs. 6 and 7.

48. James Taylor to Thomas, Jan. 12, 1854; Sept. 6, 19, 1856; and Thomas to wife, Jan. 10, 1857; all in WHTC. Statement of R.M. Henry et al., Apr. 6, 1853, M-234, 96/49–50; Taylor to CIA Manypenny, Jan. 31, 1854, M-234, 96/386; Thomas to Charles Mix, Dec. 4, 1855, M-234, 97/file designation "Cherokee T355"; Taylor to Manypenny, May 6, June 11, 1856, M-234, 98/288, 292; Taylor to SI, Aug. 21, 1856, M-234, 98/315–17; Thomas mortgages, Oct. 22, 1856, WHTP, Roll 2.

49. John A. Powell to Secretary of War Charles Conrad, Feb. 20, 1851, M-234, 116/862; Thomas to James Taylor, May 26, 1856, M-234, 98/26; T.L. Clingman to SI, June 10, 1856, M-234, 98/25; Taylor to SI McClelland, June 25, 1856, M-234, 98/300–307; Clingman to SI Jacob Thompson, Apr. 11, 1857, M-234, 98/398–99; Taylor to Thompson, Apr. 17, 1857, M-234, 98/400–404; CIA James W. Denver to Clingman, Apr. 25, 1857, M-21, 56/394.

50. Taylor to Hoke, Apr. 28, May 6, 19, 1857; William Thomas to Hoke, May 4, 1857, all in William A. Hoke Papers, SHC; Taylor to Denver, May 2, 1857, M-234, 98/644–45; Hoke to Denver, May 3, 1857, M-234, 98/453–54; Clingman to Denver, May 20, 1857, M-234, 98/409–410; William Mills to SI, n.d., received July 2, 1857, M-234, 98/509; Denver to Hoke, May 19, 1857, M-21, 56/491.

51. Thompson to Denver, July 9, 10, 1857, M-234, 98/505, 521–22; Taylor to Denver, July 14, 21, 28, 1857, M-234, 98/712, 714–16, 718–19; Taylor to Thompson, Aug. 18, 1857, M-234, 98/721–22; Denver to Taylor, July 13, 1857, M-21, 57/165; John H. Wheeler to Hoke, Sept. 3, 1857, Hoke Papers, SHC.

52. John H. Wheeler to John Hoke, Nov. 25, 1857, Hoke Papers, SHC; Thomas to wife, Jan. 3, 1858, WHTC; Thomas to Jacob Thompson, Feb. 11, 1858, M-234, 98/916–17; T.L. Clingman et al. to Thompson, Feb. 23, 1858, M-234, 98/909–10; Thomas, *Explanation of the Fund Held in Trust*; see also *Report of the North Carolina Judiciary Committee on the North Carolina Cherokees* (Raleigh, 1859), 9.

NOTES TO CHAPTER 4

1. McLoughlin and Conser, "Cherokees in Transition," 684–89, 699; Mooney, "Myths of Cherokee," 12, 157; Russell, "William Holland Thomas," 32–33, 67.

2. McLoughlin and Conser, "Cherokees in Transition," Tables 4–5, p. 685; Tables 7–8, p. 688; p. 701; Lanman, *Letters from Alleghany Mountains*, 95; Fleming, *Sketch of Life*, 54–66; Gammell, *A History of American Baptist Missions*, 323–27; petition in *Sen. Doc.* 408 (Serial 477), 21–22.

3. McLoughlin and Conser, "Cherokees in Transition," 685; see also Table 4; claim of Ginna for cabin, Aug. 8, 1843, Thomas Papers, Duke.

4. Lanman, *Letters from Alleghany Mountains*, 65–66, 84–85; Thomas, *Explanations of the Rights and Claims*, 15; see also report of Francis Dony to CIA, Nov. 17, 1874, M-234, 107/134; William McCarthy to CIA J.Q. Smith, Feb. 10, 1876, M-234, 110/285–86; David Shenck, "The Cherokees in North Carolina," *At Home and Abroad* 2 (Feb. 1882): 325.

5. Lanman, *Letters from Alleghany Mountains*, 90; Thomas, *Argument in Support of the Claims of the Cherokee Indians*, 17–18; Thomas to James Graham, Oct. 18, 1838, WHTC; Thomas to CIA George Manypenny, Sept. 23, 1853, M-234, 96/417; *Friends' Weekly Intelligencer*, Mar. 31, 1849; Shenck, "Cherokees in North Carolina," 327; Rebecca Harding Davis, "Qualla," *Lippincott's Magazine* 41 (Nov. 1875): 583.

7. Lanman, *Letters from Alleghany Mountains*, 90, 96, 101, 104; Davis, "Qualla," 582–84; Shenck, "Cherokees in North Carolina," 325, 327–28; *Friends' Weekly Intelligencer*, Mar. 31, 1849; Russell, "William Holland Thomas," 314.

8. "Present state of civilization among the Cherokee Indians of Qualla Town," accompanying letter of Thomas to William Wilkins, Mar. 3, 1845, M-234, 89/542–43.

9. Lanman, *Letters from Alleghany Mountains*, 111; Thomas, *Explanations of the Rights and Claims*, 15.

10. Russell, "William Holland Thomas," 36; Mooney, "Myths of Cherokee," 163.

11. "Present state of civilization," M-234, 89/543; Thomas to CIA William Medill, June 26, 1847, M-234, 91/520; Thomas to Medill, June 26, 1850, WHTC; Anna G. and Jack F. Kilpatrick, "Chronicles of Wolftown: Social Documents of the North Carolina Cherokees, 1850–1862," Bureau of American Ethnology *Bulletin* 196 (Washington, D.C., 1966), 33–47; 107–109. There are frequent references to the Echota Mission in *Minutes of the Annual Conferences of the Methodist Episcopal Church South* (Holston Conference), published various places, scattered issues, 1838–1873.

12. Lanman, *Letters from Alleghany Mountains*, 96.

13. *Ibid.*, 99.

14. Stringfield, handwritten historical account, p. 105, William W. Stringfield Papers, NCDAH; Kilpatrick and Kilpatrick, "Chronicles of Wolftown," 7–8.

15. McLoughlin and Conser, "Cherokees in Transition," Table 7, p. 688; "Present state of civilization," M-234, 89/543. An example of Thomas's exaggerated claims for Indian literacy is in his *Explanations of the Rights and Claims*, 15. The manner in which many Eastern Cherokees "signed" various documents

attest to their illiteracy, and most remained in that state until well after the Civil War.

16. Thomas to CIA Medill, June 26, 1847, M-234, 91/520–21; Mix to Thomas, July 5, 1851, M-21, 44/485; petition to incorporate Indian mission school, Dec. 1, 1850, M-234, 95/774–75; Thomas Diary, Jan. 23, 1852, WHTC; Russell, "William Holland Thomas," 134–35. It is likely the Methodists offered periodic instruction during the 1850s, but William Hicks, the superintendent of the Echota Mission, explained in detail some of the difficulties in establishing a permanent school. *Holston Advocate* (Knoxville, Tn.), Jan. 14, 1851.

17. See for example Thomas to James Graham, Oct. 18, 1838, WHTC; Lanman, *Letters from Alleghany Mountains*, 107–108; Mooney, "Myths of Cherokee," 163; Wilbur G. Zeigler and Ben S. Grosscup, *The Heart of the Alleghanies or Western North Carolina . . .* (Raleigh, 1883), 33–34.

18. "Present state of civilization," M-234, 89/543.

19. Thomas Diary, Oct. 2–6, 1850, WHTC; Thomas to Clingman, Dec. 8, 1850, M-234, 94/196–97.

20. G.W. Lovingood to James Taylor, Sept. 24, 1856, M-234, 98/320; Elizabeth Welch to Taylor, Oct. 21, 1856, M-234, 98/333–34. See also ch. 5.

21. Indictment of Tahquit, Mar. 8, 1856, GP 140; A.M. Burton to Gov. Thomas Bragg, Mar. 13, 1856, GP 140; see also GLB 43, pp. 414–15; Bragg to Burton, Mar. 19, 1856, GLB 43, p. 418, all in NCDAH.

22. Thomas Diary, July 2, Nov. 15, 1839, WHTC; Lanman, *Letters from Alleghany Mountains*, 94, 104; Mooney, "Myths of Cherokee," 161. *Report of the Judiciary Committee on the North Carolina Cherokees*, 1, 10, recommended allowing the Cherokees to exercise police powers within their own communities.

23. Euchella is designated as chief of Wolf Town in an affidavit of Sept. 22, 1851, M-234, 97/752; Flying Squirrel is listed as chief of Paint Town in the Mullay Roll. See also Lanman, *Letters from Alleghany Mountains*, 112–13.

24. Felix Axley to Thomas, Apr. 29, 1845, WHTC. The Thomas Papers and Letters Received by the OIA reflect little internal discord among the Eastern Cherokees during this period, though there were some caustic comments by mixed-bloods who claimed to represent Indians. And of course there were Johnson Rogers's attacks on Thomas, who was an adopted Cherokee.

25. McLoughlin and Conser, "Cherokees in Transition," Table 7, p. 688.

26. Lanman, *Letters from Alleghany Mountains*, 111; Siler to CIA Luke Lea, July 6, 1851, M-234, 95/739; Acting CIA Mix to Siler, Aug. 20, 1851, M-21, 45/81; affidavit of Raleigh Dick Thomas, June 4, 1881, M-1059, 3/82–84; Tolever Twitty to CIA, June 1, 1890, M-1059, 5/120.

27. Barnard to Gov. Edward Dudley, Apr. 6, 1840, GP 91, NCDAH.

28. Felix Axley to Thomas, Apr. 29, 1845; Aug. 10, 1846, WHTC; *Journal of the House of Commons . . .* (Raleigh, 1849), 547, 554; James Whitaker to President Taylor, Oct. 20, 1849, M-234, 93/472–73; Russell, "William Holland Thomas," 133.

29. Felix Axley to Thomas, Apr. 29, 1845, WHTC.

30. Mullay to CIA William Medill, Dec. 14, 1848, M-234, 92/279–82.

31. Lanman, *Letters from Alleghany Mountains*, 94–96.

32. *Ibid.*, 112–14.

33. Seventh U.S. Census, 1850, Haywood County, N.C., Population Schedule, 46–53, NCDAH; Thomas, *Explanations of the Rights and Claims*, 14–15; Thomas to SI Jacob Thompson, Mar. 1, 1858, M-234, 98/896–97.

34. 1850 Census, Haywood County, Population Schedule, 46–53, NCDAH; Thomas, *Explanations of the Rights and Claims*, 15.

35. Siler, comp., *The Eastern Cherokees: A Census*, 1–64.

36. *Ibid.*, 65–122; Lanman, *Letters from Alleghany Mountains*, 79; Gaston Litton, "Enrollment Record of the Eastern Band of Cherokee Indians," *North Carolina Historical Review* 17 (July 1940): 210–14.

37. Lanman, *Letters from Alleghany Mountains*, 110; Eighth U.S. Census, 1860, Jackson County, N.C., Population Schedule, M-653, 903/104–30; Schedule 4, 1860, "Productions of Agriculture," Jackson County, 33–38, NCDAH.

38. "Present state of civilization," M-234, 89/543; John Mullay to CIA William Medill, Dec. 14, 1848, M-234, 92/281; John C. Morris to CIA George Manypenny, July 14, 1855, M-234, 97/438–84; Lanman, *Letters from Alleghany Mountains*, 94; Thomas Diary, Sept. 23, 1848, WHTC; Russell, "William Holland Thomas," 136; Meetings of Cherokee council, May 20, 1859, WHTP, Roll 3.

39. *Friends' Weekly Intelligencer*, Mar. 31, 1849. The author of this may have been Charles Lanman.

40. The Senecas provide an example of a tribe, under the pressures of acculturation, shifting from a matriarchal, matrilineal society to a husband-dominated, patrilineal system. Anthony F.C. Wallace, *The Death and Rebirth of the Seneca* (New York, 1969).

41. Russell, "William Holland Thomas," 136–37, 175.

42. *Ibid.*, 137–38; Act of Jan. 10, 1845, in *Laws of the State of North Carolina, 1844—45* (Raleigh, 1845), 71–72; ch. 3, pp. 44–45; Silas H. Swetland to CIA E.S. Parker, Nov. 20, 1869, in *House Ex. Doc.*, 41 Cong., 2 Sess., No. 1 (Serial 1414, Washington, D.C., 1869), 897.

43. Ch. 3, pp. 44–45; Russell, "William Holland Thomas," 138–39.

44. Raymond D. Fogelson and Paul Kutsche, "Cherokee Economic Cooperatives: The Gadugi," in William N. Fenton and John Gulick, eds., "Symposium on Cherokee and Iroquois Culture," Bureau of American Ethnology *Bulletin* 180 (Washington, D.C., 1961), 87, 96–97; Kilpatrick and Kilpatrick, "Chronicles of Wolftown," 13, 15; John Witthoft, "Observations on Social Change among the Eastern Cherokee," in King, *Cherokee Nation*, 204–5.

45. *Letters from Alleghany Mountains*, 100–103.

46. Russell, "William Holland Thomas," 257; Thomas Diary, Sept. 27, 1849; June 1, Aug. 3, 19–20, 1850, WHTC; Thomas Lenoir to brother, June 24, 1860, Thomas Lenoir Papers, Duke University.

47. Thomas Diary, Sept. 27, 1849; June 1, Aug. 3, 1850, WHTC; Lanman, *Letters from Alleghany Mountains*, 104; Russell, "William Holland Thomas," 314; Mooney, "Myths of the Cherokee," 236.

48. Eighth U.S. Census, 1860, Jackson County, N.C., Population Schedule, M-653, 903/104–30; Schedule 4, "Productions of Agriculture," Jackson County, 33–38, NCDAH.

49. *Letters from Alleghany Mountains*, 95.

NOTES TO CHAPTER 5

1. Russell, "William Holland Thomas," 319–20, 336 (quote), 340, 351.

2. Jarrett to Thomas, July 25, 1861, Thomas Papers, Duke.

3. Edney to Gov. Clark, July 26, 1861, GP 152; A.J. Taylor to [brother], Oct. 13, 1861, GP 155; Jonathan Welch and F.M. Taylor to Gov. Clark, Oct. 17, 1861, GP 155; Thomas to Gov. Clark, Oct. 17, 1861, GP 155; all in NCDAH.

4. Thomas to Mercer Fain, Oct. 17, 1861, WHTC; R.H. Chilton to Thomas, Sept. 19, 1861, in *The War of Rebellion: A Compilation of the Official Records of the Union and Confederate Armies*, 128 vols. (Washington, D.C., 1880–1901), Ser. 1, Vol. LI, Pt. 2, p. 304; hereafter cited as *O.R.*; Russell, "William Holland Thomas," 339–40; Dial and Eliades, *Only Land I Know*, 45–46.

5. Vernon H. Crow, *Storm in the Mountains: Thomas' Confederate Legion of Cherokee Indians and Mountaineers* (Cherokee, N.C., 1982), 2.

6. Jonathan Welch and F.M. Taylor to Gov. Clark, Oct. 17, 1861, GP 155; Thomas to Gov. Clark, Oct. 8, 1861; Mar. 14, Apr. 13, 1862, GP 155, 157–58; Thomas Notebook, Jan. 1862, PC 991.1; all in NCDAH; Thomas to Gov. Zebulon B. Vance, Nov. 22, 1862, in Frontis W. Johnston, ed., *The Papers of Zebulon Baird Vance* (Raleigh, 1963–), I, 386; Russell, "William Holland Thomas," 351–52. One of many letters relating to Unionist sentiment in East Tennessee is N.W. Woodfin to Gov. Clark, Nov. 12, 1861, GP 156, NCDAH; see also Charles Faulkner Bryan, Jr., "The Civil War in East Tennessee: A Social, Political, and Economic Study," (Ph.D. diss., Univ. of Tennessee, 1978).

7. Confederate treaty with Cherokee Nation, Oct. 7, 1861, *O.R.*, Ser. 4, Vol. I, pp. 669–86; Thomas to [?], Apr. 1, 1862, Thomas Papers, Duke; Terrell to Thomas, Apr. 3, 1862; Thomas to Confederate Commissioner of Indian Affairs, Apr. 3, 1862; S.S. Scott to R.W. Johnson, May 1, 1863; all in Terrell Collection, National Anthropological Archives, Smithsonian Institution; act of July 5, 1862, in 12 *U.S. Statutes* 528.

8. Thomas to Gov. Clark, Apr. 13, 1862, GP 158, NCDAH. John W. Moore, *Roster of North Carolina Troops in the War Between the States*, 4 vols. (Raleigh: 1882) IV, 152–54, shows officers and men of both companies were mustered into service on Apr. 9, though most evidence suggests that the second company was organized a bit later. Morgan was the grandson of Gideon Morgan, who led the

Cherokees at the battle of Horseshoe Bend in 1814. The John Ross in North Carolina should not be confused with the much older Principal Chief of the Cherokee Nation.

9. Extract from letter of Apr. 15 from "Gen. Mchaffey" in *Greensborough* [*N.C.*] *Patriot*, May 8, 1862. The general referred to a "victory" at Corinth, Miss., but he obviously meant nearby Shiloh.

10. Mooney, "Myths of the Cherokee," 169–70.

11. Thomas to Gov. Clark, Apr. 17, 1862, GP 158, NCDAH; Russell, "William Holland Thomas," 355–56; James W. Terrell Reminiscences, 2–5, Terrell Papers, WCU. Two years later a newspaper commented on the Cherokees' "high degree of perfection" in drills. Extract from Asheville *News* in Columbus [Ga.] *Daily Enquirer*, May 22, 1864.

12. Russell, "William Holland Thomas," 358–61, citing Knoxville *Daily Register*, May 2, 1862; Terrell Reminiscences, 5–6. Terrell said "Ogonstoka" was Morgan's Indian name, apparently not realizing there had been a more famous personage of that name. James C. Kelley, "Oconostota," *Journal of Cherokee Studies* 3 (Fall 1979): 221–38.

13. Thomas to Clark, May 25, 1862, GP 158, NCDAH; Thomas to wife, June 25, 1862, Thomas Papers, Duke.

14. Thomas to wife, June 25, 1862, Thomas Papers, Duke; Terrell Reminiscences, 8–11, 14–15; Russell, "William Holland Thomas," 364–65; R.A. Aiken, "Eightieth Regiment," in Walter Clark, ed., *Histories of the Several Regiments and Battalions from North Carolina in the Great War 1861–'65*, 5 vols. (Goldsboro, N.C., 1901), IV, 121, said duty in East Tennessee during this period was "tiresome, thankless, disagreeable, galling and verging on the *unmanly*."

15. Terrell Reminiscences, 8, 13, 15–16; Russell, "William Holland Thomas," 364; John G. Barrett, *The Civil War in North Carolina* (Chapel Hill, 1963), 27.

16. Moore, *Roster of North Carolina Troops*, IV, 152–75, 196–216; Terrell Reminiscences; *O.R.*, Ser. 1, Vol. XVI, Pt. 2, p. 879; William W. Stringfield, "Sixty-Ninth Regiment," in Clark, *Histories of the Several Regiments*, III, 729–33; Stringfield handwritten historical account, 105–6, Stringfield Papers, NCDAH; Aiken, "Eightieth Regiment," 117–20, 124; Russell, "William Holland Thomas," 365–67; Mooney, "Myths of the Cherokee," 169. Crow, *Storm in the Mountains*, 145–47, convincingly argues that James Love's regiment, part of the Thomas Legion, was never officially designated the Sixty-Ninth.

17. Stringfield, "Sixty-Ninth Regiment," 733; Aiken, "Eightieth Regiment," 117, 119–20; Barrett, *Civil War in North Carolina*, 197; Thomas to wife, June 4, 1863, Thomas Papers, Duke; Brig-Gen. W.G.M. Davis to Gov. Vance, Jan. [n.d.] 1863, *O.R.*, Ser. 1, Vol. XVIII, pp. 810–11; *ibid.*, Vol. XXIII, Pt. 2, p. 946. Zollicoffer was on the site of present-day Bluff City, Tenn.

18. Abstract from return of District of Western North Carolina, *O.R.*, Ser. 1, Vol. XXXII, Pt. 3, p. 865; Thomas to A.T. Davidson, Jan. 22, 1864, Thomas Papers, Duke; Stringfield, "Sixty-Ninth Regiment," 737–44.

19. Barrett, *Civil War in North Carolina*, ch. 8; William Donaldson Cotton, "Appalachian North Carolina: A Political Study, 1860–1889" (Ph.D. diss. , Univ. of North Carolina, Chapel Hill, 1954), ch. 3.

20. S.S.Scott to R.W. Johnson, May 1, 1863, Terrell Collection, Smithsonian Institution; Thomas to Governor and Council of South Carolina, Feb. 28, 1864, *O.R.*, Ser. 1, Vol. LIII, Supp., pp. 313–14.

21. Palmer to Thomas, Mar. 11, 1864; Thomas to Maj.-Gen. Breckenridge, Apr. 27, 1864, both in Thomas Papers, Duke; Margaret Love to Gov. Vance, May 10, 1864, GP 177, NCDAH. As early as 1863 Thomas employed Mercer Fain to dispose of some of his lands for taxes. Thomas to Fain, June 19, 1863, WHTC.

22. Aiken, "Eightieth Regiment," 126–27.

23. "Sister Mary" to William Stringfield, Nov. 26, 1863; "Sister Mollie" to William Stringfield, Sept. 3, 1863, both in Stringfield Papers, NCDAH; Col. F.W. Graham to Col. Drake, Sept. 8, 1863, *O.R.*, Ser. 1, Vol. XXX, Pt. 3, p. 474. Stringfield was an officer of the Thomas Legion whose home was in Strawberry Plains. For a more caustic assessment of Thomas's fighting spirit, see Gov. Zebulon B. Vance to James A. Seddon, Dec. 13, 1864, *O.R.*, Ser. 1, Vol. XL, Pt. 3, p. 1253.

24. The foregoing is a composite from two accounts: Palmer's report of Dec. 11, 1863, *O.R.*, Ser. 1, Vol. XXXI, Pt. 1, pp. 438–39; and Charles H. Kirk, ed. and comp., *History of the Fifteenth Pennsylvania Volunteer Cavalry* (Philadelphia, 1906), 345–50.

25. Jennings, *Invasion of America*, 58–84.

26. Thomas A.R. Nelson, *Secession; or, Prose in Rhyme; and East Tennessee, A Poem. By an East Tennessean* (Philadelphia, 1864), 56.

27. Robert A. Crawford to Gov. Andrew Johnson, June 11, 1863, Johnson Papers, Library of Congress; Samuel W. Scott and Samuel P. Angel, *History of the Thirteenth Regiment Tennessee Volunteer Cavalry, U.S.A.* (Philadelphia, 1903; reprinted Blountville, Tenn., 1973), 321; Brig.-Gen. Samuel D. Sturgis to Brig.-Gen. E.E. Potter, Feb. 4, 1864, *O.R.*, Ser. 1, Vol. XXXII, Pt. 1, p. 137; New York *Times*, Mar. 15, 1863, p. 8. William Stringfield took particular exception to the way Scott and Angel depicted the Indians. Stringfield, historical account, 73–74.

28. Daniel Ellis, *Thrilling Adventures of Daniel Ellis, the Great Union Guide of East Tennessee . . .* (New York, 1867; rep. Johnson City, Tenn., 1974), 147–48, 426; illustration, p. 406.

29. Stringfield, "North Carolina Cherokee Indians," *North Carolina Booklet* 3 (June 1903): 20–21; Stringfield, "Sixty-Ninth Regiment," 736; Terrell Reminiscences, 7; Aiken, "Eightieth Regiment," 126, supported Stringfield's view of the Indians' behavior, saying they "were never cruel to prisoners or any one else."

30. Russell, "William Holland Thomas," 336, 358–59; Terrell Reminiscences, 6–7; extract from Asheville *News* in Columbus [Ga.] *Daily Enquirer*, May 22, 1864.

31. Extract from Bristol [Tenn.] *Advocate* in Memphis *Daily Appeal*, June 13,

1863; extract from Richmond *Enquirer* of Apr. 8 in Memphis *Daily Appeal*, Apr. 17, 1863.

32. Extract from Knoxville *Register* of Apr. 5 in Memphis *Daily Appeal*, Apr. 11, 1863; Ellis, *Thrilling Adventures*, 148. See also an Indian letter of Aug. 3, 1863, in Jack F. and Anna G. Kilpatrick, trans. and eds., *The Shadow of Sequoyah: Social Documents of the Cherokees, 1862–1964* (Norman, Okla., 1965), 11–12.

33. Barrett, *Civil War in North Carolina*, 197–98; Brig.-Gen. W.G.M. Davis to Gov. Vance, Jan. [n.d.], 1863, *O.R.*, Ser. 1, Vol. XVIII, pp. 810–11. For an excellent analysis of this incident, and the mountain society in which it occurred, see Phillip S. Paludan, *Victims: A True Story of the Civil War* (Knoxville, 1981).

34. Taylor to Lt. Col. William Walker, Nov. 1, 1863, *O.R.*, Ser. 1, Vol. XXXI, Pt. 1, p. 235; Barrett, *Civil War in North Carolina*, 199; [W.H.] Parker to [Thomas], Apr. 17, 1864, Thomas Papers, Duke

35. Mooney, "Myths of the Cherokee," 170.

36. Vance to Thomas, Nov. 4, 1863; Thomas to A.T. Davidson, Jan. 22, 1864, both in Thomas Papers, Duke; W.J. Palmer's report, Jan. 15, 1864, *O.R.*, Ser. 1, Vol. XXXII, Pt. 1, p. 75; Col. John B. Palmer to Col. G.W. Brent, Jan. 19, 1864, *ibid.*, p. 76. Vance's capture led to the court-martial of Thomas and another officer—neither the first nor last such trouble for Thomas.

37. The most complete accounts of this battle are in Washington L. Sanford, *History of the Fourteenth Illinois Cavalry and the Brigades to which it Belonged* (Chicago, 1898), 143–54; *Brownlow's Knoxville Whig and Rebel Ventilator*, Mar. 5, 1864.

38. Sturgis report, Feb. 4, 1864, *O.R.*, Ser. 1, Vol. XXXII, Pt. 1, pp. 137–38; see also Maj. John G. Foster's two reports of Feb. 7 and 21, 1864, *ibid.*, 46, 159.

39. Thomas report, Feb. 28, 1864, *ibid.*, Vol. LIII, Supp., pp. 313–14; John B. Palmer report, *ibid.*, Vol. XXXII, Pt. 2, p. 749; extract from Asheville *News* of Feb. 11 in Greensborough [N.C.] *Patriot*, Feb. 18, 1864. See also Barrett, *Civil War in North Carolina*, 232–33.

40. This same report appeared in a number of newspapers, including ones in Raleigh, Asheville, and Columbus, Ga. (*Daily Enquirer*, May 22, 1864).

41. *Brownlow's Knoxville Whig and Rebel Ventilator*, Mar. 5, 1864; Sanford, *History of Fourteenth Illinois Cavalry*, 155; Nashville *Daily Times and True Union*, Mar. 16, 1864; Mooney, "Myths of the Cherokee," 171.

42. Barrett, *Civil War in North Carolina*, 233–37; affidavit of Raleigh Dick Thomas, June 4, 1881, M-1059, 3/82–84.

43. Jack F. and Anna G. Kilpatrick, "Eastern Cherokee Folktales: Reconstructed from the Field Notes of Frans M. Olbrechts," Bureau of American Ethnology *Bulletin* 196 (Washington, D.C., 1966), No. 80, p. 430, n. 84.

44. Stringfield, "Sixty-Ninth Regiment," 744–56; Mooney, "Myths of the Cherokee," 170; Crow, *Storm in the Mountains*, chs. 7–9.

45. Russell, "William Holland Thomas," 399; Stringfield, "Sixty-Ninth Regiment," 758–59; Stringfield, "North Carolina Cherokee Indians," 14; Barrett, *Civil War in North Carolina*, 350, 364–65; W.C. Allen, *Annals of Haywood County, North Carolina* (n.p., 1935), 44–46, 81–82. Stringfield's accounts give two different dates for the fight at Soco Creek.

46. Russell, "William Holland Thomas," 399 and n. 112; Barrett, *Civil War in North Carolina*, 391–92; Stringfield, "Sixty-Ninth Regiment," 760–61; Stringfield, "North Carolina Cherokee Indians," 21–22; Allen, *Annals of Haywood County*, 83–85; Bartlett's report of May 13, 1865, *O.R.*, Ser. 1, Vol. XLIX, Pt. 2, pp. 754–55; *ibid.*, pp. 669, 710. Crow, *Storm in the Mountains*, 136–37, says the last shots were fired on May 6.

47. *O.R.*, Ser. 1, Vol. XLIX, Pt. 2, pp. 754–55.

48. Mooney, "Myths of the Cherokee," 168–69; Stringfield, "North Carolina Cherokee Indians," 19–20; Stringfield, historical account, 105.

NOTES TO CHAPTER 6

1. James Mooney and Frans M. Olbrechts, "The Swimmer Manuscript: Cherokee Sacred Formulas and Medicinal Prescriptions," Bureau of American Ethnology *Bulletin* 99 (1932), 15, 17, 39.

2. Mooney and Olbrechts, "Swimmer Manuscript," 61, 75–76; Mooney, "Myths of the Cherokee," 172; Y.J. Morris To William Thomas, Nov. 25, 1865, Thomas Papers, Duke; Joseph Keener to W.A. Graham, June 2, 1866, M-234, 100/487. The estimate of 125 deaths was derived from the R.J. Powell Census Roll, 1867, RG 75, National Archives. The Cherokees claimed that "several hundred" had died of smallpox. Quallatown Cherokees to CIA, Aug. 7, 1866, M-234, 100/893–94. The ineffectiveness of Thomas's physician may have contributed to a belief that white doctors intentionally spread disease among Indians. Mooney and Olbrechts, "Swimmer Manuscript," 39.

3. Various scraps of paper for 1866 in the Thomas Papers, Duke, attest to Thomas's supplying corn to the Cherokees during that spring and summer. For commentary on his fluctuating mental state, see Ed Fisher to Mrs. Thomas, Mar. 16, 30, 1867, WHTC; James Terrell to Dr. R.J. Powell, May 13, 1867, Thomas Papers, Duke. For Cherokee disenchantment with Thomas over the war, see John B. Jones to CIA Dennis N. Cooley, Mar. 16, 1866, M-234, 100/515; Gilbert Falls to CIA Lewis V. Bogy, Jan. 22, 1867, M-234, 101/145.

4. John B. Jones to CIA Cooley, Mar. 16, 1866, M-234, 100/513–16; Jones to CIA Francis A. Walker, July 11, 1872, M-234, 105/567–68; George W. Bushyhead to CIA Cooley, Mar. 19, 1866, M-234, 100/233–36; Gilbert Falls to CIA Bogy, Jan. 22, 1867, M-234, 101/145; Bushyhead to [CIA Ely S. Parker], Oct. 19, 1869, M-234, 102/87. See also Zeigler and Grosscup, *The Heart of the Alleghanies*, 35.

5. *Public Laws of the State of North Carolina Passed by the General Assembly at the Session of 1866* (Raleigh, 1866), 120; Worth to General Assembly, Feb. 5, 1866, GLB 53, p. 47, NCDAH.

6. *Public Laws of North Carolina . . . 1866*, 134–36.

7. *Ibid.*, 134–35; covering note for Bushyhead's power of attorney, [n.d., received Mar. 7, 1866], M-234, 100/228; Bushyhead to CIA Cooley, Mar. 19, 1866, M-234, 100/235.

8. Bushyhead to CIA Cooley, Mar. 19, 1866, M-234, 100/233–36; Cooley to Bushyhead, Mar. 21, 1866, M-21, 79/461–62.

9. Jones to CIA Cooley, Mar. 16, 1866, M-234, 100/513–16; Cooley to Jones, Mar. 21, 1866, M-21, 79/460–61; Cooley to Bushyhead, Mar. 21, 1866, M-21, 79/461–62.

10. 14 *U.S. Statutes* 799–809; Cooley to Jones, Mar. 21, 1866, M-21, 79/460–61; Cooley to W.A. Graham, June 30, 1866, M-21, 80/480.

11. Joseph Keener to W.A. Graham, June 2, 1866, M-234, 100/487–88; Cherokee petition to CIA, Aug. 7, 1866, M-234, 100/893–94; Cherokee petition to President, Sept. 12, 1866, M-234, 100/870–71; Gilbert Falls to CIA Bogy, Dec. 11, 1866, M-234, 100/481–82.

12. Bogy to Ross, Jan. 8, 1867, M-21, 82/248; Bogy to Falls, Nov. 24, 1866, M-21, 82/104.

13. W.P. Ross et al. to CIA Bogy, Jan. 27, 1867, M-234, 101/480; CIA Nathaniel G. Taylor to SI Orville H. Browning, Apr. [n.d.] 1867, M-234, 101/203–5; Bushyhead to President, Mar. 15, 1867, M-234, 101/630; R. Fields to Taylor, June 18, 1867, M-234, 101/272–73; Falls to Bogy, Jan. 22, 1867, M-234, 101/144–45; S.H. Nieman to CIA, May 14, 1867, M-234, 101/465; R.J. Powell to SI Hugh McCulloch, Jan. 23, 1867, M-234, 101/1400–1; Taylor to Browning, Apr. [n.d.] 1867, M-234, 101/200–5; Stetson and Swetland to Taylor, Apr. 2, 1867, M-234, 101/636; J. Harland to Cooley, Mar. 30, 1866, M-234, 100/497; Bushyhead telegram, Apr. 9, 1866, M-234, 100/238; Falls to Bogy, Dec. 11, 1866, M-234, 100/481–82.

14. "Constitution of 1868" in William F. Swindler, ed., *Sources and Documents of United States Constitutions*, 10 vols. (Dobbs Ferry, N.Y., 1973–79), VII, 414–30; Art. VI, Sec. 1 for voting rights.

15. Bushyhead et al. to CIA Taylor, June 9, 1868, M-234, 101/810; Joseph Henson to Preston Starrett, May 23, 1868, M-234, 101/1354; appointment of Bushyhead et al. by John W. Taylor et al., Valley Town, May 16, 1868, M-234, 101/814; appointment of Bushyhead et al. by headmen of Sand Town, May 23, 1868, M-234, 101/816; R. McBratney to Taylor, June 26, 1868, M-234, 101/1250; Powell Roll, RG 75.

16. 15 *U.S. Statutes* 228; R.J. Powell to CIA Taylor, Sept. 15, 1868, M-234, 101/1292–95.

17. Silas H. Swetland to CIA Taylor, Jan. 28, Feb. 1, 1868, M-234, 102/893–94, 902; appointments of delegates by Cheoah council, Dec. 15, 1868, M-234, 102/1021–22; approval of act of July 28, M-234, 102/997–98;

Cherokee delegation to W.B. Davis, Mar. 13, 1869, M-234, 102/782; sı Jacob D. Cox to Taylor, Mar. 20, 1869, M-234, 102/466.

18. Bushyhead et al. to cıa Taylor, June 12, 18, 1868, M-234, 101/799–801, 804; R. McBratney to Taylor, June 26, 1868, M-234, 101/1250–51; Pool to Taylor, Mar. 16, 1869, M-234, 102/758; Jackson Rogers to P.M.B. Young, Mar. 26, 1869, M-234, 102/1291–92; Lewis Downing et al. to Taylor, Mar. 12, 1869, M-234, 102/784; Downing et al. to sı, Mar. 19, 1869, M-234, 102/251; Acting cıa Charles E. Mix to Charles F. Lott, Sept. 7, 1868, M-21, 87/441; Taylor to Pool, Mar. 17, 1869, M-21, 89/338–39. For full discussion of the 1868 unratified treaty see Royce, "The Cherokee Nation of Indians," 351–56.

19. James Taylor to cıa Taylor, Nov. 7, 1868, M-234, 101/1417; petition to Pres. Johnson, Nov. 16, 1868, M-234, 101/924; cıa Taylor to James Taylor, Nov. 7, 1868, M-21, 88/246.

20. Various documents, resolutions, etc., pertaining to Cheoah council of Dec. 1868, in M-234, 102/900, 992–1031. The council justified revoking the previous powers of attorney by alluding to the war, "the changes of our relations to the Government, and the changed conditions and characters of man"—the latter an apparent reference to Thomas's mental illness. There had been an informal council at Cheoah as recently as the previous September.

21. M-234, 102/993–95; Bushyhead to cıa, Jan. 22, Feb. 8, 1868, M-234, 101/754, 763–64; R. McBratney to cıa Taylor, June 28, 1868, M-234, 101/1248–49; W.C. McCarthy to cıa E.P. Smith, Oct. 19, 1875, M-234, 109/1249.

22. References to DeWeese's and Swetland's earlier association with the Cherokees are in M-234, 101/967–71. Bushyhead to cıa, Jan. 22, Feb. 10, June 10, 1868, M-234, 101/754, 773, 813; James Taylor to cıa Taylor, July 28, 1868, M-234, 101/1389; A.H. Jones to cıa Taylor, July 11, 1868, M-234, 101/1147; John Owl et al. to [cıa] July [n.d.] 1868, M-234, 101/875; Powell to Assistant Sec. Treasury W.E. Chandler, Mar. 1, 1867, M-234, 101/1403–05. Later, Powell referred to Bushyhead, Swetland, and others as "swindlers." Powell to sı Browning, Aug. 17, 1868, M-234, 101/1285. Browning to cıa Taylor, Aug. 17, 19, 1868, M-234, 101/1157–58, 1161–62; testimony of Joseph Abbott in William S. Ball to cıa Smith, June 25, 1875, M-234, 108/283; cıa Taylor to Swetland, Nov. 10, 1868, M-21, 88/249–51.

23. The full scope of Swetland's machinations was not revealed until several years later. The following account of his activities—and those of his associates—is a composite pieced together from correspondence, testimony in court, and the reports of various investigative bodies. My interpretation is that of the Indian plaintiffs, rather than the accused, but it is a view that was sufficiently convincing for a jury to convict those involved in the schemes. A detailed discussion of the two contracts given Swetland is in the report of a special committee: Report of William Stickney et al., July [n.d.] 1875, M-234, 109/1733–42. See also deposition of William Matoy, Oct. 6, 1869, M-234, 102/165–66; Swetland to cıa Taylor, Jan. 12, 23, 1869, M-234, 102/869,

882–84. For James Blunt's story of the contracts, see Blunt to CIA Smith, Jan. 14, 1875, M-234, 108/82–87.

24. Petition of Cheoah council, Jan. 18–19, 1869, M-234, 102/1252–53, 1249–50; Swetland to CIA Taylor, Mar. 29, Apr. 7, 1869, M-234, 102/965–72, 956–63; Henry Smith to William H. Thomas, Mar. 9, 1869, Thomas Papers, Duke. Swetland's census roll is in RG 75, National Archives. An example of a number of alleged Cherokees being left off Swetland's rolls is in Tobitha Longwith to SI, Aug. 5, 1873, M-234, 106/731.

25. SI Browning to CIA Taylor, Mar. 3, 1869, M-234, 102/464; CIA Ely S. Parker to Swetland, June 9, 1869, M-234, 102/508–12. Testimony of Hugh Lambert in William S. Ball to CIA Smith, June 25, 1875, M-234, 108/280–81; Report of Stickney et al., July [n.d.] 1875, M-234, 109/1735–42; *Petition of Robert Tramper . . .* (Washington, D.C., 1876), in M-234, 111/557–59; receipt for $12,135 received by Blunt, Apr. 13, 1869, M-234, 107/824. For Blunt's version, see Blunt to CIA Smith, Jan. 14, 1875, M-234, 108/82–118. *Dictionary of American Biography* (New York, 1929), II, 399–400. Blunt did in fact perform some legal work for the Eastern Band after early 1869.

26. Swetland to CIA Parker, June 22, 30, July 2, 9, 16, 23, Aug. 9, 26, 1869, M-234, 102/1065–68, 1071, 1073–76, 1078, 1080, 1087–89, 1092, 1097–99; Sec. War to SI, June 25, 1869, M-234, 102/1263; Adj. General E.D. Townsend to SI Cox, July 3, 1869, M-234, 102/10. Despite the extortion, Bushyhead and his associates at first had praise for the disbursements of Swetland and Jocknick. Cheoah council to CIA, Aug. 20, 23, 1869, M-234, 102/71, 72–73. An indication of how their view changed is in their petition to President, Nov. 11, 1870, M-234, 103/605–6; deposition of William Matoy, Oct. 6, 1869, M-234, 102/165–66; testimony of Hugh Lambert, James Blythe, Robert Tramper, Robert Powell, John Roland, and James Terrell in William Ball to CIA Smith, June 25, 1875, M-234, 108/281–86. See also memoranda and minutes of testimony, M-234, 108/233–78.

27. Swetland to CIA Parker, Aug. 26, Nov. 20, 1869, M-234, 102/1097–99, 1121–42; *Petition of Robert Tramper . . .*, M-234, 111/557–59; complaint of Cherokee council to SI, Oct. 4, 1869, M-234, 102/169–71; testimony of James Terrell in William Ball to CIA Smith, June 25, 1875, M-234, 108/284–86; James Taylor to SI Chandler, Nov. 15, 26, 1875, M-234, 109/2172–73, 2187–90; Parker to Swetland, Jan. 25, 1870, M-21, 93/375; undated memorandum regarding Swetland at Murphy, 1869 folder, James Taylor Papers, Duke University.

28. Cherokee council to SI, Oct. 4, 1869, M-234, 102/169–71; SI Cox to A.S. Corpening, Sept. 1, 1869, M-234, 102/1295–97; Swetland to CIA, Feb. 11, 1870, M-234, 103/1088–1115; testimony of James Terrell in William Ball to CIA Smith, June 25, 1875, M-234, 108/286; Blunt to CIA Smith, Apr. 22, 1875, M-234, 108/172–73. For Swetland's troubles determining heirship, see his letter to CIA Parker, Nov. 20, 1869, in *House Ex. Doc.* 1 (Serial 1414), 896.

29. Johnston discussed various aspects of Thomas's indebtedness in a letter to him of Apr. 8, 1868, Terrell Papers, WCU. One of his concerns was that a *"Negroe & Radical Legislature"* might pass a relief or stay measure adversely affecting his rights. James Terrell discussed the land transactions in his letter to G.F. Jocknick, Jan. 16, 1870, M-234, 103/734–37. See also Joseph Henson to Preston Starrett, May 23, 1868, M-234, 101/1353–54; Terrell to CIA Parker, June 11, 1870, M-234, 103/1182–84; and agreement of William Johnston with Cherokees [Sept. 29, 1869], Taylor Papers.

30. Memorandum of [N.C.] Senate Judiciary Committee [tentatively and erroneously dated July 27, 1868], Taylor Papers. Some Indians believed from the outset that the 1868 constitution did not confer citizenship. Joseph Henson to Preston Starrett, May 23, 1868, M-234, 101/1353–54. Congressman A.H. Jones wrote James Terrell on Jan. 19, 1870, that the secretary of interior was advocating a congressional measure that would allow authorities to bring such a suit in behalf of the Eastern Cherokees. Jones was of the opinion "that much trouble is in store for Mr. Thomas and Mr. Johnson [*sic*]." Terrell Papers, WCU. Gov. Holden said that "the general understanding in the state" was that the Cherokees were citizens—though he admitted there had been no judicial decision on the matter. Holden opinion, Mar. 1, 1871, M-234, 104/1359–60.

31. Lewis Downing et al. to CIA Parker, Apr. 27, June 1, 1869, M-234, 102/283–88, 294–300; Maj. John N. Craig to CIA, Oct. 30, 1869, M-234, 102/186–91; W. Byers to CIA Taylor, Apr. 12, 1867, M-234, 101/86, reported the arrival in the Nation of 70 North Carolina Indians. See also Wardell, *Political History of the Cherokee Nation*, 242–43.

32. Thomas to chiefs of North Carolina Cherokees, Mar. 31, 1870, WHTC.

33. James Terrell to CIA Parker, June 11, 1870, M-234, 103/1183–84; Terrell to Jocknick, Jan. 21, 1870, M-234, 103/741; James Taylor to CIA Parker, Sept. 21, 1869, M-234, 102/1193–1203; James Lovingood et al. to Parker, Sept. 13, 1869, M-234, 102/12; Cheoah council to CIA, Oct. 7, 1869, M-234, 102/167–68; Macon County council to Parker, Nov. 22, 1869, M-234, 102/1287–89; Bushyhead et al. to Parker, Feb. 9, 22, 1870, M-234, 103/127–28, 136–38; Downing to Parker, Feb. 21, 1870, M-234, 103/526–27; W.P. Adair to CIA, Aug. 15, 1870, M-234, 103/19–23.

34. Bushyhead to CIA Cooley, Mar. 19, 1866, M-234, 100/236; Stetson and Swetland to SI Browning, Mar. 19, 1867, M-234, 101/628–30; Bushyhead et al. to CIA Parker, Feb. 9, 1870, M-234, 103/104. But a Cherokee council of Mar. 24, 1870, refers to him merely as "chief" (M-234, 103/991–95). Black Fox (Enola) et al. to CIA and U.S. Senate, Mar. 7, 1870, M-234, 103/147–48; instructions of Sand Town council to Bushyhead, May 27, 1870, M-234, 103/172–74.

35. 16 *U.S. Statutes* 362. Taylor gave a detailed account of his frustrations in initiating and prosecuting the suits in his report to SI Chandler, Nov. 26, 1875, M-234, 109/2187–2247.

36. John Ross to CIA Edward P. Smith, Oct. 19, 1875, M-234, 109/1218;

minutes of Cheoah council, Nov. 7, 1870, M-234, 103/595–96; preamble and resolutions of council, Nov. 7, 1870, M-234, 103/598–602; Ross and council to President, Nov. 11, 16, 1870, M-234, 103/604–8, 610–21, 592–94.

37. David Owl et al. to SI and CIA, Nov. 12, 1870, M-234, 103/988–89; Flying Squirrel to SI, Nov. 12, 1870, M-234, 103/1169–70; framework of government, Nov. 28, 1870, M-234, 104/1421–36; appointment of delegates, Dec. 6, 1870, M-234, 104/1418–19; actions of Grand Council, Jan. 16–Feb. 1, 1871, M-234, 104/1437–42.

38. Lloyd Welch et al. to CIA Parker, Feb. 20, Mar. 2, 1871, M-234, 104/1415–17, 1445–47; John Jackson et al. to William Johnston, Feb. 14, 1870, Terrell Papers, WCU. The actions of Ross and Taylor in regard to emigration and prosecution of defrauders will be covered more completely in the following pages.

39. Obadiah to Downing et al., Apr. 6, 1871, M-234, 104/369–70; John Waner et al. to Cherokee delegation, Apr. 12, 1871, M-234, 104/363–64; Downing et al. to CIA Parker, April 11, 17, 1871, M-234, 104/355–68, 371–78, 383; Brig. Gen. Alfred H. Terry to Adjutant General and response, Apr. 22, 1871, M-234, 104/49–50; Acting SI Walter H. Smith to CIA, May 17, 1871, M-234, 104/796–801; W.P. Adair and C.N. Vann to CIA, May 25, 1871, M-234, 104/70–72; Jones to Parker, June 30, 1871, M-234, 104/849–52. John Ross to SI, Apr. 15, 1871, said they left North Carolina because of a poll tax and a fraudulent contract exacted from them—less convincing reasons than the land problems. M-234, 104/1261–62.

40. Acting SI Bowen to CIA, Sept. 22, 1871, M-234, 104/984–86; SI Columbus Delano, "To the Chiefs . . . of Eastern Cherokees," Sept. 27, 1871, M-234, 109/1861–62. For Indian reform during the period see Loring Benson Priest, *Uncle Sam's Stepchildren: The Reformation of United States Indian Policy, 1865–1887* (Lincoln, Neb., 1975); Robert W. Mardock, *The Reformers and the American Indians* (Columbia, Mo., 1971); Francis Paul Prucha, *American Indian Policy in Crisis: Christian Reformers and the Indian, 1865–1900* (Norman, Okla., 1976).

41. Lang to Ross, Sept. 6, 1871, M-234, 109/1778–80; Ross to CIA E.P. Smith, Oct. 19, 1875, M-234, 109/1218–19; Flying Squirrel to CIA Walker [n.d., received Apr. 8] 1872, M-234, 105/147–51; Flying Squirrel to CIA, Oct. 12, 1874, M-234, 107/856. Francis A. Dony also disputed Ross's right to be Principal Chief. Dony to CIA, Nov. 17, 1874, M-234, 107/135.

42. SI Delano, "To the Chiefs . . . of Eastern Cherokees," Sept. 27, 1871, M-234, 109/1861; A.A. Barnes to Lang, Oct. 2, 1871, M-234, 104/1020–21; Cox to Delano, Oct. 3, 1871, M-234, 104/303; enrollment of Cherokees to be removed, Oct. 2, 1871, M-234, 104/1023–27; Delano to Acting CIA Clum, Nov. 2, 1871, M-234, 104/1008–11; Q.A. Tipton to Sec. War, Nov. 24, 1871, M-234, 104/1388–90; John Ross to Clum, Nov. 21, 1871, M-234, 104/1280. Throughout the 1870s and well into the 1880s, the Indian Office received complaints from former North Carolina Cherokees who had moved to Indian Territory.

43. Tipton to SI, Nov. 11, 14, 21, Dec. 8, 16, 23, 1871; Jan. 1, 8, 14, Feb. 11,

Mar. 16, July 13, Sept. 25, Oct. 14, 19, 1872, M-234, 104/1378, 1380, 1382, 1384, 1392, 1386; 105/980, 984, 982, 990, 1000–1001, 1010, 1012, 124–125, 1017; Tipton to Sec. War, Nov. 24, 1871, M-234, 104/1388–90; account of Tipton, M-234, 105/1003. J.M. Alexander, of Knoxville, claimed the Cherokees had appointed him emigration agent, and that Lang had erred in recognizing Tipton. Alexander to Horace Maynard, Nov. 21, 1871, M-234, 104/1207–8.

44. John Ross to W.P. Adair et al., June 4, 1872, M-234, 105/46; resolutions of Cherokee council, June 3, 1872, M-234, 105/43–45. Just a month later one of the delegates said the North Carolina Indians were making unfair demands on the Cherokee Nation. W.P. Adair to CIA Walker, July 12, 1872, M-234, 105/41–42. Though no longer a delegate, Bushyhead frequently visited Washington after 1872 to prosecute his family claims.

45. Resolution appointing Taylor, Oct. 8, 1872, M-234, 106/211–16; resolution authorizing Ross to employ attorney, Oct. 9, 1872, M-234, 107/746–49; Taylor to SI Chandler, Nov. 26, 1875, M-234, 109/2199–2200; U.S. Lusk to [?], Jan. 20, 1873, M-234, 107/802–3; Marcus Erwin to SI Delano, Feb. 11, 17, 26, 1873, M-234, 106/103–5, 107–8, 110–11; Erwin to CIA Smith, Jan. 25, 1875, M-234, 108/389–90; Delano to Acting CIA Clum, Mar. 13, 1873, M-234, 106/231–32; W.C. McCarthy to Smith, Oct. 19, 1875, M-234, 109/1252–53; Cotton, "Appalachian North Carolina," 226–27.

46. Blunt's legal defense, bitter invective, and accounts of his work for the Indians are in Blunt to CIA Smith, Jan. 14, Apr. 22, 1875, M-234, 108/81–119, 148–97 (quotation regarding Ross, 153). But he sarcastically refused to make under oath the same charges contained in these letters. Blunt to Smith, June 14, 1875, M-234, 108/206–16. See also indictment for perjury, May term, 1874, M-234, 107/827–40; William S. Ball to Smith, June 25, 1875, M-234, 108/288–89; Marcus Erwin to SI Delano, Oct. 28, 1874, M-234, 107/495–96; Erwin to Smith, Jan. 25, 1875, M-234, 108/389–94. G.F. Jocknick was also tried in North Carolina but was acquitted in 1873. Comptroller R.W. Taylor to Delano, July 17, 1873, M-234, 106/504–5.

47. SI Delano to CIA E.P. Smith, May 8, 13, June 5, 1875, M-234, 108/588–90, 595, 647–48; Blunt to Smith, June 14, Nov. 23, 1875, M-234, 108/206–16, 319–48; private memorandum [n.d., no name], regarding Blunt's fellow conspirators in government, M-234, 107/847; Taylor to SI Chandler, Nov. 26, 1875, M-234, 109/2187–2201; *Dictionary of American Biography*, II, 399–400. The three committee members were William Stickney, Henry Beard, and William C. McCarthy.

48. CIA E.P. Smith to SI, Dec. 16, 1874, in *House Ex. Doc.*, 43 Cong., 2 Sess., No. 51 (Serial 1645, Washington, D.C., 1875), 1–2; hereafter cited as *House Ex. Doc.* 51 (Serial 1645). The most complete documentation on the Cherokee lawsuit and the lands in question is in *House Ex. Doc.*, 47 Cong., 1 Sess., No. 196 (Serial 2031, Washington, D.C., 1882); hereafter cited as *House Ex. Doc.* 196 (Serial 2031).

49. James Terrell to C.M. McLoud, Jan. 4, 1878; [William Johnston?] to

Terrell, July 12, 1873, both in Terrell Papers, WCU; CIA E.P. Smith to SI, Dec. 16, 1874; Report of Arbitrators, Oct. 23, 1874, both in *House Ex. Doc.* 51 (Serial 1645), 2, 10; SI Delano to Acting CIA Clum, Apr. 30, 1873, M-234, 106/349–51.

50. CIA E.P. Smith to SI, Dec. 16, 1874; agreement to submit to arbitration, May term, 1874; Rufus Barringer to Hon. R.P. Dick, Oct. 24, 1874, all in *House Ex. Doc.* 51 (Serial 1645), 2, 5, 10–11. Valuable evidence and testimony, dated Aug. 1873, is in M-234, 109/1901–34.

51. Terrell to C.M. McLoud, Jan. 4, 1878, Terrell Papers, WCU; Francis A. Dony, "Narrative" [n.d., but late summer 1874], M-234, 107/quotation, 635; 636–37; Russell, "William Holland Thomas," 420–22.

52. Report of Arbitrators, Oct. 23, 1874, *House Ex. Doc.* 51 (Serial 1645), 6–10. The estimates of the acreage within Qualla Boundary varied considerably prior to the Temple survey of 1875. Even afterward there was disagreement, depending on whether one included certain tracts that were disputed by white claimants. See M.S. Temple to CIA E.P. Smith, Nov. 6, 1875, M-234, 109/2167–69.

53. Report of Arbitrators, Oct. 23, 1874, *House Ex. Doc.* 51 (Serial 1645); Royce, "The Cherokee Nation of Indians," n. 3 (pp. 316–18).

54. Royce, "The Cherokee Nation of Indians," n. 3 (pp. 316–18); W.C. McCarthy to [?], May 20, 1875, M-234, 109/2426–36; report of Terrell and Johnston, Nov. 15, 1875, M-234, 110/532–35; contract of Nov. 18, 1874, M-234, 110/525–28; Terrell to CIA Smith, Apr. 27, 1875, M-234, 109/1998–2010; Terrell to Thomas, Dec. 22, 1874, WHTC.

55. Resolutions of Cherokee council, Nov. 16, 1874, M-234, 107/933–40. Francis Dony was not pleased by the arbitrators' decision, believing that it did not really benefit the Indians; he thought his own descriptions of the Indians' boundaries were more exact. Dony to [CIA], Nov. 9, 1874, M-234, 107/149–50; Dony to Rufus Barringer, Nov. 18, 1874, M-234, 107/140–45.

56. Resolutions of Cherokee council, Nov. 16, 1874, M-234, 107/939; Wallace W. Rollins and Otis F. Presbrey to CIA Smith, Dec. 14, 1874, M-234, 107/809–10. The strongest case for using the 1848 money this way—and for other purposes—was in a plea of Terrell and Taylor to Smith, Dec. 24, 1874, M-234, 107/944–50. But Smith had already accepted their views, as shown in the draft of a proposed bill submitted with his letter to SI, Dec. 16, 1874, *House Ex. Doc.* 51 (Serial 1645), 4.

57. Act of June 23, 1874, in 18 *U.S. Statutes* 213; Commissioner of General Land Office S.S. Burdett to CIA Smith, July 8, 1874, M-234, 107/542–43; Burdett to F.A. Dony, July 31, 1874, M-234, 107/562–67; Dony, "Narrative," M-234, 107/591–656 (quotation, 638). Dony quickly came to view himself as an expert on Cherokee matters. See also Dony, "Report of Francis A. Dony . . ." to Commissioner General Land Office, Oct. 29, 1874, M-234, 107/568–86; Dony to [CIA], Nov. 9, 17, 1874, M-234, 107/149–50, 133–37.

58. 18 *U.S. Statutes* 447; William Johnston to CIA, Apr. 4, 1875, M-234,

108/552–53; assignment of judgments, Apr. 19, 1875, M-234, 109/1883; SI Delano to CIA E.P. Smith, June 3, 9, 1875, M-234, 108/626–27, 660–63; M.S. Temple to Smith, Nov. 6, 1875, M-234, 109/2167–69. Maps of Temple's surveys are included in *House Ex. Doc.* 196 (Serial 2031).

59. Act of Aug. 14, 1876, in 19 *U.S. Statutes* 139; Cherokee County Deed Book R. 1880–82, pp. 28–60, NCDAH; Lloyd R. Welch to CIA J.Q. Smith, Sept. 2, 1876, M-234, 110/959–62.

60. Joseph Shoards to CIA E.P. Smith, Feb. 6, 1875, M-234, 109/1634; Smith to SI, Feb. 13, 1875, M-234, 108/517–19; Smith to W.C. McCarthy, Feb. 22, 1875, M-234, 109/1878–81; Samuel W. Davidson to Smith, Mar. 30, 1875, M-234, 108/379–80; Charles F. Coffin to Smith, Apr. 13, 1875, M-234, 108/354–55; William Nicholson to Smith, Apr. 13, 1875, M-234, 109/1408, 1412; Coffin to Nicholson, Apr. 13, 1875, M-234, 109/1409–10; SI Delano to Acting CIA, May 5, 1875, M-234, 108/579.

NOTES TO CHAPTER 7

1. McCarthy described his services in his letter to CIA J.Q. Smith, Feb. 12, 1876, M-234, 110/321–42.

2. McCarthy to CIA J.Q. Smith, Jan. 22, Feb. 12, 1876, M-234, 110/252–53, 341.

3. Resolution of Cheoah council, Jan. 15, 1869, M-234, 102/1020; Swetland to CIA E.S. Parker, Aug. 26, Nov. 20, 1869, M-234, 102/1097–99, 1135; Bushyhead to CIA Parker, Oct. 19, 1869, M-234, 102/87 (quote).

4. McCarthy to CIA J.Q. Smith, Apr. 17, 1876, M-234, 110/374–78 (quote on 374). McCarthy also asked whether the Qualla Boundary came under federal laws applying to liquor sales to Indians. William Stickney did not believe liquor was a problem, but most evidence strongly suggests otherwise. Stickney report, July 31, 1875, M-234, 109/1661.

5. Report of William Stickney, July 31, 1875, M-234, 109/1655-68; George Bushyhead to CIA Dennis N. Cooley, Mar. 19, 1866, M-234, 100/234; Davis, "Qualla," 583.

6. Stickney report, July 31, 1875, M-234, 109/1655–68 (quote on 1658); McCarthy to CIA J.Q. Smith, Feb. 10, 1876, M-234, 110/285–87; Paul Brodie and James Stevenson to CIA E.P. Smith, Nov. 12, 1875, *House Ex. Doc.*, 53 Cong., 2 Sess., No. 128 (Serial 3326, Washington, D.C., 1895), 42–43; hereafter cited as *House Ex. Doc.* 128 (Serial 3326). See also Witthoft, "Observations on Social Change among the Eastern Cherokees," 202–3, 207. Special Agent John A. Sibbald and Inspector E.C. Watkins were not so pessimistic about Cherokee agriculture. Sibbald to CIA R.E. Trowbridge, Aug. 16, 1880, M-234, 112/850–51; Watkins to CIA J.Q. Smith, Dec. 18, 1875, M-234, 109/2416–17.

7. Recapitulation of Swetland Census, 1869, RG 75, National Archives. I have decided to rely on Swetland's detailed figures rather than on the federal census of 1870. See also Stickney report, July 31, 1875, M-234, 109/1665, 1667.

8. Swetland Census, 1869, RG 75; Stickney report, July 31, 1875, M-234, 109/1659, 1661; McCarthy to CIA J.W. Smith, Feb. 12, 1876, M-234, 110/ 331–32; Davis, "Qualla," 577, 581; Witthoft, "Observations on Social Change among the Eastern Cherokee," 203.

9. McCarthy to CIA E.P. Smith, Oct. 21, 1875, M-234, 109/1186; Stickney report, July 31, 1875, M-234, 109/1663–64; resolution of Cheoah council, July 15, 1875, M-234, 109/1690; Stickney to CIA E.P. Smith, Aug. 4, 1875, M-234, 109/1653–54; McCarthy to CIA J.Q. Smith, Feb. 10, 1876, M-234, 110/284–85. See also N.W. Woodfin to James Taylor, Nov. 23, 1874, M-234, 107/953–57.

10. Act of Mar. 3, 1875, in 18 *U.S. Statutes* 447; SI C. Delano to CIA E.P. Smith, Apr. 23, 1875, M-234, 108/570–71; Acting SI to CIA, Sept. 18, 1875, M-234, 108/781; SI Z. Chandler to CIA J.Q. Smith, Jan. 14, 1876, M-234, 110/143–45; McCarthy to CIA J.Q. Smith, Feb. 12, 1876, M-234, 110/324.

11. CIA E.P. Smith to McCarthy, Feb. 22, 1875, M-234, 109/1878–81 (quote on 1881); McCarthy to CIA J.Q. Smith, Feb. 12, 17, 1876, M-234, 110/324, 311; John A. Sibbald to CIA Trowbridge, July 31, 1880, M-234, 112/504–9. See also recommendation of Wallace W. Rollins to CIA E.P. Smith, Sept. 18, 1875, M-234, 109/1593–95. For discussion of the allotment policy see Prucha, *American Indian Policy in Crisis*, ch. 8; Mardock, *The Reformers and the American Indian*, 211–22.

12. McCarthy to CIA E.P. Smith, Nov. 4, Dec. 18, 1875, M-234, 109/ 1263–64, 1298–1301; McCarthy to CIA J.Q. Smith, Feb. 17, 1876, M-234, 110/311–17; Lloyd Welch and James Taylor to CIA J.Q. Smith, Mar. 24, 1876, M-234, 110/877–78, 880; John A. Sibbald to CIA Trowbridge, July 31, 1880, M-234, 112/504–9.

13. John Ross to President Grant, Nov. 16, 1870, M-234, 103/592; Ross to SI, Apr. 15, 1871, M-234, 104/1261–62; Ross et al. to SI C. Schurz, Oct. 1, 1877, and Mar. 11, 1878, M-234, 111/213, 222; Attorney General T.F. Kenan to John H. DeVaughan, Jan. 22, 1878, M-234, 111/82 (quote); Daniel Dorchester report to CIA Thomas J. Morgan, Mar. 13, 1891, p. 8, RG 75, LR.

14. John Ross et al. to SI Schurz, Mar. 11, 1878, M-234, 111/222–25. Inspector E.C. Watkins to CIA J.Q. Smith, Dec. 18, 1875, M-234, 109/2417, claimed they were citizens of North Carolina. But John DeVaughan said this was "news" to the Indians, "and they would like to know how and when it occurred." DeVaughan to CIA J.Q. Smith, Sept. 28, 1876, M-234, 110/89–90. See also Frizzell, "Legal Status of the Eastern Band of Cherokee Indians," ch. 2.

15. George Bushyhead to CIA, Oct. 19, 1869, M-234, 102/87; Davis, "Qualla," 584–85.

16. Swetland Census, 1869, RG 75. Swetland indicated whether a person

could read and write, without specifying the language. But individuals like Enola, who could read and write only in Cherokee, were recorded as being literate. Swetland listed 683 North Carolina Cherokees as literate out of 1,642—about 42%.

17. CIA E.P. Smith to SI Delano, Sept. 8, 1875, M-234, 109/1589–91; John Ross to SI Delano, Aug. 25, 1875, M-234, 109/1579–81; Ross to James Taylor, Sept. 6, 10, 12, 18, 1875, M-234, 109/2128–30, 2148–49, 2146–47, 2143–45; McCarthy to CIA J.Q. Smith, Feb. 10, 1876, M-234, 110/273–76.

18. McCarthy to CIA E.P. Smith, Oct. 21, 1875, M-234, 109/1224; McCarthy to CIA J.Q. Smith, Dec. 18, 1875, M-234, 109/1296; McCarthy to CIA J.Q. Smith, Feb. 10, Apr. 17, June 5, 1876, M-234, 110/289–95, 369–72, 420. A few students also boarded while attending the Echota Mission School.

19. McCarthy to CIA J.Q. Smith, Jan. 21, 1876, M-234, 110/239–41 (quote on 239).

20. McCarthy to CIA E.P. Smith, Oct. 19, 1875, M-234, 109/1249–55, 1167–77; Watkins to CIA J.Q. Smith, Dec. 18, 1875, M-234, 109/2418–25; Paul Stuart, *The Indian Office: Growth and Development of an American Institution, 1865–1900* (Ann Arbor, 1979), 28, 80–118.

21. McCarthy to CIA J.Q. Smith, Apr. 17, 1876, M-234, 110/375 (quote). T.F. Donaldson called Ross "an ignorant drunken Indian" who was Taylor's pawn. Donaldson to SI Schurz, Mar. 15, 1878, M-234, 111/90. Resolutions of Cheoah council, Mar. 27, 1876, M-234, 110/614–15. McCarthy said Ross held a "quasi chieftainship." McCarthy to CIA E.P. Smith, Oct. 21, 1875, M-234, 109/1216.

22. Watkins to CIA J.Q. Smith, Dec. 18, 1875, M-234, 109/2416–18; SI Chandler to CIA J.Q. Smith, Jan. 6, 28, 1876, M-234, 110/135–36, 155; Frizzell, "Legal Status of the Eastern Band of Cherokee Indians," 45–46; Bridgers, "Historical Analysis of the Legal Status of the North Carolina Cherokees," 1092.

23. McCarthy to CIA J.Q. Smith, Feb. 12, 1876, M-234, 110/321–42 (quote on 329).

24. CIA J.Q. Smith to SI, Mar. 3, 1876, M-234, 110/344–45 (quote on 345); SI Chandler to CIA J.Q. Smith, Mar. 6, 1876, M-234, 110/161; McCarthy to CIA J.Q. Smith, Mar. 23, 1876, M-234, 110/358–59.

25. McCarthy to CIA J.Q. Smith, June 5, 1876, M-234, 110/420–24. The monthly reports for the five schools are in M-234, 110/426–74. See also "Report of the condition of Cheoah Indian School," Mar. 24, 1876, M-234, 110/627–30.

26. 19 *U.S. Statutes* 176, 197–98; Welch to CIA J.Q. Smith, Aug. 21, 1876, M-234, 110/916. For an example of the attacks on McCarthy see Robert Tramper and James Taylor to SI Chandler, Apr. 17, 1876, M-234, 110/689–91.

27. Robert Tramper and James Taylor to SI Chandler, Apr. 17, Sept. 15, 21, 1876, M-234, 110/689–91, 995–97, 749–51; Lloyd Welch to SI, Mar. 6, 1878, M-234, 111/348; Second Auditor E.B. French to CIA, June 21, 1879, M-234,

111/398–400; McCarthy to CIA, Nov. 2, 1878, M-234, 111/195–99; Henry Beard to E.B. French, Apr. 17, 1880, M-234, 112/96–101; John Sibbald to CIA Trowbridge, July 31, 1880, M-234, 112/504–6.

28. Act of Mar. 3, 1877, in 19 *U.S. Statutes* 282, 291; J.D. Garner to CIA E.A. Hayt, Sept. 8, 1878, M-234, 111/118–20; SI Schurz to CIA, July 15, 1879, M-234, 111/498. For the confused state of school matters see John Ross et al. to SI Schurz, Mar. 11, 1878, M-234, 111/222–25.

29. John H. DeVaughan to E.M. Marble, Jan. 8, June 7, 18, 1878, M-234, 111/161–64, 139, 140–42; DeVaughan to C.W. Holcomb, Feb. 13, 1878, M-234, 111/84–87; J.D. Garner to CIA Hayt, Feb. 28, 1878, M-234, 111/95–96. See also Kate DeVaughan to Acting CIA Marble Sept. 20, 1880, M-234, 112/188–90; act of Cheoah council, Oct. 3, 1877, M-234, 111/355–56.

30. Garner described some of the problems of his job to CIA Hayt, June 6, 1878, M-234, 111/105–9. See also SI Schurz to CIA, July 15, 1879, M-234, 111/498; D. Atkins to R.B. Vance, July 25, 1879, M-234, 111/670–72. The schools were closed, according to one official, because "the meager results hardly warranted the expenditure." Acting CIA Brooks to John Sibbald, Aug. 3, 1880, M-234, 112/825.

31. Garner to CIA Hayt, June 6, 1878, M-234, 111/101, 109. For insight into Pratt and the institution he created, see Richard Henry Pratt, *Battlefield and Classroom: Four Decades with the American Indian, 1867–1904*, ed. and introduction by Robert M. Utley (New Haven, 1964).

32. A.J. McAlpine to R.B. Vance, Dec. 9, 1879, M-234, 112/902–4; J.A. Branner and James Atkins to CIA, Dec. 19, 1879, M-234, 111/415–16; Atkins to CIA Trowbridge, Apr. 24, 1880, M-234, 112/27–30. North Georgia Agricultural College also solicited Cherokee students. W.P. Price to SI Schurz, July 30, 1880, M-234, 112/241–42.

33. McAlpine to CIA Hayt, quoting latter, Jan. 6, 1880, M-234, 111/287–88 (quote on 287).

34. Sibbald to Acting CIA Brooks, Mar. 13, 1880, M-234, 112/374–75; Sibbald to CIA Trowbridge, Apr. 15, 1880, M-234, 112/392–400; A.J. McAlpine to CIA Trowbridge, Apr. 20, 1880, M-234, 112/301–3.

35. Braxton Craven to SI Schurz, June 29, 1880, M-234, 112/156–58; Acting CIA Brooks to Sibbald, Aug. 3, 1880, M-234, 112/822–25; Craven to Acting CIA Brooks, Aug. 9, 23, 1880, M-234, 112/160, 162; Sibbald to CIA Trowbridge, Aug. 14, 1880, M-234, 112/495–99; Fardon to Acting CIA Marble, Oct. 2, 1880, M-234, 112/224–26.

36. Fardon to Acting CIA Marble, Oct. 2, 1880, M-234, 112/228–30.

37. July 1880 report of A.J. McAlpine, M-234, 112/327; July and Aug. 1880 report of Asheville Female College, M-234, 112/39–40, 50–51.

38. Aug. 1880 report of A.J. McAlpine, M-234, 112/337.

39. A.J. McAlpine to CIA Trowbridge, July 1, 1880, M-234, 112/320–21; Sibbald to CIA Trowbridge, Aug. 14, 1880, M-234, 112/496; A.F. Fardon to Acting CIA Marble, Sept. 8, 1880, M-234, 112/207–8.

40. Oct. 1880 report of A.J. McAlpine, M-234, 112/347.

41. Taylor to A.F. Fardon, Oct. 4, 1880, M-234, 112/235; letter from Taylor's sons, M-234, 112/233–34.

42. November report of A.J. McAlpine, M-234, 112/352.

43. J.W. Bird to CIA, Sept. 5, 1880, M-234, 112/119–21; A.F. Fardon to Acting CIA Marble, Oct. 4, 1880, M-234, 112/214–22; Bird to Acting CIA Marble, Oct. 15, Dec. 4, 1880, M-234, 112/128–29, 141–43; N.J. Smith to SI and CIA, May 31, 1881; Smith to CIA Price, July 16, 1881, both in RG 75, LR.

44. Sharlotte Neely, "The Quaker Era of Cherokee Indian Education, 1880–1892," *Appalachian Journal* 2 (Summer 1975): 315–16; see also Sharlotte Neely Williams, "The Role of Formal Education among the Eastern Cherokee Indians, 1880–1971," (M.A. thesis, Univ. of North Carolina, Chapel Hill, 1971), ch. 4; N.J. Smith to CIA Hiram Price, July 16, 1881, RG 75, LR; Mooney, "Myths of the Cherokees," 175; Francis Paul Prucha, *The Churches and the Indian Schools, 1888–1912* (Lincoln, Neb., 1979), 1–40, esp. 3.

45. Neely, "The Quaker Era of Cherokee Indian Education," 316–20. There are many letters from Barnabas C. Hobbs in RG 75, LR, for the 1880s. See for example Hobbs to CIA Hiram Price, Apr. 6, 1885.

46. Neely, "The Quaker Era of Cherokee Indian Education," 317–20; Barnabas Hobbs to CIA Price, May 23, Sept. 24, Oct. 15, 1884; N.J. Smith to Price, Aug. 21, 1884, all in RG 75, LR.

47. Resolution of Cheoah council, Oct. 5, 1877, M-234, 111/381; act of Cheoah council, Oct. 6, 1877, M-234, 111/370–71.

48. W.P. Taylor to CIA, Dec. 21, 1878, M-234, 111/603–4 (quote on 603); Lockwood to CIA Hiram Price, July 17, 1882, RG 75, LR; N.J. Smith et al. to [?], Aug. 15, 1882, RG 75, LR; enactment of Cherokee council, Oct. 3, 1883, No. 18630, RG 75, LR; CIA Price to Lockwood, Dec. 2, 1884, RG 75, LS (LD), LB 131/296–97.

49. Sibbald to CIA Trowbridge, Apr. 17, Aug. 4, 1880, M-234, 112/405–17, 837–42; Acting CIA E.J. Brooks to Sibbald, June 22, 1880, M-234, 112/813–14; Henry Smith to R.B. Vance, May 26, 1880, M-234, 112/486–87; proceedings of Eastern Band, July 1880, M-234, 112/844–45, 847. The record of the 1879 council that reelected Welch is in M-234, 112/418–35. John Ross, predictably, protested Smith's election. Ross to CIA, July 5, 1880, M-234, 112/366. Welch's farewell address is in Mooney, "Myths of the Cherokee," 226–27.

50. Mooney, "Myths of the Cherokee," 178.

51. The Swetland census of 1869 shows significantly more Cherokees in North Carolina than the 1870 federal census does. I have decided to rely on Swetland's figures because he was charged exclusively with locating Indians, while federal census-takers had other responsibilities. Swetland Census, 1869, RG 75. Federal figures for 1870 showed 711 Cherokees in Swain and Jackson counties (Qualla Boundary) and 522 in Graham, Macon, and Cherokee counties. These and the 1880 totals are in John Sibbald to CIA Trowbridge, Aug. 16, 1880, M-234, 112/849–50.

52. Sharlotte Neely Williams, "Ethnicity in a Native American Community" (Ph.D. diss., Univ. of North Carolina, Chapel Hill, 1976).

53. Wardell, *Political History of the Cherokee Nation*, 243–44; CIA Price to SI, Feb. 11, 1882, in *House Ex. Doc.*, 47 Cong., 1 Sess., No. 96 (Serial 2028, Washington, D.C., 1882), 2; hereafter cited as *House Ex. Doc.* 96 (Serial 2028). Dennis Bushyhead was the son of the Rev. Jesse Bushyhead. See also Taylor to SI, Aug. 23, 1884, M-1059, 3/440–78 (quote on 474–75); John Hall et al. to SI Kirkwood, Apr. 4, 1881, RG 75, LR; Acting CIA E.L. Stevens to SI, May 24, 1882, RG 75, LS (LD), LB 96/251–56.

54. N.J. Smith to CIA Price, May 27, 1881, RG 75, LR; Cherokees to CIA Price, Jan. 19, 1882, M-1059, 2/877–84; James Taylor to CIA Price, Aug. 19, 1882, RG 75, LR; CIA Price to Samuel Gibson, May 7, 1883, RG 75, LS (LD), LB 111/391–92; Solicitor-General S.F. Phillips to President, Apr. 16, 1881, *House Ex. Doc.* 96 (Serial 2028), 4–5. See also *House Ex. Doc.*, 48 Cong., 2 Sess., No. 208 (Serial 2303, Washington, D.C., 1885); *Sen. Misc. Doc.*, 50 Cong., 1 Sess., No. 129 (Serial 2517, Washington, D.C., 1888).

55. *W.W. Rollins v. the Eastern Band of Cherokee Indians*, 87 N.C. Supreme Court 220–37. Among the countless letters, claims, and exhibits relating to this case, see A.T. and T.F. Davidson to Acting CIA Marble, Aug. 29, 1880, M-234, 112/177–83; printed reports of Rollins and Presbrey (n.d., 1875), M-234, 108/854–94. For years after the state supreme court decision, Rollins and Presbrey were attempting to collect their money. See for example CIA to SI, Mar. 30, 1888, RG 75, LS (LD), LB 171/485–89; T.F. Davidson to CIA John D.C. Atkins, Apr. 25, 1888, M-1059, 4/833–46.

56. CIA Hiram Price to R.B. Vance, June 20, 1882, RG 75, LS (LD), LB 98/82–85; J.L. Robinson et al. to CIA Price, Sept. 2, 1882, RG 75, LR; act of Aug. 7, 1882, in 22 *U.S. Statutes* 328.

57. Act of Aug. 7, 1882, in 22 *U.S. Statutes* 328; N.J. Smith to CIA Hiram Price, Dec. 13, 1882, RG 75, LR.

58. See for example Price to Hester, Dec. 30, 1882, M-1059, 3/78; affidavits and other materials, M-1059, 3/69–84; N.J. Smith to Price, Dec. 13, 1882, RG 75, LR.

59. Shenck, "The Cherokees in North Carolina," 324–25.

60. Hester Roll, 1884, RG 75.

61. Hester to CIA Hiram Price, Jan. 29, 1884, RG 75, LR; CIA Price to SI, Jan. 24, 1884, RG 75, LR. See also Mooney, "Myths of the Cherokee," 176; Witthoft, "Observations on Social Change among the Eastern Cherokees," 205–6; Sharlotte Neely, "Acculturation and Persistence among North Carolina's Eastern Band of Cherokee Indians," in Williams, *Southeastern Indians*, 165–66. The Cherokee Nation was vitally interested in Hester's census because the Band had succeeded in bringing suit for a proportionate share of the Nation's land sales and annuities.

62. For an analysis of the problem see report of Special Indian Agent Eugene W. White to CIA John D.C. Atkins, Dec. 7, 1885, M-1059, 3/1024–83 (quote

on 1039); other examples are McCarthy to CIA J.Q. Smith, Feb. 12, 1876, M-234, 110/331; Lloyd Welch to SI, Mar. 16, 1878, M-234, 111/348–39; John Sibbald to CIA Trowbridge, Aug. 16, 1880, M-234, 112/518–24.

63. Report of Eugene W. White to CIA John D.C. Atkins, Dec. 7, 1885, M-1059, 3/1027–32; CIA Hiram Price to SI, Sept. 26, 1884, RG 75, LS (LD), LB 130/103–5. The Band's difficulties retaining their lands are discussed in the next chapter.

64. Petition to Robert B. Vance [n.d., received at OIA Mar. 4, 1879], M-234, 111/651–53; James Taylor to President, Mar. 10, 1879, M-234, 111/547–55. John Ross et al. to President Hayes, July 11, 1878, M-234, 111/206–9; resolution of Yellow Hill council, Oct. 1879, M-234, 112/424. Other western Cherokees, in a neat turn of tables on the Eastern Band, claimed they were entitled to a proportionate share of the value of the North Carolina lands. W.P. Adair et al. to CIA Hayt, July 10, 1878, M-234,, 111/6–7. In 1878 and 1884 bills were introduced in Congress providing for the sale of North Carolina Cherokee lands, but neither passed. M-234, 111/10–12; M-1059, 3/407–15. See also Daniel H. Ross et al. to CIA Price, Apr. 28, 1882, RG 75, LR; Acting CIA Stevens to SI, May 29, 1882, RG 75, LS (LD), LB 96/395–97; Belva Lockwood to CIA, with petition, Mar. 14, 1883, M-1059, 2/977–84.

65. Report of Special Agent C.C. Clements, Jan. 2, 1883, in *House Ex. Doc.*, 47 Cong., 2 Sess., No. 79 (Serial 2110, Washington, D.C., 1883), 10–11. See also other relevant material in the same document.

66. Act of Mar. 3, 1883, in 22 *U.S. Statutes* 585; CIA Hiram Price to SI, Oct. 16, 1882, RG 75, LS (LD), LB 102/427–31. Smith soon hired two additional attorneys. CIA Price to SI, Mar. 21, 1883, RG 75, LS (LD), LB 109/287–90.

67. *Eastern Band of Cherokee Indians v. United States and Cherokee Nation, Commonly Called Cherokee Nation West*, in 117 *United States Reports* 288–312. The case was on appeal from the Court of Claims. See 20 *Cases Decided in the Court of Claims* 449–83.

68. 117 *United States Reports* 303, 309.

69. For comments on Taylor see Robert L. Leatherwood to CIA, Apr. 13, Nov. 14, Dec. 28, 1887, M-1059, 4/607–10, 692–94, 919–21.

70. Atkins to Smith, Apr. 27, 1886, RG 75, LS (LD), LB 147/297–98. See also B.C. Hobbs to CIA, Apr. 3, 1886, M-1059, 4/49–50; Hobbs to CIA, June 16, 1887, M-1059, 4/484–85; Oo-chun-ta to President, Sept. 15, 1886, M-1059, 4/243–44; interview of Smith in *Waynesville News*, June 10, 1886. Smith said that if the Cherokee Nation did not want them, the North Carolina Indians would like to homestead in Indian Territory. Smith to SI L.Q.C. Lamar, Mar. 1, 1887, M-1059, 4/326–27. See also memorial of Smith to President Cleveland, Apr. 6, 1887, M-1059, 4/1114–30.

71. James Mooney, "Sacred Formulas of the Cherokees," *Seventh Annual Report*, Bureau of American Ethnology (Washington, D.C., 1891), 315 (quote); Kilpatrick and Kilpatrick, "Chronicles of Wolftown," 7.

NOTES TO CHAPTER 8

1. George H. Smathers to CIA Thomas J. Morgan, Mar. 17, 1892, M-1059, 5/437.

2. White to CIA John D.C. Atkins, Dec. 7, 1885, M-1059, 3/1024–1120 (quote on 1079–80). See also Acting CIA Upshaw to Julius Holmes, Aug. 21, 1885, RG 75, LS (LD), LB 139/295–97; Robert Leatherwood to CIA, Dec. 16, 1887, M-1059, 4/700–702; N.J. Smith to CIA, n.d., received Mar. 23, 1888, M-1059, 4/1154–59; James Blythe to CIA, June 14, 1890, M-1059, 5/76–78; CIA Morgan to Blythe, Sept. 10, 1889, RG 75, LS (LD), LB 189/92–94.

3. CIA Price to Julius Holmes, Mar. 25, 1885, RG 75, LS (LD), LB 135/74–77; James Taylor et al., to SI Lamar, Apr. 16, 1885, RG 75, LR; CIA Atkins to SI, June 11, July 10, 1885, RG 75, LS (LD), LB 137/351–53, LB 138/304–6; Jesse Y. Yeates to the Attorney General, Nov. 26, 1886, M-1059, 4/543–66; George Smathers to President, n.d., received Feb. 13, 1892, M-1059, 5/368; Stilwell Saunooka et al. to SI and CIA, Oct. 5, 1892, M-1059, 5/195–96. For mention of suits by individual Indians, see Julius Holmes to CIA, Apr. 1, 1885, M-1059, 3/760.

4. For some of the many examples of these problems see Julius Holmes to CIA Price, Jan. 23, 1885, M-1059, 3/757–58; N.J. Smith to SI, Jan. 12, 1886 and Mar. 31, 1887, M-1059, 4/304–5, 329–30; Robert Leatherwood to CIA, Apr. 1, 15, 1886, and May 2, 1887, M-1059, 4/179, 5–6, 634–35; B.C. Hobbs to Atkins, Mar. 25, 1886, M-1059, 4/45–47; Atkins to Leatherwood, Mar. 25, 1886, RG 75, LS (LD), LB 146/140.

5. CIA Price to McPherson, Aug. 7, 31, 1882, RG 75, LS (LD), LB 99/455–57; LB 101/87–89; Price to McPherson, Aug. 11, 1883, RG 75, LS (LD), LB 116/20–24; CIA Atkins to N.J. Smith, Sept. 24, 1886, RG 75, LS (LD), LB 152/167–69; Acting CIA Upshaw to McPherson, Nov. 2, 1886, RG 75, LS (LD), LB 153/307–8; McPherson to Price, Aug. 27, Sept. 5, 1883, M-1059, 2/1004–8, 1010–12; act of Cherokee council, May 26, 1886, M-1059, 4/17–18; McPherson to Atkins, Sept. 27, 1886, M-1059, 4/238–39; Robert Leatherwood to CIA, Oct. 8, Nov. 14, 1886, M-1059, 4/222–27, 229.

6. P.W. Mitchell and M.C. Felmut to SI, June 30, 1892, M-1059, 5/954–60 (quote on 956).

7. For examples see Price to Smith, Aug. 11, 17, 1882, RG 75, LS (LD), LB 100/67–68, 249–52; Gibson to Price, Dec. 12, 1882, M-1059, 2/824–33; Acting SI to CIA, Jan. 13, 1885, M-1059, 3/858–59; Julius Holmes to N.J. Smith, Mar. 11, 1885, M-1059, 3/865–66; CIA Atkins to SI, Apr. 23, 1886, RG 75, LS (LD), LB 147/236–38; Atkins to SI, Feb. 8, 1887, RG 75, LS (LD), LB 156/77–80; Leatherwood to CIA, May 16, Dec. 20, 1887, M-1059, 4/640–41, 704; Andrew Spencer to CIA, Oct. 24, 1892, and Mar. 3, 1893, M-1059, 5/705–6, 1087; Acting CIA R.V. Belt to Mike Walking Stick, Feb. 9, 1891, RG 75, LS (LD), LB 211/142–43.

8. Holmes to CIA Price, Jan. 12, Nov. 23, 1885; SI Lamar to Holmes, Sept. 11, 1885; Leatherwood to CIA, Mar. 10, 1886; all in RG 75, LR.

9. See for example Leatherwood to CIA, Apr. 13, 14, Nov. 14, Dec. 28, 1887, M-1059, 4/607–10, 499–502, 692–94, 919–21; N.J. Smith to CIA Atkins, Feb. 12, 1887, M-1059, 4/321–24; Leatherwood to CIA, Apr. 7, 1888, M-1059, 4/948–54.

10. Enclosures with letter of B.C. Hobbs to CIA Price, Apr. 6, 1885; and N.J. Smith to CIA Atkins, Aug. 12, 1885, both in RG 75, LR; Hobbs to SI, Jan. 12, 1886, M-1059, 4/39–41; Hobbs to Atkins, Sept. 23, 1886, and Hobbs to [CIA?], Mar. 28, 1887, both in RG 75, LR; estimate by Hobbs of Quaker investments, Apr. 18, 1887, RG 75, LR; Daniel Dorchester report to CIA Morgan, Mar. 13, 1891, pp. 8, 14, RG 75, LR; Neely, "The Quaker Era of Cherokee Indian Education," 314–21.

11. George Smathers to CIA Morgan, Sept. 8, 1892, M-1059, 5/503 (quote): Frizzell, "Legal Status of the Eastern Band of Cherokee Indians," 55–57.

12. James Taylor et al. to SI Lamar, Apr. 16, 1885, RG 75, LR; Daniel Dorchester report to CIA Morgan, Mar. 13, 1891, p. 7, RG 75, LR; Charles C. Painter, *The Eastern Cherokees: A Report* (Philadelphia, 1888), 10, 13.

13. Mrs. Henry Spray to President, Nov. 9, 1886; John Kerr Connally to President, Nov. 10, 1886; and Daniel Dorchester report to CIA Morgan, Mar. 13, 1891, pp. 49–50, all in RG 75, LR; H.G. Osborne to CIA Atkins, Sept. 7, 1886, M-1059, 4/254–56; Deposition of John Canaught, Nov. 29, 1886, with covering letter, M-1059, 4/489–90, 504–5; Neely, "The Quaker Era of Cherokee Indian Education," 320–21; Henry Owl, "The Eastern Band of Cherokee Indians Before and After the Removal" (M.A. thesis, Univ. of North Carolina, Chapel Hill, 1929), 154–55.

14. Owl, "The Eastern Band of Cherokee Indians," 154–55; Frizzell, "Legal Status of the Eastern Band of Cherokee Indians," 59–60; Painter, *The Eastern Cherokees*, 4, 12–13. That most Indians sided with Spray is obvious in H.G. Osborne to CIA Atkins, Sept. 7, 1886, M-1059, 4/256–58.

15. H.G. Osborne to CIA Atkins, Sept. 7, 1886, M-1059, 4/254–68 (quote on 259). See also endorsement of Cherokee council, May 24, 1886, RG 75, LR; council resolution supporting Spray, Oct. 5, 1886, an enclosure in John Kerr Connally to President, Nov. 10, 1886, RG 75, LR; Hobbs to Atkins, Sept. 23, Oct. 28, 1886, RG 75, LR; Painter, *The Eastern Cherokees*, 9–12. Some Indians opposed Spray: Oo-chun-ta et al. to Attorney General A.H. Garland, Oct. 25, 1886, M-1059, 4/147–48; Jackson Blythe et al. to CIA, May 27, 1886, M-1059, 4/23.

16. N.J. Smith to CIA Atkins, Oct. 2, 1886, M-1059, 4/312–13; Painter, *The Eastern Cherokees*, 9–14; B.C. Hobbs to Atkins, June 25, July 8, 1886, RG 75, LR; Daniel Dorchester report to CIA Morgan, Mar. 13, 1891, pp. 49–50, RG 75, LR.

17. Many letters in RG 75 attest to Smith's activities in Washington during the 1880s. See also William Munn Colby, "Routes to Rainey Mountain: A Biography of James Mooney, Ethnologist" (Ph.D. diss., Univ. of Wisconsin-Madison, 1977), 55–56; Mooney, "Myths of the Cherokee," 177–78.

18. Colby, "Routes to Rainey Mountain," chs. 1–4; *Dictionary of American*

Biography, XIII, 110–11; Mooney, "Myths of the Cherokee," 11; Neil M. Judd, *The Bureau of American Ethnology: A Partial History* (Norman, Okla., 1967), 47–48.

19. Colby, "Routes to Rainey Mountain," 63–85; Mooney, "Myths of the Cherokee," 236; Mooney, "Sacred Formulas of the Cherokee," 310–12; Mooney and Olbrechts, "The Swimmer Manuscript," 1, 7.

20. Colby, "Routes to Rainey Mountain," 72, 109–10, 149–52. Mooney also obtained historical material from Thomas's daughter, Indian informants, and the works of Zeigler and Grosscup, Royce, and others. Mooney, "Myths of the Cherokee," 13, 157–81.

21. Colby, "Routes to Rainey Mountain," 90–91; Judd, *The Bureau of American Ethnology*, 49, 67. In 1913, for example, 6 of the 16 reported deaths among 2,109 members of the Band were due to tuberculosis; 35 more were believed to have the disease. *Annual Report* of CIA, 1913, in *House Doc.*, 63 Cong., 2 Sess., No. 1009 (Serial 6634, Washington, D.C., 1914), 141, 145. Trachoma was also prevalent.

22. White to CIA, Oct. 28, 1885, M-1059, 3/1006; Hart to CIA, Feb. 24, 1898, Superintendents Letterbook, FRCEP. In 1894 Thomas Potter said the greatest crime among them was "their love for liquor." *Annual Report* of CIA, 1894, *House Ex. Doc.*, 53 Cong., 3 Sess., No. 1 (Serial 3306, Washington, D.C., 1894), 397; hereafter cited as *House Ex. Doc.* 1 (Serial 3306). There is much other evidence relating to alcohol as a Cherokee problem.

23. Act of Mar. 11, 1889, in *Laws and Resolutions of the State of North Carolina . . . Session of 1889* (Raleigh, 1889), 889. See also *Journal of the House of Representatives . . . Session of 1889* (Raleigh, 1889), 338, 551, 554, 589, 709, 754, 848, 1041. For earlier commentary relating to possible incorporation, see Thomas Ruffin to Wallace Rollins, Mar. 19, 1875, M-234, 109/2338; Jesse Y. Yeates to Attorney General, Nov. 26, 1886, M-1059, 4/543–66; Cherokee memorial to President Cleveland, Apr. 6, 1887, M-1059, 4/1114–30, esp. 1117.

24. Leatherwood to CIA, Feb. 23, 1887, M-1059, 4/600–603 (quote on 602); Leatherwood to CIA, June 20, 1889, M-1059, 5/51–56; CIA Oberly to SI, Apr. 29, 1889, M-950/10–12.

25. N.J. Smith et al. to SI John Noble, n.d., M-950/7–8; Daniel Dorchester report to CIA Morgan, Mar. 13, 1891, p. 47; Henry B. Carrington to CIA, June 23, 1891, both in RG 75, LR; Henry B. Carrington, "Eastern Band of Cherokees of North Carolina," *Eleventh Census of the United States: Extra Census Bulletin* (Washington, D.C., 1892), 13–16; Frizzell, "Legal Status of the Eastern Band of Cherokee Indians," 59–60; Fred B. Bauer, *Land of the North Carolina Cherokees* (Brevard, N.C., 1970), n.p., under "The Author."

26. Smith to Morgan, Feb. 2, 1891 (quote), RG 75, LR; Morgan to Smith, Feb. 10, 1891, RG 75, LS (LD), LB 211/175; Frizzell, "Legal Status of the Eastern Band of Cherokee Indians," 59–60. A month later Smith expressed willingness to keep Quaker administration as long as the Sprays were removed. Smith et al. to Morgan, Mar. 17, 1891, RG 75, LR.

27. Jesse Reed et al. to CIA, Mar. 10, 1891 (quotes), RG 75, LR; Daniel Dorchester to CIA, Feb. 16–17, 1891, RG 75, LR; temporary report of Dorchester to CIA, Feb. 17, 1891, RG 75, LR; Smith to Morgan, Feb. 16, 27, 1891, M-1059, 5/170–71, 173–75; Prucha, *The Churches and the Indian Schools*, 10.

28. Dorchester report to CIA Morgan, Mar. 13, 1891, pp. 75–172, RG 75, LR.

29. Blythe to CIA Morgan, June 26, 1891, M-1059, 5/135–36 (quote on 137). Nearly identical remarks are in Morgan to Blythe, June 30, 1891, RG 75, LS (LD), LB 219/212. See also Stilwell Saunooka to Morgan, June 2, 1892, M-1059, 5/514; Frizzell, "Legal Status of the Eastern Band of Cherokee Indians," 59–60.

30. Smith et al. to CIA Morgan, Mar. 17, 1891; Smith to Morgan, Oct. 16, 1891, both in RG 75, LR; Smith et al. to Rep. W.T. Crawford, June 30, 1892, M-1059, 5/210–13; Neely, "The Quaker Era of Cherokee Indian Education," 320; Frizzell, "Legal Status of the Eastern Band of Cherokee Indians," 61; Carrington, "Eastern Band of Cherokees," 16.

31. *Annual Report* of CIA, 1892, in *House Ex. Doc.*, 52 Cong., 2 Sess., No. 1 (Serial 3088, Washington, D.C., 1892), 9 (quote); hereafter cited as *House Ex. Doc.* 1 (Serial 3088). See also Prucha, *The Churches and the Indian Schools*, ch. 2; Stuart, *The Indian Office*, 144–47; Acting CIA R.V. Belt to SI, May 5, 1892, RG 75, LS (LD), LB 236/476–77.

32. *House Ex. Doc.* 1 (Serial 3088), 9. See also act of Mar. 3, 1893, in 27 *U.S. Statutes* 614; Stuart, *The Indian Office*, 40.

33. Smathers to CIA Morgan, Mar. 17, 1892, M-1059, 5/434–41; Morgan to Spencer, June 15, 25, 1892, RG 75 LS (Education), LB 185/125–27, 320.

34. Spencer to CIA, Dec. 22, 27, 1892, M-1059, 5/795–97, 799; lease of land for schools, Jan. 4, 1893, M-1059, 5/1074–76; Belt to CIA Morgan, Jan. 8, 1893, M-1059, 5/803–8; Acting SI George Chandler to CIA, Feb. 1, 1893, M-1059, 5/927; Neely, "The Quaker Era of Cherokee Indian Education," 321. For Spencer's trouble with Spray, see Spencer to CIA, Mar. 23, 1893, M-1059, 5/1052–55.

35. Potter report of Sept. 10, 1894, in *House Ex. Doc.* 1 (Serial 3306), 393–96; Potter report, 1895, in *Annual Report* of CIA, 1895, *House Doc.*, 54 Cong., 1 Sess., No. 5 (Serial 3382, Washington, D.C., 1895), 386, 388; hereafter cited as *House Doc.* 5 (Serial 3382). Potter's correspondence is replete with comments on the operation of the schools. Superintendents' Letterbooks, FRCEP.

36. Potter reports in *House Ex. Doc.* 1 (Serial 3306), 394; and *House Doc.* 5 (Serial 3382), 386; Hart reports in *Annual Report* of CIA, 1897, in *House Doc.* 5 (Serial 3641), 209; and *House Doc.* 5 (Serial 3757), 219. See also Potter to William Sherrill, Nov. 27, 1894; Potter to Miss O.O. Brown, Dec. 13, 1894; Hart to Capt. R.H. Pratt, June 9, 1897; Hart to W.N. Hailmann, Jan. 25, 1898; and Hart to CIA, Feb. 10, 1898, all in Superintendents' Letterbooks, FRCEP.

37.. Action of Cherokee council, Oct. 14, 1891, M-1059, 5/353–55; George Smathers to President, n.d., received Feb. 13, 1892, M-1059, 5/370–71; contract with Kerr, enclosed with Andrew Spencer to CIA, Sept. 7, 1892, M-1059, 5/522–25; see also report of CIA, Dec. 16, 1891, RG 75, LS (LD), LB 227/256–63. Predictably, there were Cherokees who opposed such a sale. See Jackson Long et al. to CIA, July 1, 1892, M-1059, 5/203–8.

38. Ewart to SI, n.d., but returned Dec. 16, 1891, M-1059, 5/357–66; advertisement, M-1059, 5/975–77; contract with proposed terms, M-1059, 5/966–73; Acting SI Chandler to CIA, Feb. 12, 1892, M-1059, 5/347–48; CIA Morgan to James Blythe, Feb. 16, 1892, RG 75, LS (LD), LB 231/108–9. As to Ewart's doubts, see Ewart to Morgan, n.d., answered May 9; July 1, 1892, M-1059, 5/230, 256–61; Ewart to Acting CIA Belt, May 17, 1892, M-1059, 5/245.

39. Act of Aug. 4, 1892, in 27 *U.S. Statutes* 348.

40. CIA to Spencer, Aug. 13, 1892, RG 75, LS (LD), LB 242/387–88; Spencer to CIA, Sept. 7, 1892, M-1059, 5/529–33; indenture of Sept. 7, 1892, M-1059, 5/717–20; Spencer to CIA, Oct. 27, Dec. 14, 1892, M-1059, 5/680–82, 789 (quote); Belt to Spencer, Dec. 16, 1892, RG 75, LS (LD), LB 249/163 (quote). This was not the only time Belt and Commissioner Morgan directed sarcasm toward Spencer for his sense of duty, occasional querulousness, and correspondence. Both Smathers and Ewart responded to Spencer's charges by attacking him in letters to the Indian Office.

41. George Smathers to CIA, Dec. 7, 1892, M-1059, 5/492–93, 496–97; Spencer to CIA, Jan. 31, 1893, M-1059, 5/920–22; Pinchot to CIA, Jan. 31, 1893, M-1059, 5/924; Acting SI George Chandler to CIA, Feb. 10, 1893, M-1059, 5/913; CIA to Spencer, Dec. 29, 1892, RG 75, LS (LD), LB 249/431–35.

42. As early as 1892 Ewart said he had a prospective buyer. Ewart to Acting CIA Belt, Dec. 20, 1892, M-1059, 5/272–73. See also Ewart to Belt, Jan. 9, 1893, M-1059, 5/880–81; Ewart to CIA Morgan, Jan. 17, 1893, M-1059, 5/883–92; Spencer to CIA, with tribal resolutions, May 18, 1893, M-1059, 5/1094–1109; SI Smith to CIA, Sept. 6, 1893, M-1059, 5/946–48; Frizzell, "Legal Status of the Eastern Band of Cherokee Indians," 73.

43. George Smathers to R.F. Thompson, July 14, 1893, M-1059, 5/979–81; Ewart to CIA D.M. Browning, Sept. 22, Oct. 19, 1893, M-1059, 5/897–98, 900; Ewart to SI Smith, Sept. 22, 1893, M-1059, 5/870–77; contract of Boyd and Eastern Band, Sept. 28, 1893, M-1059, 6/277–31; brief of Ewart, Oct. 23, 1893, M-1059, 6/243–54. A good history of the Boyd and Smith contracts is in Assistant Attorney General John J. Hall to SI, July 25, 1894, M-1059, 6/42–64. The best account of the legal maneuverings is Frizzell, "Legal Status of the Eastern Band of Cherokee Indians," 72–81.

44. Russell, "William Holland Thomas," 405. For Thomas's last years see *ibid.*, ch. 12.

45. "Myths of the Cherokee," 13, 178.

46. For Wotherspoon's comments, see Walter L. Williams, "The Merger of Apaches with Eastern Cherokees: Qualla in 1893," *Journal of Cherokee Studies* 2 (Spring 1977): 240–45.

47. *Annual Report* of CIA, 1894, *House Ex. Doc.* 1 (Serial 3306), 81–82;

Mooney, "Myths of the Cherokee," 179; act of Aug. 23, 1894, in 28 *U.S. Statutes* 424. Later, the Band's council wanted to sell the Love tract because it was largely uninhabitable and almost inaccessible. Joseph C. Hart to CIA, June 2, 1897, M-1059, 6/362. This was finally accomplished in the early twentieth century.

48. Olney to SI, Nov. 17, 1894, M-1059, 6/77–79. In contrast, Assistant Attorney General John J. Hall had earlier written that though the Eastern Cherokees were citizens of North Carolina, "yet in all respects their contracts and the management of their property is within the supervisory control of the Department of Interior." Hall to SI, Mar. 14, 1894, M-1059, 6/26–37 (quote on 32). See also Potter to CIA, Sept. 22, Dec. 3, 1894, M-1059, 6/127–28, 145–48; briefs of Smathers and Crawford, M-1059, 6/717–46; Potter report in *House Doc.* 5 (Serial 3382), 386; Frizzell, "Legal Status of the Eastern Band of Cherokee Indians," 73–76.

49. Act of Mar. 8, 1895, in *Private Laws of the State of North Carolina . . . Session of 1895* (Raleigh, 1895), 234–40. The act of incorporation was further amended in 1897. Act of Mar. 8, 1897, in *Private Laws of the State of North Carolina . . . Session of 1897* (Raleigh, 1897), 418–24. See also Frizzell, "Legal Status of the Eastern Band of Cherokee Indians," 76–77.

50. Potter report in *House Doc.* 5 (Serial 3382), 386; comments of CIA, *ibid.*, 91–94. See also Potter to Frank T. Palmer, July 21, 1895; Potter to CIA, Mar. 18, Aug. 6, 1895; Potter to the chief of Eastern Band et al., Mar. 27, 1895, all in Superintendents' Letterbooks, FRCEP.

51. See for example Potter to C.J. Harris, Dec. 10, 1894; Potter to CIA, July 22, 1895; Potter to Frank T. Palmer, May 17, 1895, all in Superintendents' Letterbooks, FRCEP. Haddon assumed his new responsibilities in North Carolina early in September.

52. Decision of U.S. court for western district of North Carolina in equity, *United States et al. v. D.T. Boyd et al., House Doc.* 5 (Serial 3382), 632–38; Frizzell, "Legal Status of the Eastern Band of Cherokee Indians," 77–79. One of the judges contended that the Cherokees were citizens but were still wards of the United States.

53. *United States v. Boyd et al.,* 83 *Federal Reporter*, 547–56; Frizzell, "Legal Status of the Eastern Band of Cherokee Indians," 79–80.

54. Frizzell, "Legal Status of the Eastern Band of Cherokee Indians," 80–81. George Smathers favored continuing the appeal in order to define more precisely the Cherokees' status. Smathers to CIA, June 2, 1899, M-1059, 7/109–10.

55. Cherokee council to CIA and SI, Dec. 7, 1897, M-1059, 7/826–35 (quote on 831). See also Joseph C. Hart to CIA, Dec. 2, 1897, M-1059, 6/369–72; Spray report in *House Doc.* 5 (Serial 4101), 307; Frizzell, "Legal Status of the Eastern Band of Cherokee Indians," 81–83.

56. Act of Mar. 6, 1899, in *Public Laws and Resolutions of the State of North Carolina . . . Session of 1899* (Raleigh, 1899), 663; Joseph C. Hart to CIA, Nov. 17, 1897, M-1059, 6/366–67; Frizzell, "Legal Status of the Eastern Band of Cherokee Indians," 81 and ch. 3.

57. Frizzell, "Legal Status of the Eastern Band of Cherokee Indians," 71–72. See also CIA Morgan to J.L. McLeymore, June 14, 1890; Morgan to Richard H. Smith, Sept. 15, 1890, both in RG 75, LS (LD), LB 200/225–26, and LB 204/ 196–97; (?) to Morgan, Sept. 12, 1890, M-1059, 5/112–14.

58. Spencer to CIA, Oct. 27, 1892, M-1059, 5/680–82; report of Spencer in *Annual Report* of CIA, 1893, *House Ex. Doc.*, 53 Cong., 2 Sess., No. 1, (Serial 3210, Washington, D.C., 1893), 434 (quote).

59. Potter report in *House Doc.* 5 (Serial 3382), 387. Potter said that about six hundred Cherokees favored allotment, perhaps as the result of machinations of lawyers. Potter to CIA, Aug. 11, 1894, M-1059, 6/106; Potter to CIA, June 5, 1895, Superintendents' Letterbook; FRCEP. Some alleged Eastern Cherokees hoped for allotments in Indian Territory. See petition to President Cleveland and SI Smith, July 3, 1893, M-1059, 5/829–58.

60. See the comments of Henry Spray in *Annual Report* of CIA, 1902, in *House Doc.*, 57 Cong., 2 Sess., No. 5 (Serial 4458, Washington, D.C., 1903), 261.

61. In 1902 John Will said most North Carolina Cherokees wanted allotment. Will to CIA, Mar. 3, 1902, M-1059, 7/610. For an opposite view, see William W. Long to SI, Apr. 28, 1905, M-1059, 7/901–4. Perhaps the strongest stand taken in recent years for individual Cherokee property rights is Bauer, *Land of the North Carolina Cherokees*.

62. In Sept. 1899 there were 1,388 reported members of the Eastern Band, plus 96 more who were "doubtful." Henry Spray and James Blythe, enumerators, Sept. 8, 1899, M-1059, 7/294–97.

63. Henry Spray report of Aug. 27, 1900, in *House Doc.* 5 (Serial 4101), 307; J.A. Holmes to CIA, Sept. 11, 1900, M-1059, 7/219. Michael Frome, *Strangers in High Places: The Story of the Great Smoky Mountains* (New York, 1966), ch. 14.

64. "Myths of the Cherokee," 236–37 (quote on 237).

BIBLIOGRAPHY

MANUSCRIPTS

Theodore W. Brevard Papers. North Carolina Division of Archives and History, Raleigh.

Nathaniel C. Browder Papers. Western Carolina University, Cullowhee, N.C.

Cherokee-related materials from National Archives. Microfilm rolls. Newspapers and Microforms Department, Duke University, Durham, N.C.

Fain Family Papers. Western Carolina University, Cullowhee, N.C.

Governors Letter Books. North Carolina Division of Archives and History, Raleigh.

Governors Papers. North Carolina Division of Archives and History, Raleigh.

Duff Green Papers. Southern Historical Collection, University of North Carolina, Chapel Hill.

William Hoke Papers. Southern Historical Collection, University of North Carolina, Chapel Hill.

David Hutchison Papers. York County Library, Rock Hill, S.C.

Andrew Johnson Papers. Library of Congress.

John H. Knapp Papers. North Carolina Division of Archives and History, Raleigh.

Legislative Papers. North Carolina Division of Archives and History, Raleigh.

Thomas Lenoir Papers. Duke University, Durham, N.C.

Museum of the Cherokee Indian, Archives. Cherokee, N.C.

Secretary of State Papers. North Carolina Division of Archives and History, Raleigh.

Jacob Siler Papers. Southern Historical Collection, University of North Carolina, Chapel Hill.

William W. Stringfield, historical account, Stringfield Papers. North Carolina Division of Archives and History, Raleigh.

William W. Stringfield Papers. North Carolina Division of Archives and History, Raleigh.

William W. Stringfield Papers. Western Carolina University, Cullowhee, N.C.

David L. Swain Papers. North Carolina Division of Archives and History, Raleigh.

James Taylor Papers. Duke University, Durham, N.C.

James W. Terrell Collection. MS 1926, National Anthropological Archives, Smithsonian Institution, Washington, D.C.

James W. Terrell Papers. Duke University, Durham, N.C.

James W. Terrell Papers. North Carolina Division of Archives and History, Raleigh.

James W. Terrell Papers. Western Carolina University, Cullowhee, N.C.

James W. Terrell Reminiscences, Terrell Papers. Western Carolina University, Cullhowhee, N.C.

William Holland Thomas Collection (and Additions). Western Carolina University, Cullowhee, N.C.

William Holland Thomas Papers, Duke University, Durham, N.C.

William Holland Thomas Papers. 4 Microfilm Rolls. Newspapers and Microforms Department, Duke University, Durham, N.C.

William Holland Thomas Paper and Notebook. North Carolina Division of Archives and History, Raleigh.

William Holland Thomas, "Supplementary Report of Cherokee Indians Remaining in N.C., 1835–1840." Museum of the Cherokee Indian, Cherokee, N.C.

William Holland Thomas III Papers. Western Carolina University, Cullowhee, N.C.

United States. Federal Records Center, East Point, Ga.

Circuit Court Records, Western District of North Carolina, Asheville.

Equity Case 701. *Cherokee Indians v. W.H. Thomas et al.* and *U.S. and Cherokee Indians v. W.H. Thomas et al.*

Record Group 75. Records of the Bureau of Indian Affairs.

Cherokee Indian Agency. Administrative Records. Enumeration and Enrollment Records. Censuses, 1894–1905.

Cherokee Indian Agency. General Records. Correspondence, Chronological file, 1890–1914.

Cherokee Indian Agency. Superintendents' Letterbooks, 1892–1901.

United States. National Archives, Washington, D.C.
Record Group 29. Records of the Bureau of the Census.
Microcopy 653. Population Schedules of the Eighth U.S. Census, 1860.
Microcopy 704. Population Schedules of the Sixth U.S. Census, 1840.
Record Group 75. Records of the Bureau of Indian Affairs.
"Cherokee Valuations N.C. 1836 Welch and Garrett [*sic*]," Cherokee Property Valuations, 1835–1839.
Joseph G. Hester Census Roll, 1884.
Letters Received by the Office of Indian Affairs, 1881–1900.
Letters Sent by the Office of Indian Affairs, 1881–1900.
Microcopy 21. Letters Sent by the Office of Indian Affairs, 1824–1881.
Microcopy 234. Letters Received by the Office of Indian Affairs, 1824–1881.
Microcopy 348. Report Books of the Office of Indian Affairs, 1838–1885.
Microcopy 574. Special Files of the Office of Indian Affairs, 1807–1904.
Microcopy 950. Interior Department Appointment Papers: North Carolina, 1849–1892.
Microcopy 1059. Selected Letters Received by the Office of Indian Affairs Relating to the Cherokees of North Carolina, 1851–1905.
R.J. Powell Census and Payment Roll, 1867.
Records of the Fourth Board of Cherokee Commissioners.
Silas H. Swetland Census and Payment Rolls, 1869.
Record Group 94. Records of the Adjutant General's Office.
Letters Received, Main Series, 1822–1860.
Microcopy 401. Compiled Service Records of Volunteer Union Soldiers Who Served in Organizations from the State of North Carolina.
United States. North Carolina Division of Archives and History.
Seventh U.S. Census, 1850, North Carolina.
Eighth U.S. Census, 1860, North Carolina.
Zebulon Vance Papers, Personal Collection. North Carolina Division of Archives and History, Raleigh.
Walker Family Collection. Western Carolina University, Cullowhee, N.C.

Stephen Whitaker Papers. North Carolina Division of Archives and History, Raleigh.

John Williams Papers. North Carolina Division of Archives and History, Raleigh.

PRINTED COLLECTIONS, SERIES, AND DOCUMENTS

American State Papers. 38 vols. Washington, D.C., 1832–1861.

Congressional Globe. 46 vols. in 111. Washington, D.C., 1834–1873.

Gales, Joseph. *Register of Debates in Congress. . . .* 14 vols. in 29. Washington, D.C., 1825–1837.

Hamilton, J.G. de Roulhac, ed. *The Correspondence of Jonathan Worth.* 2 vols. Raleigh, N.C., 1909.

Hamilton, J.G. de Roulhac, and Max R. Williams, eds. *The Papers of William Alexander Graham.* 6 vols. Raleigh, N.C., 1957–1976.

Johnston, Frontis W., ed. *The Papers of Zebulon Vance.* Raleigh, N.C., 1963–.

Kappler, Charles J. *Indian Affairs: Laws and Treaties.* 5 vols. Washington, D.C., 1904–1941.

Kilpatrick, Jack F. and Anna G., eds. *The Shadow of Sequoyah: Social Documents of the Cherokees, 1862–1964.* Norman, Okla., 1965.

Minutes of the Annual Conferences of the Methodist Episcopal Church South (Holston Conference), published various places, scattered issues, 1838–1873.

Moore, John W. *Roster of North Carolina Troops in the War Between the States.* 4 vols. Raleigh, N.C., 1882.

North Carolina.
Journals of the Senate and House of Commons of the General Assembly of the State of North Carolina.
North Carolina Supreme Court.
Private Laws of the State of North Carolina.
Public Laws of the State of North Carolina.
Report of the North Carolina Judiciary Committee on the North Carolina Cherokees. Raleigh, 1859.

Richardson, James D., ed. *A Compilation of the Messages and Papers of the Presidents: 1789–1897.* 10 vols. Washington, D.C., 1896–1899.

Siler, David W., comp. *The Eastern Cherokees: A Census of the Cherokee Nation in North Carolina, Tennessee, Alabama and Georgia in 1851.* Cottonport, La., 1972.

Swindler, William F., ed. *Sources and Documents of United States Constitutions*. 10 vols. Dobbs Ferry, N.Y., 1973–1979.

Thomas, William Holland. *Argument in Support of the Claims of the Cherokee Indians. . . .* Washington, D.C., 1839.

———. *Explanation of the Fund Held in Trust by the United States for the North Carolina Cherokees*. Washington, D.C. 1858.

———. *Explanations of the Rights and Claims of the Cherokee Indians*. Washington, D.C., 1851; facsimile reprint, Asheville, N.C., 1947.

———. *A Letter to the Commissioner of Indian Affairs upon Claims of the Indians Remaining in the States East*. Washington, D.C., 1853.

Tolbert, Noble, J., ed. *The Papers of John Willis Ellis*. 2 vols. Raleigh, N.C., 1964.

Tyner, James W., ed. *Those Who Cried: The 16,000*. n.p., 1974.

United States.

Cases Decided in the Court of Claims.

Federal Reporter.

U.S. Congress:

Commissioners of Indian Affairs, Annual Reports, 1838–1915.

25 Cong., 2 Sess., *Sen. Doc. 120: Report of the Secretary of War . . . in relation to the Cherokee Treaty of 1835* (Serial 315, Washington, D.C., 1838).

25 Cong., 2 Sess., *House Doc. 453: . . . correspondence between the War Department and Major General Scott* (Serial 331, Washington, D.C., 1838).

25 Cong., 3 Sess., *House Doc. 224: Cherokee Indians in North Carolina* (Serial 348, Washington, D.C., 1839).

26 Cong., 1 Sess., *House Doc. 2: Report of the Commissioner of Indian Affairs* (Serial 363, Washington, D.C. 1839).

27 Cong., 2 Sess., *House Report 1098: Removal of the Cherokees West of the Mississippi* (Serial 411, Washington, D.C., 1842).

27 Cong., 3 Sess., *House Report 288: Removal of the Cherokees, & c.* (Serial 429, Washington, D.C., 1843).

28 Cong., 1 Sess., *House Doc. 234: Memorial of the "Treaty Party" of the Cherokee Indians* (Serial 443, Washington, D.C., 1844).

28 Cong., 2 Sess., *Sen. Doc. 90: Memorial of the Cherokee Indians who have become citizens of the State of North Carolina* (Serial 451, Washington, D.C. 1845).

29 Cong., 1 Sess., *Sen. Doc. 298: Message . . . relative to the internal feuds among the Cherokees* (Serial 474, Washington, D.C., 1846).

29 Cong., 1 Sess., *Sen. Doc. 301: Documents in relation to difficulties*

existing in the Cherokee Nation . . . (Serial 474, Washington, D.C., 1846).

29 Cong., 1 Sess., *Sen. Doc.* 408: *Memorial of the Cherokee Indians residing in North Carolina* . . . (Serial 477, Washington, D.C., 1846).

30 Cong., 1 Sess., *House Report 632: Cherokee Indians in North Carolina* (Serial 526, Washington, D.C., 1848).

32 Cong., 1 Sess., *House Misc. Doc.* 64: . . . *amount of money paid William H. Thomas for and on account of the Cherokees of North Carolina* (Serial 652, Washington, D.C., 1852).

33 Cong., 1 Sess., *House Ex. Doc.* 85: *Cherokees East and West of the Mississippi* . . . (Serial 723, Washington, D.C., 1854).

36 Cong., 1 Sess., *Sen. Misc. Doc.* 61: *Memorial* . . . *praying that the President be authorized to purchase that portion* . . . *known as the "neutral land"* (Serial 1038, Washington, D.C., 1860).

40 Cong., 2 Sess., *House Ex. Doc.* 141: *Letter* . . . *relative to payment of interest to Cherokee Indians in North Carolina* . . . (Serial 1337, Washington, D.C., 1868).

40 Cong., 3 Sess., *Sen. Ex. Doc.* 25: . . . *appropriation required to pay the expenses of a special agent to take the census of the North Carolina Cherokees* (Serial 1360, Washington, D.C., 1869).

41 Cong., 2 Sess., *House Ex. Doc.* 1: *Report of the Commissioner of Indian Affairs* (Serial 1414, Washington, D.C., 1870).

43 Cong., 2 Sess., *House Ex. Doc.* 51: *Letter* . . . *relative to the lands of the North Carolina or eastern band of the Cherokee Indians* (Serial 1645, Washington, D.C., 1875).

43 Cong., 2 Sess., *House Ex. Doc.* 169: . . . *an estimate of appropriation* . . . *to institute and prosecute suits against the present and former agents of the Eastern Band* . . . (Serial 1648, Washington, D.C., 1875).

45 Cong., 2 Sess., *House Report 466: Eastern Band of Cherokee Indians* (Serial 1823, Washington, D.C., 1878).

45 Cong., 3 Sess., *House Misc. Doc.* 17: *Remonstrance of the Principal Chief and Delegates of the Cherokee Nation of Indians* (Serial 1861, Washington, D.C., 1879).

47 Cong., 1 Sess., *Sen. Ex. Doc.* 179: . . . *payment of certain legal services rendered to the Cherokee Indians in North Carolina* . . . (Serial 1991, Washington, D.C., 1882).

47 Cong., 1 Sess., *House Ex. Doc.* 96: *Removal of Eastern Cherokee Indians* (Serial 2028, Washington, D.C., 1882).

47 Cong., 1 Sess., *House Ex. Doc.* 196: *Letter . . . relative to the lands and funds of the Eastern Band of North Carolina Cherokees* (Serial 2031, Washington, D.C., 1882).

47 Cong., 2 Sess., *House Ex. Doc.* 79: *. . . report . . . in reference to the differences between the Eastern and Western bands of Cherokee Indians* (Serial 2028, Washington, D.C., 1882).

48 Cong., 1 Sess., *Sen. Ex. Doc.* 135: *. . . preliminary report . . . concerning roll of the Cherokee Indians east of the Mississippi River* (Serial 2167, Washington, D.C., 1884).

48 Cong., 1 Sess., *House Report* 827: *Eastern Band of Cherokee Indians of North Carolina* (Serial 2255, Washington, D.C., 1884).

48 Cong., 2 Sess., *House Ex. Doc.* 208: *. . . estimate . . . for subsistence and removal of certain Eastern Cherokee Indians* (Serial 2303, Washington, D.C., 1885).

49 Cong., 1 Sess., *House Report* 539: *Eastern and Western bands of Cherokee Indians* (Serial 2436, Washington, D.C., 1886).

49 Cong., 2 Sess., *Sen. Report* 1680: *. . . the bill (S 375) to refer the claims of the Eastern and Western Bands of the Cherokee Indians to the Court of Claims . . .* (Serial 2456, Washington, D.C., 1887).

50 Cong., 1 Sess., *Sen. Misc. Doc.* 129: *Memorial in behalf of certain Cherokee Indians* (Serial 2517, Washington, D.C., 1888).

50 Cong., 2 Sess., *House Ex. Doc.* 36: *. . . appropriation for legal proceedings in behalf of the Eastern Band of Cherokee Indians . . .* (Serial 2651, Washington, D.C., 1889).

51 Cong., 1 Sess., *House Ex. Doc.* 1: *Report of the Commissioner of Indian Affairs* (Serial 2841, Washington, D.C., 1891).

52 Cong., 1 Sess., *Sen. Ex. Doc.* 135: *. . . bill for the relief of the Eastern Band of Cherokee Indians* (Serial 2901, Washington, D.C., 1892).

52 Cong., 1 Sess., *Sen. Report* 1064: [*. . . relative to S. 3402, for the relief of the Eastern Band of Cherokees*] (Serial 2915, Washington, D.C., 1892).

52 Cong., 1 Sess., *House Report* 1871: *. . . relative to H.R. 9482, for the relief of the Eastern Band of Cherokees* (Serial 3048, Washington, D.C., 1892).

52 Cong., 2 Sess., *House Ex. Doc.* 1: *Report of the Commissioner of Indian Affairs* (Serial 3088, Washington, D.C., 1892).

53 Cong., 2 Sess., *House Ex. Doc.* 1: *Report of the Commissioner of Indian Affairs* (Serial 3210, Washington, D.C., 1895).

53 Cong., 2 Sess., *House Ex. Doc.* 128: *Eastern Band of Cherokees v. W.H. Thomas et al.* (Serial 3226, Washington, D.C., 1895).

53 Cong., 3 Sess., *House Ex. Doc.* 1: *Report of the Commissioner of Indian Affairs* (Serial 3306, Washington, D.C., 1894).

53 Cong., 3 Sess., *House Ex. Doc.* 312: *Removal of Eastern Band of Cherokee Indians* (Serial 3324, Washington, D.C., 1895).

54 Cong., 1 Sess., *House Doc.* 5: *Report of the commissioner of Indian Affairs* (Serial 3382, Washington, D.C., 1896).

54 Cong., 2 Sess., *Sen. Doc.* 144: *The Catawba Tribe of Indians* (Serial 3471, Washington, D.C., 1897).

55 Cong., 2 Sess., *House Doc.* 5: *Report of the Commissioner of Indian Affairs* (Serial 3641, Washington, D.C., 1897).

55 Cong., 3 Sess., *House Doc.* 5: *Report of the Commissioner of Indian Affairs* (Serial 3757, Washington, D.C., 1898).

56 Cong., 2 Sess., *House Doc.* 5: *Report of the Commissioner of Indian Affairs* (Serial 4101, Washington, D.C., 1900).

57 Cong., 2 Sess., *House Doc.* 5: *Report of the Commissioner of Indian Affairs* (Serial 4458, Washington, D.C., 1903).

63 Cong., 2 Sess., *House Doc.* 1009: *Report of the Commissioner of Indian Affairs* (Serial 6634, Washington, D.C., 1914).

United States Reports.

United States Statutes at Large.

The War of the Rebellion: A Compilation of the Official Records of the Union and Confederate Armies. 128 vol. Washington, D.C., 1880–1901.

BOOKS AND MEMOIRS

Adair, James. *Adair's History of the American Indian*, ed. Samuel Cole Williams. Johnson City, Tenn., 1930.

Allen, W.C. *The Annals of Haywood County, North Carolina.* n.p., 1935.

Arthur, John Preston. *Western North Carolina: A History (From 1730 to 1913).* Raleigh, 1914.

Barrett, John G. *The Civil War in North Carolina.* Chapel Hill, 1963.

Bauer, Fred B. *Land of the North Carolina Cherokees.* Brevard, N.C., 1970.

Berkhofer, Robert F., Jr. *The White Man's Indian.* New York, 1978.

Browder, Nathaniel C. *The Cherokee Indians and Those Who Came After: Notes for a History of Cherokee County, North Carolina, 1835–1860.* Hayesville, N.C., 1973.

Brown, Douglas S. *The Catawba Indians: The People of the River*. Columbia, S.C., 1966.

Brown, John P. *Old Frontiers: The Story of the Cherokee Indians from Earliest Times to the Date of their Removal to the West, 1838*. Kingsport, Tenn., 1938.

Carter, Samuel, III. *Cherokee Sunset, A Nation Betrayed: A Narrative of Travail and Triumph, Persecution and Exile*. Garden City, N.Y., 1976.

Cashion, Jerry Clyde. *Fort Butler and the Cherokee Indian Removal from North Carolina*. Raleigh, 1970.

Clark, Walter, ed. *Histories of the Several Regiments and Battalions from North Carolina in the Great War 1861–'65*. 5 vols. Goldsboro, N.C., 1901.

Corkran, David H. *The Cherokee Frontier: Conflict and Survival, 1740–1762*. Norman, Okla., 1962.

Crow, Vernon H., *Storm in the Mountains: Thomas' Confederate Legion of Cherokee Indians and Mountaineers*. Cherokee, N.C., 1982.

Dial, Adolph L., and David K. Eliades. *The Only Land I Know: A History of the Lumbee Indians*. San Francisco, 1975.

Elliott, Charles W. *Winfield Scott: The Soldier and the Man*. New York, 1937.

Ellis, Daniel. *Thrilling Adventures of Daniel Ellis, the Great Union Guide of East Tennessee. . . .* New York, 1867; reprinted Johnson City, Tenn., 1974.

Fitzgerald, Mary N. *The Cherokee and His Smoky Mountain Legends*. 3d ed. Asheville, N.C., 1946.

Fleming, Robert. *Sketch of the Life of Elder Humphrey Posey, First Baptist Missionary to the Cherokee Indians. . . .* Philadelphia, 1852.

Foreman, Grant. *The Five Civilized Tribes*. Norman, Okla., 1934.

———. *Indian Removal: The Emigration of the Five Civilized Tribes of Indians*. Norman, Okla., 1953.

Freel, Margaret. *Our Heritage: The People of Cherokee County, North Carolina, 1540–1955*. Asheville, N.C., 1956.

Frome, Michael. *Strangers in High Places: The Story of the Great Smoky Mountains*. Garden City, N.Y., 1966.

Gammel, William, *A History of American Baptist Missions . . . .* Boston, 1849.

Gearing, Fred. *Priests and Warriors: Social Structures for Cherokee Politics in the 18th Century*. Menasha, Wis., 1962.

Gilbert, William H., Jr. *The Eastern Cherokees*. Washington, D.C., 1943.

Gulick, John. *Cherokees at the Crossroads*. Chapel Hill, 1960.

Hudson, Charles M. *The Catawba Nation*. Athens, Ga., 1970.
———. *The Southeastern Indians*. Knoxville, 1976.
Hunter, Kermit. *Unto These Hills: A Drama of the Cherokees*. Chapel Hill, 1950.
Jahoda, Gloria. *The Trail of Tears*. New York, 1975.
Jennings, Francis. *The Invasion of America: Indians, Colonialism, and the Cant of Conquest*. Chapel Hill, 1975.
Judd, Neil M. *The Bureau of American Ethnology: A Partial History*. Norman, Okla., 1967.
Kephart, Horace. *The Cherokees of the Smoky Mountains: A Little Band That has Stood Against the White Tide for Three Hundred Years*. Ithaca, N.Y., 1936.
———. *Our Southern Highlanders*. New York, 1913.
King, Duane H., ed. *The Cherokee Indian Nation: A Troubled History*. Knoxville, 1979.
Kirk, Charles H., ed. and comp. *History of the Fifteenth Pennsylvania Volunteer Cavalry*. Philadelphia, 1906.
Kvasnicka, Robert M., and Herman J. Viola, eds. *The Commissioners of Indian Affairs, 1824–1977*. Lincoln, Neb., 1979.
Lanman, Charles. *Letters from the Alleghany Mountains*. New York, 1849.
Malone, Henry Thompson. *Cherokees of the Old South: A People in Transition*. Athens, Ga., 1956.
Mansfield, Edward D. *The Life of General Winfield Scott*. New York, 1846.
Mardock, Robert W. *The Reformers and the American Indians*. Columbia, Mo., 1971.
McCall, George Archibald. *Letters from the Frontier: Written during a Period of Thirty Years' Service in the Army of the United States*. Philadelphia, 1868.
Milling, Chapman J. *Red Carolinians*. Chapel Hill, 1940.
Mooney, James. "Myths of the Cherokee," *Nineteenth Annual Report* of the Bureau of American Ethnology. Washington, D.C., 1900. Pt. 1.
———. "Sacred Formulas of the Cherokee," *Seventh Annual Report* of the Bureau of American Ethnology. Washington, D.C., 1891.
Moulton, Gary M. *John Ross: Cherokee Chief*. Athens, Ga., 1978.
Nash, Gary B. *Red, White and Black: The Peoples of Early America*. Englewood Cliffs, N.J., 1974.
Nelson, Thomas A.R. *Secession: or, Prose in Rhyme; and East Tennessee, A Poem. By an East Tennessean*. Philadelphia, 1864.
O'Donnell, James, III. *The Cherokees of North Carolina in the American Revolution*. Raleigh, 1977.
———. *Southern Indians in the American Revolution*. Knoxville, 1973.

Painter, Charles C. *The Eastern Cherokees: A Report*. Philadelphia, 1888.

Palmer, William J. *Letters 1853–1863, Gen'l. Wm. J. Palmer*, comp. Isaac H. Clothier. Philadelphia, 1906.

Paludan, Phillip S. *Victims: A True Story of the Civil War*. Knoxville, 1981.

Perdue, Theda, ed. *Cherokee Editor: The Writings of Elias Boudinot*. Knoxville, 1983.

―――. *Slavery and the Evolution of Cherokee Society, 1540–1866*. Knoxville, 1979.

Pomeroy, Kenneth B., and James G. Yoho. *North Carolina Lands: Ownership, Use, and Management of Forest and Related Lands*. Washington, D.C., 1964.

Pratt, Richard Henry. *Battlefield and Classroom: Four Decades with the American Indian, 1867–1904*, ed. and intro. Robert M. Utley. New Haven, 1964.

Priest, Loring Benson. *Uncle Sam's Stepchildren: The Reformation of United States Indian Policy, 1865–1887*. Lincoln, 1975.

Prucha, Francis Paul. *American Indian Policy in Crisis: Christian Reformers and the Indian, 1865–1900*. Norman, Okla., 1976.

―――. *American Indian Policy in the Formative Years: The Indian Trade and Intercourse Acts, 1790–1834*. Cambridge, Mass., 1962.

―――. *The Churches and the Indian Schools, 1888–1912*. Lincoln, Neb., 1979.

Reid, John Phillip. *A Better Kind of Hatchet: Law, Trade and Diplomacy in the Cherokee Nation During the Early Years of European Contact*. University Park, Pa., 1976.

―――. *A Law of Blood: The Primitive Law of the Cherokee Nation*. New York, 1970.

Rights, Douglas L. *The American Indian in North Carolina*. 2d ed. Winston Salem, N.C., 1957.

Royce, Charles. "The Cherokee Nation of Indians," *Fifth Annual Report* of the Bureau of American Ethnology. Washington, D.C., 1887.

Sanford, Washington L. *History of the Fourteenth Illinois Cavalry and the Brigades to which it Belonged*. Chicago, 1898.

Satz, Ronald N. *American Indian Policy in the Jacksonian Era*. Lincoln, Neb., 1975.

Scott, Samuel W., and Samuel P. Angel. *History of the Thirteenth Regiment Tennessee Volunteer Cavalry, U.S.A.* Philadelphia, 1903; reprinted Blountville, Tenn., 1973.

Scott, Winfield. *Memoirs of Lieut.-General Scott, LL.D.* 2 vols. New York, 1864.

Sheehan, Bernard. *Seeds of Extinction: Jeffersonian Philanthropy and the American Indian*. Chapel Hill, 1973.

Smathers, George H. *The History of Land Titles in Western North Carolina*. Asheville, N.C., 1938.

Smith, Arthur D.H. *Old Fuss and Feathers* . . . . New York, 1937.

Smith, W.R.L. *The Story of the Cherokees*. Cleveland, Tenn., 1928.

Starkey, Marion L. *The Cherokee Nation*. New York, 1946.

Strickland, Rennard. *Fire and the Spirits: Cherokee Law from Clan to Courts*. Norman, Okla., 1975.

Stuart, Paul. *The Indian Office: Growth and Development of an American Institution, 1865–1900*. Ann Arbor, 1979.

Walker, Robert Sparks. *Torchlights to the Cherokees: The Brainerd Mission*. New York, 1931.

Wallace, Anthony F.C. *The Death and Rebirth of the Seneca*. New York, 1969.

Wardell, Morris L. *A Political History of the Cherokee Nation, 1838–1907*. Norman, Okla., 1938.

Washburn, Wilcomb. *The Indian in America*. New York, 1975.

Wetmore, Ruth Y. *First on the Land: The North Carolina Indians*. Winston Salem, N.C., 1975.

Wilkins, Thurman. *Cherokee Tragedy: The Story of the Ridge Family and the Decimation of a People*. New York, 1970.

Williams, Walter L., ed. *Southeastern Indians Since the Removal Era*. Athens, Ga., 1979.

Woodward, Grace Steele. *The Cherokees*. Norman, Okla., 1963.

Young, Mary E. *Redskins, Ruffleshirts and Rednecks: Indian Allotments in Alabama and Mississippi, 1830–1860*. Norman, Okla., 1961.

Zeigler, Wilbur G., and Ben S. Grosscup. *The Heart of the Alleghanies or Western North Carolina*. . . . Raleigh, 1883.

ARTICLES

Aiken, R.A. "Eightieth Regiment." In Clark, *Histories of the Several Regiments and Battalions*, IV, 117–28.

Avery, Sarah L. "Colonel William Holland Thomas." *North Carolina University Magazine* 29 (May 1899):291–95.

Bloom, Leonard. "The Acculturation of the Eastern Cherokee: Historical Aspects." *North Carolina Historical Review* 19 (Oct. 1942): 323–58.

Bridgers, Ben Oshel. "An Historical Analysis of the Legal Status of the

North Carolina Cherokees." *North Carolina Law Review* 58 (Aug. 1980): 1075–1131.

―――. "A Legal Digest of the North Carolina Cherokees." *Journal of Cherokee Studies* 4 (Winter 1979): 21–43.

Burke, Joseph C. "The Cherokee Cases: A Study in Law, Politics, and Morality." *Stanford Law Review* 21 (Feb. 1969): 500–531.

Carrington, Henry B. "Eastern Band of Cherokees of North Carolina." *Eleventh Census of the United States: Extra Census Bulletin*. Washington, D.C., 1892. Pp. 11–21.

Conser, Walter H. Jr. "John Ross and the Cherokee Resistance Campaigns, 1833–1838." *Journal of Southern History* 44 (May 1978), 191–212.

Corkran, David H. "Cherokee Pre-History." *North Carolina Historical Review* 34 (Oct. 1957): 455–66.

Covington, James W. "Proposed Catawba Indian Removal, 1848." *South Carolina Historical and Geneological Magazine* 55 (Jan. 1954): 42–47.

Davis, Kenneth Penn. "Chaos in the Indian Country: The Cherokee Nation, 1828–35." In King, *Cherokee Nation*, 129–47.

―――. "The Cherokee Removal, 1835–1838." *Tennessee Historical Quarterly* 32 (Winter 1973): 311–31.

Davis, Rebecca Harding. "Qualla." *Lippincott's Magazine of Popular Literature and Science* 41 (Nov. 1875): 576–86.

Dickens, Roy S., Jr. "The Origins and Development of Cherokee Culture." In King, *Cherokee Nation*, 3–32.

Donaldson, Thomas F. "Eastern Band of Cherokees of North Carolina and Eastern Cherokees." *Eleventh Census of the United States: Extra Census Bulletin*. Washington, D.C., 1892. Pp. 7–9.

Finger, John R. "The Abortive Second Cherokee Removal, 1841–1844." *Journal of Southern History* 47 (May 1981): 207–26.

―――. "The North Carolina Cherokees, 1838–1866: Traditionalism, Progressivism, and the Affirmation of State Citizenship." *Journal of Cherokee Studies* 5 (Spring 1980): 17–29.

―――. "The Saga of Tsali: Legend Versus Reality." *North Carolina Historical Review* 56 (Winter 1979): 1–18.

Fogelson, Raymond D., and Paul Kutsche. "Cherokee Economic Cooperatives: The Gadugi." In William N. Fenton and John Gulick, eds., "Symposium on Cherokee and Iroquois Culture." Bureau of American Ethnology *Bulletin* 180 (1961): 87–123.

French, Laurence, and Renitia Bertoluzzi. "The Drunken Indian Stereotype and the Eastern Cherokees." *Appalachian Journal* 2 (Summer 1975): 322–44.

Harmon, George D. "The North Carolina Cherokees and the New Echota Treaty of 1835." *North Carolina Historical Review* 6 (July 1929): 237–53.

Hudson, Charles M. "The Catawba Indians of South Carolina: A Question of Ethnic Survival." In Williams, *Southeastern Indians*, 110–20.

————. "Utkena: A Cherokee Anomalous Monster." *Journal of Cherokee Studies* 3 (Spring 1978): 62–75.

Iobst, Richard W. "William Holland Thomas and the Cherokee Claims." In King, *Cherokee Nation*, 181–201.

Kelley, James C. "Oconostota," *Journal of Cherokee Studies* 3 (Fall 1979): 221–38.

Kilpatrick, Jack F., and Anna C. "Chronicles of Wolftown: Social Documents of the North Carolina Cherokees, 1850–1862." Bureau of American Ethnology *Bulletin* 196 (1966): 1–111.

————. "Eastern Cherokee Folktales: Reconstructed from the Field Notes of Frans M. Olbrechts." Bureau of American Ethnology *Bulletin* 196 (1966): 379–447.

King, Duane H. "The Origin of the Eastern Cherokees as a Social and Political Entity." In King, *Cherokee Nation*, 164–80.

King, Duane H., and E. Raymond Evans, "Tsali: The Man Behind the Legend," *Journal of Cherokee Studies* 4 (Fall 1979): 194–201.

King, Duane H., and Laura H. "The Mythico-Religious Origin of the Cherokees." *Appalachian Journal* 2 (Summer 1975): 258–64.

Kupferer, Harriet J. "The Isolated Eastern Cherokee." *Midcontinent American Studies Journal* 6 (Fall, 1975): 124–34.

————. "The 'Principal People,' 1960: A Study of Cultural and Social Groups of the Eastern Cherokee." Bureau of American Ethnology *Bulletin* 196 (1966): 215–325.

Kutsche, Paul. "The Tsali Legend: Culture Heroes and Historiography." *Ethnohistory* 10 (Fall 1963): 329–57.

Lambert, Robert S. "The Oconaluftee Valley, 1800–1860: A Study of the Sources for Mountain History." *North Carolina Historical Review* 35 (Oct. 1958): 415–26.

Litton, Gaston. "Enrollment Records of the Eastern Band of Cherokee Indians." *North Carolina Historical Review* 17 (July 1940): 199–231.

McLoughlin, William G. "Thomas Jefferson and the Beginning of Cherokee Nationalism, 1806 to 1809." *William and Mary Quarterly* 3d ser. 32 (Oct. 1975): 547–80.

McLoughlin, William G., and Walter H. Conser, Jr. "The Cherokees in Transition: A Statistical Analysis of the Federal Cherokee Census of 1835." *Journal of American History* 64 (Dec. 1977): 678–703.

Metcalf, P. Richard. "Who Should Rule at Home? Native American Politics and Indian-White Relations." *Journal of American History* 61 (Dec. 1974), 651–65.

Mooney, James, and Frans M. Olbrechts. "The Swimmer Manuscript: Cherokee Sacred Formulas and Medicinal Prescriptions." Bureau of American Ethnology *Bulletin* 99 (1932): 1–319.

Nash, Gary B. "The Image of the Indians in the Southern Colonial Mind." *William and Mary Quarterly* 3d ser. 29 (Apr. 1972): 197–230.

Neely, Sharlotte. "Acculturation and Persistence among North Carolina's Eastern Band of Cherokee Indians." In Williams, *Southeastern Indians*, 154–73.

————. "The Quaker Era of Cherokee Indian Education, 1880–1892." *Appalachian Journal* 2 (Summer 1975): 314–22.

North Carolina Commission of Indian Affairs. "A Historical Perspective about the Indians of North Carolina and an Overview of the Commission of Indian Affairs." *North Carolina Historical Review* 56 (Spring 1979): 177–87.

Perdue, Theda. "Cherokee Planters: The Development of Plantation Slavery Before Removal." In King, *Cherokee Nation*, 110–23.

————. "Rising from the Ashes: The *Cherokee Phoenix* as an Ethnohistorical Source." *Ethnohistory* 24 (Summer 1977): 207–17.

Persico, V. Richard, Jr. "Early Nineteenth Century Cherokee Political Organization." In King, *Cherokee Nation*, 92–109.

Prucha, Francis P. "American Indian Policy in the 1840s: Visions of Reform." In John G. Clark, ed., *The Frontier Challenge: Responses to the Trans-Mississippi West*. Lawrence, Kan., 1971. Pp. 81–110.

————. "Andrew Jackson's Indian Policy: A Reassessment." *Journal of American History* 56 (Dec. 1969): 527–39.

Reed, Gerard. "Postremoval Factionalism in the Cherokee Nation." In King, *Cherokee Nation*, 148–63.

Reid, John Phillip. "The European Perspective and Cherokee Law." *Appalachian Journal* 2 (Summer 1975): 286–93.

————. "A Perilous Rule: The Law of International Homicide." In King, *Cherokee Nation*, 33–45.

Robertson, H.G. "The Eastern Band of Cherokee Indians, From 1835 to 1893." *North Carolina University Magazine* 31 (Apr. 1901): 173–80.

Russell, Mattie. "Devil in the Smokies: The White Man's Nature and the Indian's Fate." *South Atlantic Quarterly* 73 (Winter 1974): 53–69.

Shenck, David. "The Cherokees in North Carolina." *At Home and Abroad* 2 (Feb. 1882): 321–31.

Stringfield, William W. "North Carolina Cherokee Indians." *The North Carolina Booklet* 3 (July 1903): 5–24.

―――. "Sixty-Ninth Regiment." In Clark, *Histories of the Several Regiments and Battalions*, III, 729–61.

Wetmore, Ruth Y. "The Role of the Indian in North Carolina History." *North Carolina Historical Review* 56 (Spring 1979): 162–76.

Williams, Walter L. "The Merger of Apaches with Eastern Cherokees: Qualla in 1893." *Journal of Cherokee Studies* 2 (Spring 1977): 240–45.

―――. "Patterns in the History of the Remaining Southeastern Indians, 1840–1975." In Williams, *Southeastern Indians*, 193–207.

Wilms, Douglas C. "Cherokee Settlement Patterns in Nineteenth Century Georgia." *Southeastern Geographer* 14 (May 1974): 46–53.

Witthoft, John. "Observations on Social Change among the Eastern Cherokees." In King, *Cherokee Nation*, 202–22.

Young, Mary. "The Cherokee Nation: Mirror of the Republic." *American Quarterly* 33 (Winter 1981): 502– 24.

Young, Virginia D. "A Sketch of the Cherokee People on the Indian Reservation of North Carolina." *Woman's Progress* (Jan. 1894): 169–74.

NEWSPAPERS

Brownlow's Knoxville Whig and Rebel Ventilator, 1863–1866.

Daily Appeal (Memphis), Apr. 11, 17, June 13, 1863.

Daily Enquirer (Columbus, Ga.), May 22, 1864.

Daily Register (Knoxville), 1862.

Daily Times and True Union (Nashville), Mar. 16, 1864.

Friends' Weekly Intelligencer, (Philadelphia), Mar. 31, 1849.

Greensborough [N.C.] Patriot, May 8, 1862; Feb. 18, 1864.

Holston Christian Advocate (Knoxville), 1851–1854.

Keowee [S.C.] Courier, Dec. 8, 1849.

National Intelligencer (Washington, D.C.), 1838–1839.

New York *Times*, Mar. 15, 1863.

Niles' National Register (Baltimore), 1838–1839.

Palmetto-State Banner, (Columbia, S.C.), Aug. 30, 1849.

DISSERTATIONS, THESES, AND OTHER UNPUBLISHED MANUSCRIPTS

Bryan, Charles Faulkner, Jr. "The Civil War in East Tennessee: A Social, Political, and Economic Study." Ph.D. dissertation, University of Tennessee, 1978.

Cashion, Jerry Clyde. "Cherokee Removal from North Carolina." 1966 typescript.

Colby, William Munn. "Routes to Rainey Mountain: A Biography of James Mooney, Ethnologist." Ph.D. dissertation, University of Wisconsin, Madison, 1977.

Cotton, William Donaldson. "Appalachian North Carolina: A Political Study, 1860–1889." Ph.D. dissertation, University of North Carolina, Chapel Hill, 1954.

Frizzell, George E. "The Legal Status of the Eastern Band of Cherokee Indians." M.A. thesis, Western Carolina University, 1981.

Owl, Henry M. "The Eastern Band of Cherokee Indians Before and After the Removal." M.A. thesis, University of North Carolina, Chapel Hill, 1929.

Redman, Susan M. "United States Indian Policy and the Eastern Cherokees 1838–1889." M.A. thesis, University of Cincinnati, 1980.

Russell, Mattie U. "William Holland Thomas, White Chief of the North Carolina Cherokees." Ph.D. dissertation, Duke University, 1956.

Williams, Sharlotte Neely. "Ethnicity in a Native American Community." Ph.D. dissertation, University of North Carolina, Chapel Hill, 1976.

———. "The Role of Formal Education among the Eastern Cherokee Indians, 1880–1971." M.A. thesis, University of North Carolina, Chapel Hill, 1971.

INDEX

Abbott, Joseph, 108

Acculturation: of pre-removal Cherokees, 8–10, 13–14, 16, 18, 20; of Cherokees East in 1839, 29; of North Carolina Cherokees, 42, 60–81; promotion of by education, 133–39; observed by James Mooney, 153; relation of federal authority to, 170; by 1900, 176, 178. *See also* Education

Adair, James, 5

Agriculture: among pre-removal Cherokees, 4, 7–8; among North Carolina Cherokees, 11, 14, 60–63,70, 80–81; among North Carolina Cherokees after Civil War, 127; livestock, 127–28; model farms, 127–28; primitive nature of, 148; use of suitable land, 175

Alabama Cherokees: population of in 1835, 16; in 1839, 29; census of, 52; farms of, 60; population in 1851, 71; population as per Hester Roll, 143

Alcohol: problems of, 11; temperance, 14, 42, 65–66; post-Civil War problems with, 102; William McCarthy's views on, 126–27; related to murder, 132; drunken student, 136–37; consistent problem of, 155, 220n. 22; Nimrod Smith accused of drunkenness, 156–57; related to idleness, 169. *See also* Health

Allotment: private reservations under 1817 and 1819 treaties, 10–11; reservations under Treaty of New Echota, 17; claims for private reservations, 31; as U.S. policy, 129; U.S. considers it for North Carolina Cherokees, 175, 224 n. 59. *See also* Lands

American Baptist Board of Home Missions, 125–26

Anighisgi, 97

Apache Indians, 171

Asbury, Francis, 14

Asheville: occupied by federal forces, 97; *passim*

Asheville Female College, 135–37. *See also* Education

Askew, John, 109–110

Astoogatogeh, 91

Atkins, John D. C., 146, 151

Axley, Felix: opposes removal, 38–39; agent, 46; helps with Mullay Roll, 48; comments on Cherokees, 69

Ayunini. *See* Swimmer

Ballplay: criticized, 68; described, 74, 80; in Civil War, 94; revived, 174, 178

Balsam Mountains, 3, 176

Barnard, Andrew, 68

Barringer, Rufus, 119–20

Barter: in Cherokee economy, 128

Bartlett, William C., 97–98

Belt, R. V., 162, 170

Big Cove: Cherokee settlement at, 67; school at, 131, 133, 150; timber in, 149; *See also* Quallatown Cherokees

Bird, J. W., 138

Bird Town: Cherokee settlement at, 67; statistics on, 71; school at, 131, 150; state land grants at, 147. *See also* Quallatown Cherokees

Black Fox. *See* Enola

Blaine, James G., 150–51

Blunt, James G.: intrigues of, 109–10;

242

Blunt, James G. (Cont.)
denounced, 114; indicted and tried,
117–18; mentioned, 126, 132, 134
Blythe, James: assists James Mooney,
153; appointed agent, 156; opposes
Nimrod Smith, 156–57; dismissed,
158, 162; mentioned, 171; attacked,
172–73. *See also* Factionalism
Board of Cherokee Commissioners: under
Treaty of New Echota, 35–37, 46
Board of Indian Commissioners, 115
Bogy, Lewis V., 104
Boudinot, Elias, 8, 16
Boyd, David L., 170–74
Bragg, Thomas, 50, 55
Brown, Thomas C., 138
Bryson, Goldman, 66, 94
Bryson City (Charleston), N.C.: 3, 25,
132, 146, 149, 176
Buffalo Town (Cheoah). *See* Cheoah
Cherokees
Bureau of American Ethnology, 152
Burnside, Ambrose, 87, 89
Bushyhead, Dennis (Principal Chief of
Cherokee Nation), 140, 143, 216 n. 53
Bushyhead, George (Principal Chief of
Eastern Band): claims in Washington,
58; post-Civil War leadership, 102–
108; denounced by William Thomas,
112; calls self Principal Chief, 113;
mentioned, 116; attacked, 117; on
liquor problem, 127. *See also* Fac-
tionalism
Bushyhead, Jesse (The Reverend),
13–14, 21, 216 n. 53

Carlisle Institute: founded, 135; Chero-
kee students attend, 162, 169, 178
Cartoogechaye Creek, 21, 71
Catawba Indians: join North Carolina
Cherokees, 42–44; removal of from
North Carolina, 47–48; intermarry
with Cherokees, 43, 68
Cathcart Tract: Timber on, 169–72
Chandler, Zachariah, 132–33
Chapman, Alfred, 52–54
Charleston. *See* Bryson City (Charleston),
N.C.
"Charley." *See* Tsali

Cheoah Boundary, 51, 121–22, 125
Cheoah Cherokees: represented by William Thomas, 17; oppose removal, 18;
remain along Cheoah river, 29; authorized to form company, 44–45, 73;
uncertain status of, 51–52; mentioned, 69, 85; statistics on, 71; hold
tribal councils, 107–108, 113–14;
payments to, 110; James Obadiah,
headman of, 115; faction among,
115–17; land problems of, 121; schools
among, 128, 130–131, 133. *See also*
North Carolina Cherokees; Quallatown Cherokees; Snowbird Community; Valley River Cherokees
Cherokee, town of (Yellow Hill): first
mentioned, 22; called Yellow Hill,
67; near Echota Mission, 126; schools
at, 131, 138–39, 150–51; capital at,
139; Hester Roll read at, 143
Cherokee Company, 44–45, 73–74. *See
also* Gadugi
Cherokee County, 35, *passim*
Cherokee Nation: established, 8; opposes
removal, 14–16; removal of, 21, 28;
factionalism in, 28–29; claims in behalf of, 31; possible removal of North
Carolina Cherokees to, 31–39; returnees from, 49; conflicting land claims
with Eastern Band, 56, 58, 106–107;
supports consolidation with Eastern
Band, 58, 104, 112–13, 140; receives
Eastern Cherokees, 116–17; lawsuit
against, 143, 145. *See also* North
Carolina Cherokees
Cherokees, pre-removal: origins and
legends, 3–4; Lower Towns, 3; Middle Towns, 3, 10; Upper (Overhill
Towns), 3; Out Towns, 3, 6, 10; trade
and relations with British, 4–6; economy, 4, 7; political system, 4–5; family and kinship, 5; blood revenge, 5;
clans, 5; relations with U.S., 6–8,
10, 15–18. *See also* Acculturation
Chickasaw Indians, 4
Chinoque. *See* Owl, John
Choctaw Indians, 4
Chota, 5
Citizenship: of Quallatown Indians,

Citizenship (*Cont.*)
10–11, 16–19; U.S. attitudes toward that of Cherokees, 31–32; arguments of William Thomas concerning, 41–42; uncertainty regarding, 49–52, 55–56; as related to Cherokee service in military, 83; not implied in right of residency, 102; uncertainty over, 105; denied, 111–12; dispute over, 129–30, 212 n. 14; within Cherokee Nation, 140; Supreme Court decision in regard to, 145–46; confusion over, 147; claimed for Cherokees, 169–70; discussed in lawsuit, 172–74; uncertainty regarding after lawsuit, 174–75. *See also* North Carolina, State of; United States, relations with North Carolina Cherokees; Voting
Civil War: and Cherokees, 82–100; William Thomas organizes fighting force, 82–87; opposition to in western North Carolina, 87–88; Cherokee battle at Gatlinburg, 89–90; savage Indian stereotype during, 90–93; Cherokees against bushwhackers, 93–94; Cherokee captives taken to Knoxville, 96; Unionist Cherokees, 96–97; Thomas Legion surrenders, 97–98; effects on Cherokees, 98, 100–102
Clark, Henry T., 86
Clements, C. C., 145
Cleveland, Grover, 150–51
Clingman, Thomas L., 38, 53, 58
Clothing: Cherokee, 62
Colvard, Calvin A., 128, 130–31
Common Fund of Eastern Band: creation and use of, 122, 125, 128, 130, 132; use of changed by law, 133–134, 148; used for education, 150, 151–52; authorized for paying back taxes, 169–70
Cooley, Dennis N., 103–104
Cox, David C. (low-ranking official), 115
Cox, Jacob D. (Commissioner of Indian Affairs), 110
Craven, Braxton, 136
Crawford, Samuel J. (Cherokee attorney), 145

Crawford, T. Hartley (Commissioner of Indian Affairs), 29, 32, 34, 36–39, 41
Creek Indians: mentioned, 4, 14; war with U.S. and Cherokees, 7, 84
Crime: among North Carolina Cherokees, 66–67; assaults, 127; murder, 132. *See also* Trespassing
Cudjo, 71
Cuming, Alexander, 4–5, 116
Cunning Deer, 66
Currey, Benjamin F., 17

Dances, 64, 69, 80
Davidson, Francis M., 95
Davis, George Barber, 13
Davis, Jefferson, 82–83
Davis, Rebecca Harding, 130, 137
Dawes Severalty Act. *See* Allotment
DeSoto, Hernando, 4
Deaderick, James W., 38–39
Deep Creek, 25, *passim*
Denver, James W., 58–59
DeVaughan, John, 134
DeVaughan, Kate, 134
DeWeese, John T., 108–109, 117
Dickson, Harry M., 172–74
Dillard, John H. (arbitrator), 119
Dillard, John L. (Cherokee attorney), 11
Dony, Francis A., 122
Dorchester, Daniel, 157
Downing, Lewis, 112–13, 115
Dragging Canoe, 84
Drowning Bear. *See* Yonaguska
Dudley, Edward B., 18, 20, 29

Eastern Band of Cherokees. *See* North Carolina Cherokees
Eastern Cherokees (Cherokees East). *See* Alabama Cherokees; Cheoah Cherokees; Georgia Cherokees; North Carolina Cherokees; Quallatown Cherokees; Tennessee Cherokees; Valley River Cherokees
Eaton, William, Jr., 51–52
Echota Mission: founded, 63; services at, 63–64; near Cherokee, 126; school at, 135, 150, 197 n. 16. *See also* Education; Religion
Edney, B. M., 82

Education: of pre-removal Cherokees, 8;
lack of among North Carolina Cherokees, 60; literacy, 64–65, 130; U.S.
provides for, 125–26; schools among
North Carolina Cherokees, 130–31;
poverty of students, 131; collapse of
schools, 133; common fund used for,
133–34; state supervision of, 134; fac-
tional disputes concerning, 134–35;
sending Cherokees to colleges, 135–
37; Quaker schools, 138–39; discrim-
ination against blacks, 143; under
Quakers, 149–52; training school at
Cherokee, 150–51; Quaker problems
concerning, 156–58; U.S. takes over
Cherokee schools, 158, 162; federal
programs, 162, 169; changes brought
by, 178. *See also* Acculturation; Carlisle Institute; Hampton Institute;
Haskell Institute
Ellis, Daniel, 91–93
Enola: preacher, shaman, and official,
64–65, 80; in Civil War, 84, 100;
suspicion of mixed-bloods, 107; denies
legitimacy of Cheoah council, 113;
land commissioner, 125; property of,
128; critic of William McCarthy, 132;
supposed chief, 140; dies, 146
Erwin, Marcus, 117
Euchella: takes private allotment, 10–11;
role in Tsali episode, 24–28; chief of
Wolf Town, 67; described by Charles
Lanman, 70; property of, 71
Euchella v. Welsh, 11, 50
Ewart, H. G., 169–70, 172–73

Factionalism: in Cherokee Nation,
28–29; among North Carolina Cherokees after Civil War, 100, 102–104;
George Bushyhead and James Taylor
faction, 107–108; John Ross-Taylor
faction, 112–18; confronting William
McCarthy, 125–26; McCarthy becomes involved, 131–32; Nimrod
Smith becomes dominant, 139–40,
142; as problem in 1880s and 1890s,
147; Smith versus Henry Spray and
James Blythe, 156–58. *See also* Harmony Ethic; Political Developments
Falls, Gilbert, 104–105

Family and kinship: discussed, 5; role of
women, 5, 60, 71–72
Fardon, A. F., 136
Fillmore, Millard, 53
Fishing: in Cherokee economy, 7, 60, 62
Flint District, Indian Territory, 112
Flying Squirrel: pursues Tsali, 24; claims
to be Yonaguska's successor, 31; chief
of Paint Town, 67; property of, 71,
128; suspicious of mixed-bloods, 107;
denies legitimacy of Cheoah council,
113; elected Principal Chief, 114, 116;
mentioned, 131
Food: kind and preparation of, 62
Fort Cass, 22, 24
Fort Loudoun, 5
Foster, William S., 23–28
Fourteenth Amendment, 105
Franklin, N. C., 36
Frauds. *See* Blunt, James G.; Rogers,
Johnson K.; Swetland, Silas H.
Friends Normal School of Maryville,
Tennessee, 135, 138–39, 156

Gadugi, 73–74. *See also* Cherokee Company
Garner, J. D., 134–35, 138
George II, 5
Georgia: demand for Indian lands, 8–9,
14–16. *See also* Removal
Georgia Cherokees: number in 1835, 16;
in 1839, 29; move to North Carolina,
49; census of, 52; farms of, 60; popu-
lation of in 1851, 71; U.S. seeks in-
formation about, 104; claim share of
lands, 106; some wish to emigrate,
112–13; livestock of, 128; vote for
Lloyd Welch, 132; population as per
Hester Roll, 143
Geronimo, 171
Gibson, Samuel G.: appointed agent,
142–43; wants sale of timber, 149
The Gilded Age, 108
Ginseng, 11
Graham, James (Congressman), 29, 34–35
Graham, William A. (Governor), 45
Graham County, 121, *passim*
Grant, Ulysses S.: petition to, 114; In-
dian Peace Policy, 115; promises to
help removal, 116

Great Smoky Mountains, 3, 20, 62
Great Smoky Mountains National Park, 90, 176
Green, Benjamin, 45–47, 52–53
Green, Duff (Benjamin Green's father), 45–47, 52–53
Green corn ceremonies, 80

Haddon, Julian, 162, 173
Hadley, Simon, 158
Hampton Institute, 162, 169, 178
Harmony Ethic, 68, 100, 102, 117. *See also* Factionalism
Harrison, Benjamin, 152, 156, 169–70
Hart, Joseph C., 155, 162, 169
Haskell Institute, 162, 169
Hayes, George W., 52, 82–83
Hayt, Ezra A., 135
Haywood County, 37, *passim*
Health: of Cherokees during Civil War, 86, 88; smallpox, 101; lice, 137; tuberculosis, 155. *See also* Alcohol
Henson Family, 71
Hester, Joseph G., 142–43, 155
Hester Roll: Indians question accuracy of, 143
Hindman, Thomas C., 31–34, 36
Hiwassee River, 13, *passim*
Hobbs, Barnabas C., 138, 150, 158
Hog Bite, 21, 71
Hoke, John, 58–59
Holden, W. W., 111
Holmes, Julius L., 149
Hopewell. *See* Treaty of
Horseshoe Bend, Battle of, 7–8, 37
Housing: Cherokee, 8, 61
Hunting: in Cherokee economy, 4, 7, 10, 60–62

Indian Civilization Fund, 65, 140
Indian Policy, U.S.: land acquisition and civilization, 6–7; federal programs, 7; change in regard to Cherokees, 35–36. *See also* Allotment; Education; Removal; United States, relations with North Carolina Cherokees
Indian Rights Association, 152
Indian Territory. *See* Cherokee Nation

Intermarriage: with Catawba Indians, 43, 68; with whites, 68, 143; with blacks, 97, 143
Iroquois Indians, 3

Jackson, Alfred E. (Confederate General), 87
Jackson, Andrew (General and President), 7–8, 15–17
Jackson, John (Cherokee), 114
Jackson County, 82, *passim*
James, Horace, 125
Jarrett, G. T., 82
Jarrett, Nimrod S. (U.S. appraisal agent), 18
Jefferson, Thomas, 7
Jenkins, Jonas, 27
Jocknick, G. F., 109–10
Johnson, Andrew: denounces Confederate Indians, 90–91; receives petition, 107
Johnston, Thomas D., 119, 121
Johnston, William (father of Thomas D. Johnston), 110–11, 113–14, 119–21, 125
Jones, Evan, 13, 15
Jones, John B., 103
Junaluska: and Andrew Jackson, 7–8; returns from Cherokee Nation, 49; becomes citizen, 49, 51; mentioned, 71, 82, 84, 91
Junaluska Zouaves, 82–83

Kerr, D. W., 169
Killian, M., 20
King, J. W., 38
Kirk, George W., 96–97
Kituwha, 3
Knoxville: Cherokees visit during Civil War, 85–86, 93; captured by Union forces, 87, 89; Cherokee captives taken to, 96, 101
Knoxville Register, 93
Knoxville Whig and Rebel Ventilator, 96

Labor: Cherokees a source of, 14, 128
Lambert, Hugh, 114

Lands: acquired by Thomas for Cherokees, 17, 21, 29, 32, 34, 44; possible sale to Catawba Indians, 42–43; at Quallatown, 44–45; at Cheoah, 51–52; threatened by William Thomas's indebtedness, 110–12; lawsuits concerning, 119–21; decision of arbitrators concerning, 120–21; survey of, 122, 125; U.S. acquires for Cherokees, 125, 128; trespassing, 143–44, 147–49, 176; some Cherokees advocate sale of, 145; dispute over those of Cherokee Nation, 145; and incorporation of Eastern Band, 155; redemption of Qualla Boundary, 169–70; settlement regarding trespassers, 171–72; problems of allotment, 175. *See also* Timber; Trespassing
Lang, John D., 115–16
Lanman, Charles: describes Tsali's execution, 27, 70; observes Cherokee religion, 63–64; idealizes Quallatown, 69–70, 81; describes ballplay, 74, 80
Larned, C. H., 23, 25
Lea, Albert M. (Acting Secretary of War), 31–32, 34
Lea, Luke (Commissioner of Indian Affairs), 52–54
Leatherwood, Robert L., 149, 156
Legends: concerning Cherokee origins, 3–4; oral tradition, 101
Literacy. *See* Education
Little Tennessee River, 3, *passim*
Lockwood, Belva A., 139
Logan, John A., 151
Loudon, Tenn., 115–16, 140
Love, James R., 97, 171–72
Love, Margaret, 88
Lufty Indians. *See* Quallatown Indians
Lumbee Indians: status, 50; in Civil War, 83

McCall, George A., 25
McCarthy, William C.: appointed agent, 125–26; advocates temperance, 126–27; wants model farms, 128–29; pays Cherokee taxes, 129; sets up schools, 130–31; involved with factions, 131–32; protests closing of agency, 132–

McCarthy, William C. (*Cont.*)
33; accused, 134; mentioned, 142; on trespassers, 144
Macedonia. *See* Echota Mission
McMillen, Joseph W., 18
Macon County, 25, *passim*
McPherson, Theodore H. N., 148
Manney, Mary A., 131
Martin, James G., 97
Mason, William T., 172–74
Medill, William C., 48
Mineral resources, 148
Mix, Charles E., 65
Monroe, James, 8
Moody, J. M., 173
Mooney, James: and Tsali legend, 21–22, 27–28; and Indian preparations for war, 85; and Unionist Cherokees, 96; background and relationship with Nimrod Smith, 152–53, 171; work among Cherokees, 153, 155; views expressed in "Myths of the Cherokee," 176, 178
Morehead, J. M., 43
Morgan, George Washington (Confederate officer), 84–85
Morgan, Thomas J. (Commissioner of Indian Affairs), 157–58
Moytoy, 5, 116
Mullay, John C.: takes census, 48–49; views on Quallatown, 69
Mullay Roll, 49, 55; used by Confederates, 84; basis for Swetland Roll, 109; enrollees of move, 112
Murphy, town of, 33, *passim*

Nantahala River, 11, *passim*
Nelson, Thomas A. R., 90
Neutral Lands, 56, 58, 106
New Echota, Ga., 8. *See also* Treaty of
Nikwasi Mound, 4
"Noble Savage" stereotype, 70
North Carolina, State of: act of 1783, 6; *Euchella v. Welsh,* 11; opposes Cherokee residency, 15; uncertainty over Cherokee citizenship, 18–19; regarding possible Cherokee hostility, 20; attitudes toward Cherokees, 29; committee on Indian removal, 37–38;

North Carolina (*Cont.*)
gives tacit permission for Cherokees to stay, 41–42; authorizes Cherokees to form company, 44–45; and uncertain Cherokee status, 49–52; equivocation of, 55–56, 59; and Cherokee military service, 83; recognizes Cherokee residency, 102–103; and Cherokee right to sue, 111–12; taxation of Cherokees, 129–30; and Cherokee schools, 134; state supreme court decision, 142; law abetting trespassing, 144; Cherokees supposed citizens of, 145–46; taxation of Cherokees, 148; 1868 constitution allows Cherokee voting, 150; 1889 incorporation of Eastern Band, 155–56; act of 1895, 172–73; uncertainty concerning Cherokees, 174–75. *See also* Citizenship; North Carolina Cherokees

North Carolina Cherokees: relations with state, 6; treaties of 1817 and 1819, 10; Quallatown Indians, 11, 13–14; missionaries among, 13–14; and removal, 16–19, 20–21; Tsali episode, 21–28; avoid removal, 28–40; uncertain status, 41–59; Catawbas among, 42–44; relations with U.S., 45–49; other Cherokees join, 49; right to vote, 49–50; relations with blacks, 50; Cheoah Cherokees, 51–52; payments to, 52–55; wish to remain, 55; relations with Cherokee Nation, 56, 58; economy of, 60–62; acculturation of, 60–81; education among, 64–65; harmony ethic among, 68; Quallatown Indians, 69–71; clan restrictions, 72; marriage patterns, 72; role of women among, 72; Cherokee Company, 73–74; ballplay among, 74, 80; Civil War among, 82–100; post-war troubles, 102–105; recognized as tribe, 105; request U.S. aid, 106; dispute over Neutral Lands, 106–107; face loss of lands, 110–12; involved in law suits, 111–13, 118–21; first referred to as Eastern Band, 113; problems of, 126–27; economy, 127–28; taxes and citizenship, 129–30; education of, 130–39; Nimrod Smith and factionalism, 139–40, 142; sued by

North Carolina Cherokees (*Cont.*)
Wallace Rollins, 142; Hester Roll, 143; inability to bring suit, 144; 1886 Supreme Court decision, 145–46; confused status, 147; Justice Department sues in behalf of, 148; Quaker education, 149–152; James Mooney among, 152–53, 155; incorporate as Eastern Band, 155–56; factionalism among, 156–57; U.S. takes over schools of, 158, 162, 169; challenge federal authority, 169–74; continuing uncertain status, 174–75; situation as of 1900, 176, 178. *See also* Acculturation; Cheoah Cherokees; Citizenship; Civil War; Education; Factionalism; Quallatown Cherokees; Removal; Thomas, William Holland; Valley River Cherokees

Nunnehi, 4

Obadiah, James, 115
Oconaluftee Indians. *See* Quallatown Indians
Oconaluftee River, 10, *passim*
Oconostota, 84–85
Office of Indian Affairs. *See* United States, relations with North Carolina Cherokees
Old Settlers, 10
Olney, Richard, 172
Oochella. *See* Euchella
Oosawih, 86
Osborne, H. G., 151–52
Owl, David, 114
Owl, John (Valley River Cherokee leader), 48–49, 114

Paint Town: settlement at, 67; statistics on, 70. *See also* Quallatown Cherokees
Painter, Charles C., 152
Palmer, John B. (Confederate officer), 88
Palmer, William Jackson (Union officer), 89–90, 95
Panther family, 71
Per capita payments: claims for, 31; confirmed in 1846 treaty, 46; on basis of Siler Roll, 52–54
Pinchot, Gifford, 170
Political developments: Cherokee Nation

Political developments (*Cont.*)
organized, 8, 15; Cherokee town governments in North Carolina, 67–68;
1868 Cheoah council and constitution,
107–108, 140; 1869 Cheoah council,
113, 126–27; 1870 Cheoah council,
113–14; 1870 Quallatown council,
114; 1872 Cheoah council, 117; 1874
Cheoah council, 121–22; 1875 Quallatown council, 131–32; 1877 Cheoah
council, 139; 1880 as transition, 139;
Cherokee voters desert Democrats,
150–51; Nimrod Smith loses election,
158; new leadership challenges federal
authority, 169–74. *See also* Factionalism; North Carolina, State of;
United States, relations with North
Carolina Cherokees
Polk, James K., 46
Pool, John, 106
Population: of Cherokees in 1835, 16; in
1839, 28–29, 187n. 33; as per Mullay
Roll, 49; as per 1850 census, 70; as
per Siler Roll, 52, 70–71; as per 1860
census, 80–81; as per Swetland Roll,
109, 140; at Quallatown, 140; as per
1880 census, 140; as per Hester Roll,
143; in 1900, 176
Porter, James M., 39
Posey, Humphrey, 13
Potter, Thomas W.: federal official, 162;
and opponents, 172–73; views on allotment, 175
Powell, John Wesley (head of Bureau of
American Ethnology), 152–53
Powell, R. J. (prepares Cherokee Roll),
105
Pratt, Richard Henry, 135, 169
Presbrey, Otis F., 142
Price, Hiram, 149
Progressivism. *See* Acculturation

Quakers: John D. Lang, 115; interest in
education, 125; J. D. Garner, 134–
35; establish Cherokee schools, 138–
39; program of education, 149–50; alleged influence on Indian voting,
150–51; schools attacked, 151–52;
Henry Spray and factionalism, 156–
58; end association with Cherokee

Quakers (*Cont.*)
Schools, 158. *See also* Education;
Hobbs, Barnabas; Spray, Henry
Qualla Boundary: first mentioned, 22;
established, 44; extent of, 120; surveyed, 125; *passim. See also* Quallatown
Cherokees
Quallatown Cherokees: settlement at
Quallatown, 11; relations with William Thomas, 13; religion and culture, 14; and Treaty of New Echota,
16–18; claim to be citizens and wish
to remain in North Carolina, 18–19;
suspected of being hostile, 20; assist
in removal, 24–27; Indians told to
join with, 26; population of, 28–29;
Thomas chief of, 31; council of, 34;
petition to state, 37; wish to remain,
41–42; organize Cherokee Company,
44–45, 73–74; owe taxes, 51; disbursement among, 53; hunting
among, 62; religion of, 63–64; temperance among, 64–66; crime among,
66–67; establish towns, 67; statistics
on, 70–71; economy among, 72–73;
ballplay among, 74, 80; in Civil War,
82–100; attitudes concerning
Thomas, 102; comprise a faction, 107;
payments among, 109–10; hold council, 114, 116; lands of, 120–22, 125;
farms and livestock of, 127–28; education of, 130–31; faction of, 139–40;
population of, 140; timber of, 149;
training school among, 150–51. *See
also* Big Cove; Bird Town; Cheoah
Cherokees; Cherokee, Town of; North
Carolina Cherokees; Paint Town; Valley River Cherokees; Wolf Town

Railroad, 149, 176
Raper, Jesse, 128
Raper family, 71
Reconstruction, 129
Reid, David S., 51–52
Religion: missionaries, 8, 13–14; Christianity, 60–61, 63–64; Cherokee services in Knoxville, 85–86; prevalence
of Baptists and Methodists, 151. *See
also* Acculturation; Education; Quakers

Removal: as U.S. policy, 7–8, 10; Georgia's demands for, 14–15; act of 1830, 15; North Carolina's attitude toward, 15; 1838 removal, 20–28; inquiries regarding, 29; efforts of 1841–44, 31–40; Congress asks about costs of, 35; efforts of 1856–57, 58–59; to Cherokee Nation, proposed, 103–105; of some Cherokees, 112–13; attitudes of factions toward, 114–15; of Obadiah group, 115–17; of 1880, 140; suggested, 146

Ridge, John, 16

Ridge, Major, 16

Robbinsville, 128, *passim*

Robinson, James, 36–38

Rogers, Johnson K.: Cherokee agent, 46; attacks William Thomas and others, 52–54; misleads Cherokees, 53–54; mentioned, 71

Rogers, William, 36

Rollins, Wallace W.: hired as tribal attorney, 117–18; sues Eastern Band, 142, 146; fails to record Cherokee titles, 144

Ross, John (Principal Chief of Cherokee Nation): defends Cherokee rights, 8–9, 15–16; sends condolences to Winfield Scott, 23; leader of faction, 28; argues for claims, 31; opponent of William Thomas, 32–33; agrees to accept Cherokees East, 35–36

Ross, John (supposed Principal Chief of Eastern Band): in Civil War, 84; succeeds George Bushyhead, 113; supposedly becomes Principal Chief, 115–16; faction leader, 117–18, 131, 139–40; implication of in murder, 132; attacks William McCarthy, 132–33; characterized, 118, 134, 213 n. 21; moves to Cherokee Nation, 140. *See also* Factionalism

Ross, W. P. (Principal Chief of Cherokee Nation), 104

Ruffin, Thomas, 119

Salola. *See* Squirrel

Sand Town, Macon County, N.C.: Cherokee community of, 85; mentioned, 103; payments at, 110; George

Sand Town (*Cont.*)
Bushyhead headman of, 113; John Jackson of, 114

Saunooka, Stillwell, 158

Savage Indian stereotype: 9–10, 68; during Civil War, 90–93

Schurz, Carl, 135

Scott, Winfield: arrives in Southeast, 20; undertakes removal, 21; involved in Tsali episode, 21–27

Sectionalism, as factor in Cherokee status, 56, 59

Seminole War, 20, 28

Sequoyah, 8, 130

Severalty. *See* Allotment

Shelton Laurel, North Carolina, 94

Sibbald, John A., 135–37, 139

Siler, David W., 52, 68, 70–71, 143

Siler Roll, 52, 54, 68, 70–71, 143

Smathers, George H.: assists U.S. in Cherokee litigation, 158; influence of among Cherokees, 170; Cherokee attorney, 172–73; attacked, 172–73

Smith, Andrew Jackson (Second Lieutenant, U.S. Army), 22–23, 25

Smith, Edward P. (Commissioner of Indian Affairs), 122, 129–30

Smith, Henry (father of Nimrod J. Smith), 114, 128, 139

Smith, John Q. (Commissioner of Indian Affairs), 133

Smith, Nimrod J. (Principal Chief of Eastern Band): mentioned, 114; becomes Principal Chief, 139; background, 140; opposes aiding malcontents, 142; assertiveness of, 142; favors sale of outlying lands, 145; considers removal, 146; sells timber in Big Cove, 149; leads Indians into Republican camp, 150–51; defends Henry Spray, 152; relationship with James Mooney, 152–53; opposes Spray and James Blythe, 156–58; death of, 171; mentioned, 169, 173. *See also* Factionalism

Smith, W. C. (purchaser of Cherokee Timber), 170–71

Smithsonian Institution, 152

Soco Creek, 11, *passim*

Snowbird Community, 140

Snowbird Gap: school at, 150

Spencer, Andrew (Superintendent of Cherokee Schools): appointed, 162; attacks George Smathers and Henry Spray, 170; views on allotment, 175

Spencer, John C. (Secretary of War), 35

Spoliations: claims for, 31

Spray, Henry: superintendent of Quaker schools, 138; educational work, 150; alleged influence on Indian voting, 150–51; and critics, 152; assists James Mooney, 153; opposes Nimrod Smith, 156–57; refuses to vacate Cherokee schools, 158, 162; opposed by Andrew Spencer, 162, 170; mentioned, 171; attacked, 172–73; U.S. superintendent of schools for Cherokees, 174, 178. *See also* Factionalism

Squirrel, 63, 68

Starrett, Preston, 46; and family, 71

Stickney, William, 127–28

Strawberry Plains: Cherokees camp at in Civil War, 86–87; retreat from, 89

Stringfield, William: on Cherokee religion, 64; on Cherokee scalping, 91–92

Sturgis, Samuel D., 95

Swain County, 126, *passim*

Swetland census, 127–28, 130, 140

Swetland, Silas H.: prepares census and payment roll, 108–109; intrigues with James Blunt, 109–10; denounced, 114; mentioned, 111, 113, 117, 127

Swimmer: learns traditional lore, 80; in Civil War, 84–85, 100; difficult times for, 146; friend of James Mooney, 153; and changes in Cherokee society, 176, 178

Tahquit, 66–67

Taxation: of Cherokee land, 51; delinquent land taxes, 129, 147–48; poll tax, 129, 150; large tract sold for back taxes, 169; may use common fund for paying taxes, 169–70; selling timber for paying taxes, 169–70; continues after important lawsuit, 174. *See also* North Carolina, State of

Taylor, C. H. (Cherokee Civil War officer), 94

Taylor, David (father of James T[a]), 71

Taylor, David, 137

Taylor, James (Cherokee agent and faction leader): in Washington, 58; supports removal, 58–59; mentioned, 71; serves in Civil War, 84; post-war leader, 102; helps organize Cheoah council, 107; denounced by William Thomas, 112; removal agent, 112–13; faction leader, 117–18; characterized, 118, 134; land commissioner, 122, 125; critic of William McCarthy, 132–33; faction leader, 139–40; moves to Indian Territory, 140, 142; criticizes U.S., 145; approves Supreme Court decision, 146; opposes federal agents, 149; accusations of, 152. *See also* Factionalism

Taylor, Zachary (General and President), 48–49

Tecumseh, 97

Temple, M. S., 122, 125

Tennessee Cherokees: number of in 1835, 16; in 1839, 29; move to North Carolina, 49; census of, 52; farms of, 60; population of in 1851, 71; livestock of, 128; vote for Lloyd Welch, 132; population as per Hester Roll, 143

Terrell, James W.: to make annual payments, 54–55; possible agent to enroll Cherokees, 58; in Civil War, 84–85; on Cherokee scalping, 93; defendant, 111, 119–21; land commissioner, 121–22; target of murder attempt, 132; aids James Mooney, 153

Terry, Alfred, 115

Thomas, William Holland: background, 11, 13; Cherokee adviser, 13; merchant for Cherokees, 13, 62; encourages Quallatown Indians, 14; represents Cherokees in Washington, 17, 31; asks Indians if they wish to remain, 18; responds to charges, 20; role in Tsali episode, 21–28; buys land for Cherokees, 21, 29, 32, 34, 44; de facto successor of Yonaguska, 31; agent to disburse funds, 31, 44; attacked by Thomas Hindman, 32–34;

Thomas, William Holland (*Cont.*)
opposes removal efforts, 38–39; supports Cherokee citizenship, 41–42, 49–50, 55–56; and Catawbas, 42–43, 47; wants transportation and subsistence funds, 44, 47; organizes company, 44–45, 73–74; associate of Benjamin and Duff Green, 45; and treaty of 1846, 46–47; and John Mullay, 48–49; in politics, 49–50, 58; and Indian taxation, 51, 129; and Cheoah Indians, 51–52; attacked by Johnson Rogers, 52–54; relationship with James Terrell, 54–55; and lands of Cherokee Nation, 56, 58; indebtedness of, 58; and removal efforts, 58–59; idealizes Quallatown Cherokees, 62–63, 69–70, 81; and conversion of Cherokees, 63–64; and education of Cherokees, 64–65; seeks to apprehend criminals, 66–67; encourages Cherokee settlements, 67; influence among Valley River Cherokees, 69; advocates Christian marriage, 72; uses ballplay for electioneering, 80; member of secession convention, 82–83; promotes use of Cherokees in war, 83–86; leader of Thomas Legion, 86–100; mental illness of, 98, 101, 107, 119–20; no longer undisputed Cherokee leader, 101–103; powers of attorney revoked, 107; lands sold for indebtedness, 110–111; denounces foes, 112; sued, 119–21, 148; praised by Cherokees, 121–22; political influence of on Indians, 151; aids James Mooney, 153; death and assessment of, 171

Thomas Legion: organized, 86–87; campaigns, 87–98; mentioned, 140

Thompson, Jacob, 59

Timber: Nimrod Smith approves cutting of, 142; cutting of on outlying lands, 147–48; extent of, 148–49; sale of, 149; sale of on Cathcart Tract, 169–72; lawsuit regarding, 172–74. *See also* Lands

Timson, John: joins Valley Town church, 13; freeholder of North Carolina, 18;

Timson, John (*Cont.*)
works for removal, 33–39; helps with census, 48; murder of, 66, 94

Tipton, Q. A., 116–17

Tourism, 176

Trade: with British, 4–5; with William Thomas, 62

Traditionalism. *See* Acculturation

Transportation and Subsistence Fund: under Treaty of New Echota, 36–37, 44; under act of 1848, 47, 54–55, 59, 103–105, 108, 112, 115; diversion of, 122, 125, 128. *See also* Common Fund of Eastern Band

Treaty: of Hopewell, 6; of 1817, 10–11, 41; of 1819, 10–11, 41; of New Echota, 16–17, 20, 29, 35, 38, 41, 46, 48, 51–52; of March 1840 (with Catawbas), 42; of 1846, 46–47, 52; of July 1866, 104; of July 1868 (unratified), 106–107. *See also* United States, relations with North Carolina Cherokees

Treaty party, 17, 28, 44

Trespassing. *See* Lands; Timber

Trinity College, 135–36, 139, 169. *See also* Education

Tsaladihi. *See* Smith, Nimrod J.

Tsali: legend of, 21–28; assessment of his role, 28; mentioned, 67; and Charles Lanman, 70

Tuckasegee River, 10, *passim*

Turner, Nat, 50

Tuscarora Indians, 6

Tyler, John, 32–34, 39–40

Unaguskie, 85–86

United States, relations with North Carolina Cherokees: conference with William Thomas, 17; appraisal agents, 17–18; removal efforts, 20–40; uncertain relationship, 41; claims, 44; claims and legislation, 44–47; Mullay Roll, 48–49; Siler Roll and per capita payments, 52–54; transportation and subsistence money, 54–55; renewed removal efforts, 58–59; education, 65; Civil War, 82–100; possibility of postwar re-

United States (*Cont.*)
moval, 103–104; Eastern Cherokees recognized as distinct tribe, 105; U.S. responsibility, 105–108; Swetland Roll, 108–10; legal suits regarding Cherokees, 113, 117–21; removal of 1871–72, 115–17; William McCarthy appointed, 125–26; wardship, 130; U.S. inspections, 132, 134; closing of agency, 132–34; removal of 1880, 140; U.S. jurisdiction affirmed, 142; Samuel Gibson appointed, 142; protection of Cherokee lands, 143–44; Cherokees criticize U.S., 144–45; Eastern Band sues U.S., 145–46; 1886 Supreme Court decision, 145–46; U.S. restricts sale of timber, 149; complaints of agents, 149; U.S. critical of Quakers, 151–52; U.S. disapproves of Nimrod Smith, 157–58; U.S. takes over schools, abolishes agency, 158, 162; functions of U.S. school superintendents, 162, 169; U.S. authority challenged, 169–71; money to settle claims, 171–72; U.S. sues to maintain authority, 172–74; uncertain status of Cherokees, 174; allotment, 175; Great Smoky Mountains National Park, 176. *See also* Allotment; Citizenship; Civil War; Education; Removal
Unto These Hills, 22
Utkena, 3
Utsala. *See* Euchella

Valley River Cherokees: in 1839, 29; visited by Thomas Hindman, 33; denounce removal, 38–39; attitudes toward census, 48–49; Christian converts, 63; intermarriage among, 68; William Thomas's influence among, 69; statistics on, 71; C. H. Taylor, 94; advocate guardianship, 105; property among, 127–28. *See also* Cheoah Cherokees; North Carolina Cherokees; Quallatown Cherokees
Valley Town mission, 13–14, 66
Vance, Robert B., 94–95, 132–33
Voting: of North Carolina Cherokees,

Voting (*Cont.*)
49–50; allowed Cherokees, 130, 147; of Indians and related Quaker problems, 150–51; in 1890 election, 156; denied in 1900, 174–75

Wachucha, 27
Walker, Felix, 11, 13
Wardship. *See* United States, relations with North Carolina Cherokees
Washington, 26, 186n. 22
Wasituna. *See* Washington
Watkins, E. C., 132
Waynesville, N.C., 13, *passim*
Weaverville College, 135–37. *See also* Education
Webster, N.C., 176
Welch, Elizabeth, 128
Welch, John (Valley River Cherokee), 33
Welch, Lloyd (Principal Chief of Eastern Band): denounced, 114; succeeds Flying Squirrel, 131–32; denies need of agent, 133; supported by J. D. Garner, 134; consolidates power, dies, 139; mentioned, 140. *See also* Factionalism
Welch, William (U.S. appraisal agent), 17–18
Western Yearly Meeting of Indiana, 138. *See also* Quakers
White, Eugene W., 147–48, 155
Wolf Town: settlement at, 67; statistics on, 70–71. *See also* Quallatown Cherokees
Wool, John, 14, 20–21
Worcester v. Georgia, 16
Worth, Jonathan, 102
Wotherspoon, W. W., 171

Yellow Hill. *See* Cherokee, town of
Yonaguska: takes private allotment, 10–11; adopts William Thomas, 13; advocates temperance, 14, 42, 65–66; opposes removal, 18, 21, 31; role in Tsali episode, 27; discovers Alum Cave, 62; attitude toward Christianity, 63; property of, 71; mentioned, 102, 126

Zollicoffer, Tenn., 87, 93